The Act of Teaching:

Reflections on a Basic Human Act

Gabriel Moran

Folio Avenue Publishing Service
2031 Union Street, Suite 6,
San Francisco CA 94123 415-869-8834 (866-365-4628)
www.folioavenue.com

The Act of Teaching
Copyright © 2019 Gabriel Moran

Printed in the United States of America.

ISBN: Paperback: 978-1-951193-34-8

eBook: 978-1-951193-36-2

This book is a revision of *Showing How: The Act of Teaching*. Valley Forge, PA: Trinity International, 1997.

Contents

Introduction

Does the world need another book on teaching? There already seems to be a surfeit of books on the topic. But, there are very few books on the activity of teaching itself. I am not referring to this year's publishing lists. I am making the claim about several thousand years of writing.

There are books on "teaching world history," "teaching geometry to tenth graders," or "teaching in urban schools," and endless other books that include the word teaching in the title. This book is on teaching itself. The value of such an inquiry will be up to the reader to judge.

It is a puzzling fact that there is so little writing on the nature of teaching itself. Philosophers whose task includes reflecting on important aspects of human life are mostly silent about the activity of teaching. Even those philosophers who show interest in education seem to assume that teaching does not need explicit attention.

John Dewey is rightfully hailed as one of the greatest thinkers in United States history. He wrote dozens of books over a span of sixty years in which he drew a close relation between education and philosophy. Yet it is difficult to pin down even part of an essay in which Dewey spells out his assumptions about the nature of teaching.

Philosophers do make assumptions about teaching. All human beings do. Of course, it would be exhausting and impossible to unearth our assumptions about numerous things that we do. But teaching is an activity that is found among all people (and other animals) and seems to be indispensable for acquiring human skills and knowledge. Reflection upon the nature of teaching might be helpful for understanding our relation to other people and to our environment.

i

The question of teaching is rightly associated with education. It does not follow, however, that asking about the nature of teaching belongs exclusively to an academic discipline called education or to individuals called educators. This book asks, what is the meaning of "to teach?" The answer is mainly philosophical. To some people that might suggest that the question is impractical. However, a philosophy that examines how people speak and how their actions are guided by the assumptions in their language could prove to be very practical.

It is important to know at the start what can and cannot be expected from an inquiry such as this one. We are accustomed to think that if a problem exists what we need is a solution. In most areas of modern science, we have a right to ask for a solution. In some areas of human life, however, what we can hope to find is a way of speaking and thinking that offers a better approach than competing alternatives. That is, there are philosophical traditions, each of which presumably offers valid insights into the human condition.

This book isolates the question of teaching for examining how people speak about teaching and what else is assumed by that way of speaking. I present evidence to support a way of speaking about teaching that is more comprehensive and consistent than the alternatives.

For example, one of John Dewey's assumptions about teaching is shared by the authors of most books on teaching in modern times. Teaching is what people called teachers do in schools. Most writers make a sweeping gesture toward parents ("our most important teachers") and then parents are not mentioned again.

Parents and other possible teachers are allowed a little informal or metaphorical share in the word teach, but it is clear who "the teachers" are. If we believed that parents are teachers, we would not have "parent teacher associations." We would have associations of parental teachers and schoolteachers.

This book is not an attack on schoolteachers; that is the last thing they need. But they are not helped by being given an overwhelming job of being *the* teacher while the other teachers in society complain that the teachers have not succeeded in turning out intelligent, knowledgeable, and well-behaved human specimens.

One of the aims of this book is to give some help to people who work in classrooms. At present, they are trying to construct the roof of a house when at best the house has a shaky foundation and incomplete frame. My insistence on not equating teaching with what schoolteachers do is for the sake of the schoolteacher, as well as for the many other teachers that our language neglects.

I have spent fifty-five years in a classroom in the role of teacher which includes the title of professor. That does not qualify me to write a book on teaching although it has given me a great deal of material for reflection on the possibilities and limitations of classroom instruction. In every one of those fifty-five years I have asked myself: What am I supposed to do in this room that justifies the great expenditure of time by the people gathered here? When I taught in a private university I had to add: What can I do that justifies the outrageous tuition these students are paying to be in this room?

In the course of this book, I will mention things that I learned as a classroom instructor, either by trial and error or by the indispensable help of colleagues and friends. However, I learned more about the nature of school teaching from being in the role of student rather than professor. The twenty years from first grade to PhD gave me plenty to reflect on, concerning what is effective and what is not effective about teaching.

Nearly all the school instructors I had were good and dedicated people but many of them did not seem to know how to do their job. I can sympathize with them, having discovered that the job is not easy. Nonetheless, either they needed help to do their work or they should have been in a different line of work.

I would draw one general conclusion about school teaching: the higher up it goes, the worse it gets. If a teacher does not know what he or she is doing with a group of eight-year-olds in a school room, the teacher will quickly discover his or her failure. In contrast, there are professors who drone on year after year. They moved from one side of the desk to the other and have never given much thought to what it means to teach. Great scholars do not always make good teachers.

One of the best teachers I have had in my life was my wife, Maria. She taught me all kinds of things, including how to teach in school. She had spent more than a dozen years teaching band and choir to ten-year-old boys. That will teach you how to teach in school or break you. When she eventually moved on to be a professor, people marveled at how good she was at teaching. In addition to her natural talents she had learned about the nature of teaching by the kind of experience that every university professor could profit from.

University professors are paid much more than first-grade teachers. If teaching skill were the criterion, the salary scale would be turned upside down. College professors can easily deceive themselves into thinking that teaching consists in reading their brilliant lecture to a few dozen or a few hundred people who are sitting quietly in front of them.

But if the students do not agree to sit still for more than a few minutes, a teacher must be aware of other factors in teaching than his or her delivering a speech. This principle might be extended to suggest that the place to begin the study of teaching might be when the "student" has not yet learned to speak, or to do much else for himself or herself.

That principle would mean that the most obvious place to reflect on teaching is what a mother does with a newborn infant. The absence of philosophical reflection on what can be learned about teaching from the teaching of infants is not surprising. Most books on philosophy have been written by men. However, that is not an excuse. They could pay attention to earliest childhood and listen to parents, especially mothers, about how to teach everything that they teach their infants.

In Alison Gopnik's brilliant book, *The Philosophical Baby*, she says that when she consulted the index of the thousands of pages of the *Encyclopedia of Philosophy,* she found no references to babies, infants, families, parents, mothers and fathers, and only four to children." She notes that in a later edition of the *Encyclopedia* there are references to essays on young children.[1] However, there has been no major reorientation of philosophy.

Consider two classics on teaching for their references to the family. Jacques Barzun writes in the first chapter of *Teacher in America*: "The odd thing is that almost everybody is a teacher at some time or other during his life. Besides Socrates and Jesus, the great teachers of mankind are mankind itself – your parents and mine."[2] He does not explain why this is an "odd thing" instead of one of the most important facts about teaching. Instead, after this sentence praising parents, the book does not return to them.

Gilbert Highet's *The Art of Teaching* also has one paragraph on parents in a chapter entitled "Teaching in Ordinary Life." This chapter is the last one in the book although it would seem to fit logically as the first chapter. In any case, the 240 pages which are on (school) teaching are untouched by "teaching in ordinary life."[3]

Sometimes the attitude to parental teaching is condescending or even offensive. Steven Pinker writes in *The Language Instinct:* "First, let us do away with the folklore that parents teach their children language….Many parents (and some psychologists who should know better) think that mothers provide children with implicit lessons. These lessons take the form of a special speech variety called Motherese."[4] Pinker is right that parents do not teach their children by providing lessons or speaking in a special dialect. They teach language to their child in the way that parents teach, that is, by actions expressing care for the child, talking with the child, and talking with each other.

Pinker is undoubtedly using a different meaning of teaching than I am. I assume he thinks that his meaning is better than the one I am offering. I wish to present evidence in this book that my meaning of teaching is better grounded historically and has more fruitful possibilities in its use. Since his meaning of teaching excludes parents teaching their children many things, including language, I think it is an unhelpful choice.

Children learn because they are taught. If they grow up in an English-speaking community, they learn to speak English; if they grow up in a Chinese-speaking community, they learn to speak Chinese. The teachers are the parents along with everybody and everything in their community.

To teach and "to teach"

What I ask of the reader in this book is something that many people find difficult to do, namely, to suspend temporarily the identification between an idea and a word for that idea. I am exploring the meaning of "to teach" while distinguishing that meaning from the idea that the term is usually identified with. I argue for a meaning of the verb to teach that differs from the way it is most often used by people who write about teaching.

It is difficult for any of us to become reflective about the language we use. Most of the time we are not consciously aware of ambiguities in the words we are using. That attitude is necessary so that we are not tongue-tied in carrying on every conversation. But occasionally someone may challenge what we say by using a different meaning for a word than the meaning that we have assumed is the obvious meaning. We are puzzled or we start arguing.

I vividly recall reading an essay in a college freshman class. that said all philosophical problems are arguments about words. I thought that was a ridiculous trivializing of arguments about important questions in life. Surely people differ in their ideas about politics, economics, success, sex, religion and many other things.

I was unaware that many thinkers in the early twentieth century had begun to probe language as not only the way we communicate but also what obstructs our communication. This examination of language has not died down; it has intensified throughout the twentieth and twenty-first centuries.

I will occasionally call upon some of the important thinkers that raised questions about language. Perhaps at the beginning of the parade is Friedrich Nietzsche who many people have heard of but are unsure what he is famous for. His main importance here is that he made explicit a skepticism about language. Not only do our words hide our motives and desires from other people; words can mask our intentions even from ourselves. He was writing about the "unconscious" before Sigmund Freud developed that idea.[5]

The philosopher who began writing shortly after Nietzsche and is most helpful for dealing with the problem that Nietzsche identified is Ludwig Wittgenstein. Like most of us when we are unreflective, Wittgenstein began with the assumption that our knowledge consists of ideas to which we attach appropriate names. But he came to realize that many of our words do not correspond to any object outside our minds.[6]

For example, the word nature is one of the most ambiguous words in our language, in part because there is no object that corresponds to that word. "Nature" was coined or invented at a moment in the distant past; it became a useful word for scientists, philosophers and others. Do people know what they mean by "nature" and also what the person they are talking to means by "nature."

There cannot be a useful discussion of nature unless people agree on the meaning of the word. Two great scholars in the 1930s identified sixty-six meanings for the word nature.[7] Even if they exaggerated and there are only forty-six or six meanings, how can we have a discussion of nature? Who decides what the right meaning is?

Wittgenstein is best known for coining the phrase "language game" to indicate that conversations in any area of life operate as a game with rules which we might or might not be aware of, and by using words whose meanings are agreed upon. Wittgenstein writes: "It is what human beings say that is true and false; and they agree in the language they use."[8]

This attention to language may seem to lead to a cloud of abstractions but the opposite is true. We are forced to reflect on what comes out of our mouths and to dig deeper into both human history and our own history. It is ideas that are abstractions lifted from the things that we encounter or that we invent. Another person's ideas are not directly available to us. But words are out in public between us.

At the beginning of any course I taught, I would say to students: "By walking through the door to this classroom you give me a license to examine your words. If you are not willing to grant me that license, I advise you not to take this course. I care about how you speak and how you use words when you write. I do not care what you think. You can think anything you like." Ultimately, of course, I did care about what they thought but I had no direct access to their ideas. I had a right only to examine their words. It was up to them to decide if they would change their ideas.

Who decides what any of our words mean? An isolated word does not have a meaning; it has a meaning in the context in which it is used. Most dictionaries are not much help if they simply tell us that one word is equivalent to another. The "definition" of a word is overrated. A definition only limits the meaning of a word to a particular context (or game) that the writers of the dictionary have decided is the right context. Our most important words have been used in dozens or hundreds of contexts.

The most helpful dictionaries are modeled on the Oxford English Dictionary which provides the different meanings of a word by examples that show its use throughout history. It is no help when someone says there are four or fourteen meanings of a word and he or she is choosing to use one of those meanings. What a speaker stipulates as the meaning of the word does not prevent other meanings from being conveyed to a listener.

Anybody can try to make any word mean anything. If they get enough people to agree with them, that meaning will become part of the language. But if the proposed meaning has no basis in the history of the term, the attempt to introduce a new meaning will probably fail.

For the meanings of a term I refer to the history of the word and its current geography of usage. If one can discover the etymology of a word, that meaning is always revealing although never definitive. It is fascinating to learn that one person decided that a new word was needed and that he or she succeeded in getting the word accepted into the language. With most of our basic and important words their origins are lost to human memory. Did someone first use the words love, fear, food, blood, bones, and die? Yes, but in a world a long time ago.

The word teach and its equivalent in other languages is not as basic as many of those other important words, but it has surely been around for millennia. It is therefore impossible to trace the complete history of the word's meaning. However, there is still plenty of history for examining how the word teaching has been used, especially during the time when thinkers have called attention to the meaning of the word.

The following chapters contrast two traditions for the meaning of teaching. The hallmark of the first tradition is that teaching and learning are separable activities. The result is that teachers and learners are separate populations. The teachers are a special group of people who are trained to provide explanations to a group of learners or pupils who can understand such lessons. What could be more obvious: the teachers teach, the learners learn. The two activities are different in kind. The teachers can only make their best effort to share what they know; it is up to the pupils to make the effort to understand.

The hallmark of the second tradition is that teaching-learning is a single activity seen from opposite ends. The potential teachers are everyone and everything. The learners need to have an organism capable of responding to teaching although they do not need the ability to grasp explanations. The most obvious case of teaching-learning is a mother and a newborn infant. The mother teaches by everything that she does; the infant is open to the entire universe, but its learning is controlled by a focus on the mother's body.

This second tradition of teaching is capable of embracing elements from the first tradition. It includes the complete range of human languages used from teaching an infant to teaching a physicist. Human speech is always set within a physical and social context and a nonhuman environment. The glory of human beings is their language, but they must never forget that they share characteristics with other animals who might have something to teach humans.

Part I of this book examines the historical upheavals when moral questions about teaching have surfaced. The two traditions for the use of the word teach are identified. Then the second meaning of "teach" is illustrated with examples of teaching by bodily movement.

Part II describes teaching when language is the main vehicle of teaching. This section describes the various games in which language is used. Those uses include languages to achieve a teacher's purpose, to remove obstacles that prevent achieving that purpose, or to engage in conversation.

Part III explores the institutional settings in which teaching occurs. One of those educational forms, the school, is given special attention. The last chapter returns to the issue of teaching as a moral activity.

Part One

Chapter One: The Dilemma of Teaching

This chapter describes the first tradition of teaching in which to teach and to learn are separate processes. It is not historically the first tradition, but it is the one that dominates the philosophical assumptions about teaching until today.

Teaching has undoubtedly been practiced so long as human beings have existed. And presumably there were always questions and problems with teaching. But the general situation was one in which fathers taught their sons, mothers taught their daughters, craftsmen taught apprentices, religious leaders taught their successors, and friends taught friends. There was not usually an expectation that the next generation would be living in a very different world. Our word tradition means "to hand on" and that can express the way ancient people lived.

The Tradition of Teaching and Learning

The first tradition of teaching which follows can be linked to three moments when the nature of teaching became a philosophical issue. The first moment was in ancient Greece when philosophy began. The questions raised were who had a right to be teaching and what can they teach? The second moment was an extended period in the seventeenth and eighteen centuries as the new sciences blossomed. Does anyone know how to teach this avalanche of new material to the wider society? The third moment had a focus in the 1960s, but it has continued to the present. Just when science and technology had seemed to triumph, a skepticism showed up that called everything into question. Philosophy had begun with a search for how to separate truth from falsehood. Today, large numbers of people doubt that anything is true or at least that no one who claims to be teaching can be trusted to know the truth.

1

The Ancient Dilemma

The era that we identify in Greek history as the beginning of philosophy is the fourth century B.C.E. Knowledge gathered in the new medium of writing involved new thinking about how teaching occurs. Socrates, teacher of Plato and in part fictionalized by him, emerged as a challenger to a group of people who claimed to be teachers. "Sophists" is a claim of wisdom by a group of men who claimed to be able to teach their wisdom to other people. Socrates, in contrast, made no claim to possess a wisdom that could be taught to others.[1]

Socrates is sometimes said to be the founder of our modern ideal of a teacher. But he remains a complex and mysterious character. We piece together his thinking from the early dialogues of Plato and a few other references in Xenophon and Aristophanes.

What is evident in almost every reference to teaching in Plato's Socratic dialogues is the moral issue at stake. I do not mean only that the question of teaching is often posed in the context of asking if anyone can teach virtue? Rather, the claim to possess knowledge and to be able to impart such knowledge to other people is seen as a claim to moral superiority. If the claim cannot be sustained, then the "teachers" are not technical failures but moral frauds.

The argument between Socrates and the Sophists is told to us in a one-sided way with Socrates as the hero. Some twentieth-century scholars raised the question of whether Socrates's opponents might not have something worthwhile to teach us about teaching. For example, the Sophist Protagoras speaks eloquently about the whole community teaching people through its laws; punishment, according to Protagoras, is intelligible only if it functions as a form of teaching. Socrates may be a great teacher, but might it be that his form of teaching presupposes a form of teaching that is communal and nonverbal? [2]

On a textual level, the case could be made that Socrates rejects teaching and teachers. For example, in the *Apology*, Socrates says, "I counted Evenus fortunate indeed if he really does possess that art and teaches for such a modest fee. For my own part, at any rate, I would be puffed up with vanity and pride if I had such knowledge. But fellow Athenians, I just don't have it."[3]

Socrates is saying here that he does not possess knowledge that he could impart to others. Such statements need to be read in the context of the irony that abounds in Socrates' speech. Socrates might be said to have founded our modern meaning of irony: saying one thing while giving a signal that the opposite is true. In this instance, the first sentence is laced with irony: the huge fee that Evenus charges for his teaching would be a modest fee, Socrates says, if he really could teach what he claims to teach.

The moral dilemma that Socrates was wrestling with and could not resolve by a straightforward answer was, who anoints anyone as "teacher" and gives that person the right to teach? Who gave that person or persons the right to have their word assumed to be true and beyond challenge?

The issue of whether Socrates "teaches" is well summed up by Gregory Vlastos: "In the conventional sense, where to 'teach' is simply to transfer knowledge from the teacher's to the learner's mind, Socrates means what he says: that sort of teaching he does not do. But in the sense which *he* would give to 'teaching' – engaging would-be learners in elencthic argument to make them aware of their own ignorance and enable them to discover for themselves the truth the teacher has held back – in that sense of 'teaching' Socrates would want to say he is a teacher, the only true teacher."[4]

3

In our day, as in Socrates's time, there is perhaps a "conventional" sense of teaching as transferring knowledge from the teacher's mind to the student's mind. Given any sustained reflection on the matter, it becomes apparent that such a transfer is impossible. In Socrates's sense of teaching, all that a teacher can do is show the students that they are ignorant and challenge them to discover the truth for themselves.

The point of the exercise was to get people to recognize their own ignorance with the result that they would search for the truth on their own or from another source besides people claiming to teach knowledge. The effect, whether Plato and Socrates intended it, was to introduce skepticism, a word that simply means questioning, but came to mean doubt about all claims to authority and truth. In this new world, the individual was set loose from many restrictions of familial and tribal ways. That was a liberation for the individual but a new burden on him to find his own way. It was mainly a male story; women's lives changed but not so drastically.

What some people take from Socrates is that teaching is impossible and that each of us must discover the truth for ourselves. The people who are called teachers are doing something which is not only ineffective but immoral. Probably in every decade of every century someone makes the great discovery that there is no such thing as teaching. He or she announces to the world a new finding: No one can teach anyone anything.[5] The irony in Socrates is lost and his only message is that to teach or rather claim to teach is fraudulent.

The Modern Crisis

What came to be called "the scientific revolution" spread throughout the European-controlled world during the seventeenth and eighteenth centuries. The early founders of this "modern age" would probably be surprised that we have a problem with

4

teaching. Science, it was assumed, would answer how teaching is accomplished. Surely teaching was a minor problem compared to the problems of astronomy and physics.

One of the scientists of the "new education," Johann Comenius (1592-1670), wrote: "As soon as we have succeeded in finding the proper method, it will be no harder to teach schoolboys in any number desired, than with the help of the printing press to cover a thousand sheets daily with the neatest writing."[6]

We find here one of the favorite metaphors for teaching in modern times: writing on a slate or, printing on paper. This metaphor for teaching is attacked by humanistic critics of education. To be fair to Comenius, he is commenting here on teaching large groups instead of small groups, not on what teaching is. For the most part, his writing on teaching is not posed in mechanical terms. In fact, the term that dominates almost every page of his educational writings is "natural." Comenius and others after him believed that teaching will be easy once the laws of nature have been discovered; education is simply a following of nature.

The metaphor for teaching as writing on a slate was fixed by John Locke (1632-1704) who was one of the most influential thinkers in the late seventeenth century. He was not a scientist but like any thinker of the time he was influenced by the new sciences. His book *Some Thoughts Concerning Education* became the standard handbook for teachers.

Education was based on the authority that adults have over children. Teaching did not seem complicated within this context. Adults who were appointed as teachers had the authority to instruct children in what they had to know about this new world. He questioned the harsh treatment of children, but he still assumed that "corporal punishment" is sometimes needed.[7]

Locke is usually classified as an empiricist philosopher. That means he assumed that all knowledge comes through the senses. That can sound like the medieval principle of knowledge that "nothing is in the intellect that was not first in the senses." However, as Thomas Aquinas adds, "except the intellect itself." The intellect was empty to start with but it was an active power to receive knowledge. Thomas compares the teacher to a physician who is trying to heal a patient. Whatever skills and medicines the physician possesses, he must still rely on the healing power inherent to the body itself. Locke's empiricism, in contrast, has the teacher trying to deliver knowledge to an intellect that is an empty slate.

Locke's metaphor of teaching as writing on a tablet is one that teachers say that they reject. In practice, however, that seems to describe what many teachers try to do. Even when schoolteachers rearrange the chairs, use lots of technology, and invite questions, they still seem to have as their ultimate end that knowledge is imprinted on the student's mind.

As noted earlier, the higher you go in schools the more naïve is the idea of teaching. Absent much struggle with the paradoxes of Socrates, teachers in high schools fall back on trying to fill up Locke's empty slate. And it is even more common in college to find professors who view students as empty vessels or blank slates.

The writer who took on John Locke's dominance in education was Jean-Jacques Rousseau (1712-1778). The two men agreed on many things, but Rousseau rightly saw himself as offering a different and richer view of education, including the nature of teaching. Unfortunately, that is not the widely held view of Rousseau. He is appealed to as an opponent of teaching whose philosophy was to let children follow their own nature and discover what they wish to know.

Rousseau's 1762 book, *Emile,* is a brilliant work that embodies all our modern problems of politics, science, religion and education.[8] The book is not much read outside schools of education and it is questionable how well it is read there. In the philosophy of education syllabus, I was given to teach, there were three main characters. Socrates presented the problem; Rousseau offered a seductive but totally unreal solution; John Dewey provided the answer with his progressive education.

Emile is a complicated work. I taught the book dozens of times (that is, I read the book with students and tried to help them understand it) and each time I learned something new. I suspect that people who confidently summarize in a paragraph what the book is about have never engaged the whole book. The last book within the book is on the education of the girl Sophie. This part of *Emile* is often omitted because some women students find it offensive. And yet it is a main key to understanding the whole work.

One of the confusing things for today's reader of *Emile* is that Rousseau drew an opposition between "man" and "nature," with his sympathies on the side of "nature." But the contemporary reader can misread this choice to mean that the nonhuman world (nature) provides the path for a boy to follow. By "nature," Rousseau means the individual as opposed to "man" by which he means the social world. The boy Emile is prepared to defend himself against the corruptions of politics and society.[9]

One of Rousseau's great strengths was to distinguish different stages of life and corresponding different stages of education. A person's nature dictates a different approach at each stage of life. When people quote *Emile,* it is usually from the first book that is about the young child. Emile has a tutor whose job is to oversee the education of Emile. Until Emile is about six years old the tutor's job is to see that "nothing is done" – except to protect the

7

child against anyone interfering with nature's plan. "Teaching" does not begin until about age six and it continues until about age sixteen. Rousseau ridicules people who argue with a child, but he declares that the boy of about six does have the capacity to reason about things which are in his immediate interest. The tutor's job is to provide experiences that develop the boy's reasoning power.

It is not until about age twelve that Emile is fully reasonable and can then be instructed about the way that the world is, especially through the natural sciences. At this stage when Emile's reason has developed, the tutor's role has changed. "This is the time of labors, of instruction, of study. And note that it is not I who arbitrarily make this choice. It is nature itself that points to it."

Emile has no friends his age. He needs to be shielded from society which is corrupt. Eventually the tutor must fall back as society's sex, religion, and politics come to bear. The desperate hope is that Emile's individuality will then be strong enough to withstand the assault of these social forces.

The curriculum is guided by the child's interests. But the tutor is the one who knows what is best; it is he alone who knows where the process is leading. The system is authoritarian, but as all authoritarians know, the trick is to hide the coercive power in what appears to be complete liberty. When a conflict does arise, Rousseau's advice to the tutor is brutally realistic: "Let him know only that he is weak and you are strong and that from your respective situation he lies at your mercy....Let the bridle which constrains him be compulsion not authority."[10] There is sweet reasonableness on the part of the teacher, because if necessary, the child can be intimidated or shamed by sheer power.

A problem with Rousseau's framing of teaching is that the teacher is male and so is the student; or at least the main part of *Emile* is about the education of the boy Emile; the girl Sophie appears only in the last of the five books.[11] To his credit, Rousseau was aware of an important question here: the possible differences between boys and girls in education.

Emile is educated to become an "autonomous man." Sophie's education is to prepare her to be the mother of Emile's children and the manager of his home. While Emile is supposedly becoming independent, he will in fact be dependent on his partner for all of life's earthly necessities. In public, the man is powerful, in private the woman is; but this relation of public man and private woman does not produce two whole human beings.

It is interesting to note that Sophie is more easily taught than Emile and will never have to rebel against teaching. Women were thought to be closer to "nature." Mothers were to teach their daughters sewing, cleaning, cooking, caring for infants. The powers that are exercised pertain to nurturing bodily functions. In religion, Sophie does not have to be shielded as Emile is, nor is she ever provided with the deistic system that he is given to digest. Religion is the comfortable set of attitudes and practices that the mother will maintain and pass on to her daughter.

In a novel written after *Emile*, Rousseau admitted that the project of Emile's education might fail. In the novel, Sophie rebels against her role and becomes sexually promiscuous; Emile goes through various hardships and ends up a loner. The lack of an integral relation between Emile and Sophie reveals that Emile's education is at least as deficient as Sophie's.[12]

Mary Wollstonecraft's opposition to Rousseau in *Vindication of the Rights of Woman* (1792) is dominated by "reason." Her contention is that women can be every bit as reasonable as men. She writes: "Children cannot be taught too early to submit to reason ... for to submit to reason is to submit to the nature of things."[13] Wollstonecraft gives short shrift to all the "womanly" things that occupy Sophie's upbringing. Jane Martin points out that much of what Sophie is taught are necessities of human life.

9

They are not things that can be or should be transcended in the name of reason."[14]

Women insist today that girls can be the equal to boys in the use of reason. The evidence of recent decades overwhelmingly supports that contention. But is the production of reasonable individuals a sufficiently rich ideal for education.

The way that Sophie is taught by her mother might be relevant to the teaching of Emile. Both boys and girls need to learn to take care of the body's functioning as well as how to think clearly and deeply. Perhaps if Emile were taught in a way that incorporated how and what Sophie were taught, he would not have to rebel against his tutor to become an autonomous man.

Instead of a combination of Emile and Sophie becoming the ideal of education, the autonomous man became the model of an enlightened age. At the end of the eighteenth century, Immanuel Kant announced as the motto of the enlightenment: "Have courage to use your own reason. Enlightenment is man's release from his self-incurred tutelage. Tutelage is man's inability to make use of his understanding without direction from another."[15] Tutelage or teaching is the mark of a child; to be an adult is to have had the courage to escape from teaching and to make one's own decisions without direction from another.

Kant's challenge to modern man to "come of age" was enthusiastically received by generations of young people. But is this escape from tutelage realistic? "It is, in fact, the hallmark of the adolescent to suppose there is no further need of teaching. To be an adult is to have discovered, often at great cost, the depth and the permanence of the need to set ourselves at school."[16] The author is not saying that all adults need to go to school but that the dependence on teaching, which is obvious in schools for children, never ceases to be important for a human being. We can "set

10

ourselves at school" every day without entering a building called a school.

In the nineteenth century, Johann Pestalozzi, in his novel *Leonard and Gertrude,* presented the mother Gertrude as the model for teaching.[17] That was a big leap for any man to take. It brought out many qualities that had not been associated with teaching. Pestalozzi had some influence on schools in the United States, softening the harsh rigor of the schoolmasters.

Starting in the 1840s, the reversal from men to women in public school teaching gave a boost to Pestalozzi's influence on schoolteachers. A problem remains, however, in trying to bring the mother's form of teaching directly into the school. Perhaps in kindergarten and early grades of elementary school, the model is appropriate. But academic teaching of older children and adults involves other qualities than the form of teaching that is appropriate in the home.

1960-The Present

There is a discernible line from *Emile* to the contemporary educational scene. Even the big reformers, including John Dewey, leave most of the picture of *Emile* intact. Teaching does not seriously exist before a child is approaching the age of reason. Children are then isolated in a special place with a group of adults called teachers. Children are instructed on how things are until they are ready to go into "the real world," a phrase that even schoolteachers use.

Up to the 1950s the minority of young people who went on to college did not experience it as dramatically different from high school. The male college teachers (who preferred to be called professor or doctor) taught abstract subject matter to the young men who were happy to have the privilege of another four years of school and were not inclined to rebel.

11

A convergence of factors in the 1960 began to challenge this picture but the rebels seldom challenged the language and the assumptions that have been in place since at least the eighteenth century. Teachers are people who work in school. Schools are places set aside for children to occupy much of their day. Some places have "pre-school" which as the term indicates is still controlled by the model of school. "Adult education," despite the attempt of theorists to create a different model largely remained a continuation of the image of school and the schoolteacher.

When rebellion began in the 1960s the easiest route was to oppose teachers and teaching. The teachers in school are not giving us "the real stuff." That might be true; the school staff are not "the teachers"' they are schoolteachers whose job is to provide instruction in what can be learned in school. Today's world requires some sophisticated knowledge for learners to navigate the sciences, economics, technology and social science. Schools are places for specialized learning directed by specialized teachers.

In the 1960s the country was struggling with major changes, starting with the movement for racial equality and after that a women's movement that challenged every institution. What united these and other movements was opposition to the United States war in Vietnam.

An expanded college population became skeptical about all kinds of authority. Colleges were often on the receiving end of the anger of young people even though their bigger problem was government authority. The supposed wisdom of their elders was called into question and with that a doubt about teaching.

In the 1960s there was an explosion of books on education with particular emphasis on teaching. I will cite a sample of books that struggled with what teaching is. Some of them did have helpful suggestions for improving the teaching in schools but their main bent was attacking teaching as a power play from which students needed to be liberated.

That is true even of a writer such as John Holt whose first book, *Why Children Fail,* was a beautifully detailed study of a better way to teach elementary school students. But Holt's frustration at the bad teaching in schools led him to became more radical in his criticism of the school itself and its teaching.[18].

Psychology, which had played a role in educational reforms since the 1890s took center stage in the 1960s, with an assumption that the relation between teaching and learning is best understood through the dynamics of adult-child psychology.

One of the most popular writers of the decade was Carl Rogers whose "client-centered psychology" took particular aim at the power that adults have over children by teaching. Rogers wrote that "we should do away with teachers" and replace them with "facilitators, giving freedom and life and the opportunity to learn to students." He concluded, "When I try to teach, as I do sometimes, I am appalled by the results, which seem a little more than inconsequential, because sometimes the teaching seems to succeed. When this happens, I find the results are damaging. I am only interested in being a learner."[19]

An assault on teaching that came from a different direction was in a book entitled *Summerhill* by the school's founder and overseer, A.S. Neill. He made no secret about his attitude to teaching: "I refuse to be classified as a teacher. Think what a tin god a teacher really is. He is the center of the picture; he commands, and he is obeyed."[20] The book painted an idyllic picture of a school that got rid of teaching and allowed students to run the school and carry out their own education.

Summerhill purported to be a school with total freedom, but it could also be viewed as a closed system in which the school was run by an authoritarian leader who made all the big decisions while the children were free to do what they wished within the system. There were numerous attempts to create imitations of Summerhill that usually ended in chaos if there were no rules except ones that children invented.

One of the most interesting and popular books of the decade was entitled *Teaching as a Subversive Activity*. The title was a little misleading because the author, Neil Postman, was encouraging teachers to side with the students who were demanding that schools be aware of students' views and the changing landscape of communication media. Postman had been one of the first people to realize the good and bad potential of television for education.

Postman was keenly aware that education can be not only subversive but must also affirm what is useful from the past. Postman's many subsequent books made clear this conservative element in his educational thinking. But enthusiastic supporters of subverting teaching neglected the follow-up[21].

At the end of the 1960s, one of the most popular speakers in the country was Ivan Illich. After analyzing many institutions, Illich hit upon the school as the linchpin of oppression. His prescription for liberation was contained in the small tract, *De-Schooling Society*.[22] The end of the 1960s – with its relentless rebellion on college campuses – was primed for Illich's message.

The message Illich stated most succinctly was "to teach is to corrupt." During the short time in which he was hailed as prophet and liberator, large audiences of schoolteachers listened to his attacks on teaching, andthen dutifully filed back

14

into their classrooms and continued to teach. Those who agreed with his thesis presumably felt more guilty than before for morally subverting the young.

Illich's failure to make any relevant distinctions regarding "teach," "teaching," "teacher," and "schoolteacher" undermined the possibility of his saying something helpful about education in general and about the meaning of "to teach" in particular. Illich's typical opposition was between teaching and learning; more teaching meant less learning, hence the passionate attack upon teaching.

Many students were receptive to the message that the teachers should get out of the way and let students choose their own educational path. Surprisingly, some college professors agreed with the students. College faculty had recently expanded to meet the demand of a larger student population.

There were not only more professors but professors with a new mix of gender and color. Until the 1960s the image of the professor was a mature gentleman who had the leisure to study his well-defined subject of interest and which for a few hours of the week he put forth to a select body of young men. When the students rebelled, some of the new professors sided with them much to the horror of most of the settled profession.

In a short time, the direct attack upon teaching died down but the relation between professor and students would never be the same. College students today are not trying to get rid of teachers, but they often rebel against particular elements in the curriculum, especially concerning politics and sex. The result is what conservatives long feared and not exactly what liberals were aiming for. Student skepticism reaches down into the high schools and even the elementary school. The schoolteacher's voice is only one among a multitude of voices that young people have at hand.

The questioning of authority which had been there since Socrates's time was now omnipresent.

The attitude of some people both within and outside schools is to dismiss all this agonizing over education and get back to the simple fact: teaching consists of adults telling children what is so. If that is not working, either the teachers are not doing their job, or the students have something wrong with them and probably need more discipline.

Despite the revolution in media of communication and talk about lifelong learning, the words teacher and teaching, unless qualified, are assumed to refer to teachers in elementary and high schools. Perhaps if the framework for the meanings of teacher and teach were not confined to the school, it could lead to a different awareness of how learning occurs both outside and inside schools. We might pay more attention to the whole environment in which people of every age learn.

An interesting development of recent decades has blurred some of the clear lines that placed children in schools in contrast to adults who have left behind schoolbooks and schoolteachers. A student not so long ago was assumed to be a child of about six to seventeen years of age. A minority stayed on for four more years in college. That picture has changed considerably. Students, these days, can come in all ages. Until the 1960s there had been a bias against adults as learners.

An adult education movement that was blossoming in the 1960s and 1970s took aim at this bias. Together with many other forces in society, including better studies of learning, it undermined the bias against older people. Some theorists had tried to establish the basis of adult education by contrasting the "self-directed learning" of adults to the teacher-directed learning of children. Children were subjected to pedagogy; adults were said to be learn by "andragogy." An international conference on adult education stated, "In adult education practice it was now widely accepted that the concepts of 'student' and 'teacher' were inadequate. Instead of 'teacher,' the word 'guide' or 'counselor' or 'animateur' were increasingly being used."[23]

If adults continue to learn throughout their lives and if they might be enrolled in a systematic course of study, why is there anything called adult education with its own separate vocabulary. What has emerged is a continuity of education throughout life – starting at birth. There is a need for numerous variations in the way that education is made available and is engaged in by people. Age is one, but only one, of the factors that is part of the educational mix.

Most textbooks on "teacher preparation" or "teacher training" eliminate a wider, deeper meaning of "to teach" on page 1. They plunge into explaining all the activities that a schoolteacher must confront. The ethical problem of teaching, which has been present with us since Socrates and exacerbated by modern conditions of education, is beyond the limits of what can be addressed. Perhaps most of what is in the textbooks on teacher preparation is true, but these books need a sound grounding for the basic meaning of "to teach" so that schoolteachers have a realistic and fighting chance.

The act of teaching is still identified with the rational activity of an individual called "the teacher." In this tradition, to teach is to intend to teach. Such a circular statement may not seem to get very far, but it does specify what is under the teacher's control. What teachers must do is "make an effort" to have something happen with their pupils. The teacher can only teach – intend something. It is up to the students to engage in a different activity called learning.

There is an admirable modesty in this attitude. Philosophers and religious thinkers have counseled humility on the part of the human teacher. Unfortunately, however, the modern emphasis on intention takes place within an individualism that

17

only recognizes the subjective world of the individual and the external facts of perception. Thus, the result of equating intention with teaching is not humility for teachers but a reduction of teaching to a subjective world. Whether teaching has any connection to a "real world" of fact and accomplishment is beyond anyone's control.

In the tradition discussed in the following chapter, intention emerges only at the center of physical interactions and social relations. Human intention can alter what is already occurring, but one must attend to all the elements of a situation rather than only to one's intention.

Chapter Two: The Tradition of Teach-Learn

This chapter introduces the second tradition of teaching. The chapters after this one will show the implications for this meaning of teaching. The hallmark for this tradition, which sets it in contrast to the meaning of teaching laid out in the previous chapter, is that teach-learn is a single activity viewed from opposite ends. The proof that teaching occurs is learning. Conversely, learning indicates that teaching has occurred.

This tradition does not have a great many philosophers who have explicitly affirmed this meaning although I will cite a few thinkers who can be listed in its support. What this tradition does have is most of the human race on its side. This meaning of teaching goes back long before Socrates and has never been interrupted.

Teach-learn has been overshadowed in modern times by educational institutions and educational practices that assume the first tradition of teaching in which intention and explanations are the main notes of teaching. For the past seventy-five years this tradition of teaching and learning has been challenged from several directions but until there are basic changes in how teaching is spoken about, a different tradition of teach-learn cannot fully emerge.

In this second tradition, to teach is to show someone how to do something. Most comprehensively, to teach is to show someone how to live and how to die. In ordinary English, "showing how" includes aural, oral, and tactile relations. The smallest child who is trying to tie a shoelace or drink through a straw knows exactly what he or she is asking for by the words, "Show me how to do that."

This meaning does not include the idea of "intention." The exclusion of intention as necessary to teaching has the effect of including as potential teachers inanimate objects and nonhuman

19

animals. It also addresses the concern that has occupied philosophy and psychology since Nietzsche and Freud. What we do and say may have important effects even when we do not intend them.

A teacher in a classroom teaches more than he or she is aware; the students are learning things but not necessarily what the teacher is intending that they learn. Most literature on teaching goes its way as if Nietzsche, Freud, and twentieth-century thought have not occurred. The conscious intention of anyone cannot be taken at face value; context must be examined.

Nietzsche's statement more than a century ago unmasks the trust in intention: "The suspicion has arisen that the decisive value of an action resides in precisely that which is *not intentional* in it, and that all that is in it which is intentional, all of it that can be seen, known, "conscious," still belongs to its surface and skin – which like every skin, betrays something but *conceals* still more."[24]

In many areas of life, we have learned the point that Nietzsche is making here. If someone is accused of making a bigoted statement, the first line of defense is usually, "But I didn't intend to offend." Far from ending the matter, the fact that the bigoted statement was *not* intended makes it more serious. The bigotry is embedded in the subconscious and unconscious, in history and culture, in symbols and institutions. If bigotry could be eliminated just by changing an individual's intentions, the task would be relatively easy. But we must get at what is behind intention, or underneath intention. Nietzsche and Freud were themselves getting behind the reasonable thinking and conscious intention of eighteenth- and nineteenth-century thinkers. They contacted an older wisdom that knew what the road to hell is paved with.

The story of the unintended is not always about the dark, duplicitous, and evil doings of human beings. In the case of teaching, most of the story is about the good and joyful teaching of human beings, teaching in which intention plays at most an indirect part. Much of the daily teaching in small affairs as well as historic teaching across the generations is not intended. Thus, the literature on education that equates teaching with intention simply eliminates from examination most of what is taught.

This meaning of "teach" uses the verb "to show how" not the verb "to show." "Showing" is almost exclusively visual in meaning. Showing someone *how to do* something requires more senses than the visual. It very often involves body in contact with body. John Dewey uses the example of teaching someone to swim. It cannot be done by showing the potential learner a picture of someone swimming or even by the teacher swimming. The teacher must get in the pool and hold on to the learner while he or she practices moving arms and legs. Precise instructions must accompany the movements of the body. The teacher must repeat the directions and the learner must repeat the actions until success is achieved by teacher and learner.

Teach-learn is a single action from opposite perspectives. The teacher and the learner succeed together or fail together. We learn because we have been taught by something or someone. In a *Peanuts* cartoon Lucy says, "I taught Snoopy how to sing." Charlie Brown objects that Snoopy can't sing, Lucy replies: "I taught him to sing; I did not say he learned to sing." No one comes into the living room and announces: "I taught Jimmy to ride the bicycle, but he did not learn." Instead, he might say: "I tried to teach Jimmy but he did not learn."

There could be multiple reasons why the attempt at teaching failed. The temptation for the teacher is to assume that there is some defect or lack of effort on the part of the learner. That could be true but the teacher would do well to examine not only his or her knowledge of and intention to teach the skill but the steps by which the attempted teaching proceeded.

Teachers throughout the centuries have wished to pass on some knowledge or skill to learners. The learner needs to have a capacity to learn. Sentient animals and humans of any age qualify as having that capacity. A stone would not qualify as a potential learner nor would a tree (as far as we know).

Parents have always taught their children and they still do. Most parents discover that what they taught their children was not mainly what they intended to teach. Nothing is a more powerful teaching for a child than the way parents interact with each other. How parents act may be a more powerful teacher than what they tell their children.

To the question whether teaching and learning necessarily go together, most educational writers in recent decades give a negative answer. They are countering what they see as the naive fallacy of an earlier era. Their point of reference is the attempt during the first half of the twentieth century to develop a "science" of teacher effectiveness.[25] Mountains of data were collected to discover which behaviors on the part of the teacher would cause learning in the pupil.

As often happens with reactions, critics of that earlier movement accepted the main terms of what was being criticized. In this case, the question was still posed as a causal relation between school teaching and learning. Because studies had failed to prove any causal relation between the behavior of the schoolteacher and the student's learning, teaching and learning were declared to be totally separable activities. A more radical criticism would have asked a different kind of question. For a start, it would not have equated teaching with the activities of schoolteachers.

Books in the philosophy of education presume that people who say that teaching and learning go together have made a naive error of logic. They are guilty of a "category mistake." Gilbert Ryle was the philosopher who was regularly invoked to explain this error. We have confused a "task verb," such as kicking a soccer ball, and an "achievement verb," such as scoring a goal.[26]

A more fruitful comparison of teaching to kicking a soccer ball would be a comparison to hitting a baseball. Baseball calls its task verb "to hit the ball" It calls its achievement verb "to get a hit." No baseball fan is confused by this seeming equivocation. Achieving a hit requires the batter to hit; there is continuity between the task and the achievement. However, hitting the ball does not always achieve getting a hit because there are other factors that are involved. The batter can improve his approach to hitting and increase his number of hits. However, his intention to improve his hitting can actually get in the way of achieving a hit. The cruel thing about baseball is that the batter may hit the ball 400 feet and not get a hit; the next batter may hit the ball 30 feet while trying to get out of the way and find he has achieved a hit. The patient player, the only ones who last, know that with a smooth swing the hits will come in the course of a season. But on a particular day, the connection between "hitting" and "a hit" is partially controlled by the batter but also by fate, luck, or the fallible judgment of the official scorer.

Some days the would-be teacher feels he has hit well but he does not make a hit with the students. He does not naively confuse the two meanings of hit. Why he did not succeed on a particular day may be unclear. The teacher may wish to examine not only what he or she says in the classroom but other factors which have been beyond the teacher's awareness. The teacher may wish to try harder or possibly try softer.

Aristotle speaks of teaching-learning as an example of his agent/patient relation. That is, there is a single "actualization" which can be viewed from opposite ends: "the actualization of x in y and the actualization of y through the action of x." There is only one activity (or motion) and it occurs in the student.[27] Aristotle may be overly optimistic about the ability of the individual teacher to bring about this actualizing of the learner's power. Presumably he recognized the common case where the individual teacher, despite his intention, fails to bring about this movement.

The student in school might not learn what the teacher teaches because the student is always engaging more than one teacher. David Elkind comments on what is called the slow learner, "the one who does not acquire the curriculum at a 'normal' rate." However, as Elkind notes, "the slow learner is fast to learn that he is slow." Elkind writes, "Once we acknowledge that children are learning something all of the time, even if it is not what we set out to teach them – then we have considerably broadened our options for reaching children and directing their mental growth."[28]

It is important to recognize that in addition to always learning, the child is always being taught. In the case of the "slow learner," the child does not invent or imagine something that is not there. The child learns what he or she is taught. Plenty of things in the child's environment teach the child that he or she has been judged "slow." Some of that teaching may come from the behavior of the adult at the front of the room.

In some conscious ways, and more so in unconscious ways, the school instructor conveys an attitude that the slow learner quickly grasps. A system of tests, grades, rewards, and punishments confirms to the child where he or she fits. Keeping the term "to teach" here is important. The child is not only learning but is systematically being *taught* that he or she is a slow learner. Only by recognizing that teaching is occurring are we led to examine the teaching, and perhaps to change some of it.

The Teacher: Everything

In this tradition of teach-learn, everything in the universe is a potential teacher. Because teaching does not have to include intention and explanation, nonhuman things, including inanimate objects, can be a teacher to humans. In fact, it seems likely that most teaching is by what are called natural objects. The question is whether humans are willing and open to learning from the world around them. When I used to say fifty years ago that we ought to pay attention to what the ocean can teach us, people thought that was just a figure of speech. Today there are many people who realize that the ocean is teaching us urgent lessons. Other people still dismiss the ocean's teaching.

In Michael Oakeshott's essay, "Learning and Teaching," he allows that we might learn from a book or the sea, and we might be self-directed in our learning. But then he asserts, "To say that the book, the sky or the sea has taught us anything, or that we have taught ourselves, is to speak in the language of unfortunate metaphor."[29]

Oakeshott does not explain why the metaphor is "unfortunate." More basic is his dismissal of these cases as "metaphor" instead of the genuine sense of teaching. Each of the cases that he cites deserves comment. Sea and sky are perhaps of a piece. Books are different, and the self as teacher raises further complications.

Does it make any sense to say that the sea teaches us? Obviously if teaching requires either a human intention to teach or a teacher to provide explanations, then there is nothing to discuss. But if "to teach" means to show someone how to live and how to die, then the sea as teacher is not a vague figure of speech. It is just about the biggest and most powerful teacher on earth.

When the sea speaks, humans had better listen. The ocean conveys, as nothing else does, our most elemental relation to life's forces; it was not by chance that Freud called the sense of connection to everything the "oceanic" feeling. The sea's enveloping power undermines all our feelings of strength and security. Few things are more soothing than the gentle roll of waves onto the shore; few things are more terrifying than a hurricane-driven sea.

No doubt some people would say that the sea has never taught them anything. Many people live relatively far from the sea and cannot engage it regularly. They cannot absorb its daily lessons, even though the human race is subjected to its potential teaching every minute of the day. Some people are fortunate enough to listen to the sea daily. They learn from the moods of the ocean that change each day. A crowded summer beach is not to be disparaged, but to learn from the sea one must contemplate it in winter bleakness and in all the transitions between summer and winter.

As for Oakeshott's second example of books as teachers, one does not have to reach far at all. The book is the closest we can get to most of our human teachers, living and dead. Surely, there is nothing vague or outlandish in saying, "Aristotle has taught me ... " by which we mean Aristotle's books. I think Erasmus went too far when he claimed that reading the New Testament provides closer contact with Jesus than what the disciples of Jesus experienced in the first century.[30] Erasmus's point is that we get to know a person best through *listening* to his or her words. That is often, if not always, more enlightening than simply looking at them.

It is significant that when referring to Plato's *Republic* we use the verb in the present tense: "Plato says in Book II .... " Plato is dead and does not say anything, but the Plato embodied in the text is present and is still a great teacher. I would proudly say I have been taught by Thomas Aquinas, Ludwig Wittgenstein, and Hannah Arendt. They are real people, real teachers, although I never met them and have only their words on paper. I am surprised that Oakeshott rejects the book as teacher; even in a highly interpersonal image of teaching in which words are the medium, the book fits right into that image, only a step removed from the human teacher in the flesh.

Oakshott's third example, the self as teacher of the self, does raise problems. The phrase "self-taught" is often used as an attack on teaching. There are times when a person can be both the subject of the act of teaching ("I" as teaching) and the indirect object of the teaching ("me" as taught). An "outside" teacher (human or nonhuman) provides the beginning pattern of how to do something; the teacher within takes it from there.

But the claim to be a self-taught person can be blind. The claim that I and only I am the source of the learning is to be oblivious to all the people and books, not to mention the sea and sky, that give direction, resources, and substance to my learning. Self-taught learning is not likely to include political debates, social reconstruction, or examination of institutional power.

When the phrase "self-taught man" means that someone is an avid reader or has had the initiative to learn carpentry, TV repair, skiing, or making money in the bond market, admiration may be in order. If the phrase is used boastfully to mean he trusted no one, listened to no one, and had no need to learn from others, then the self-taught, self-made man, is living an illusion that could collapse at any time. Anyone who is truly governed from the center of the self knows that the self can use all the teaching help it can get.

By referring to the sea as a teacher, it may seem that what we have recognized in human activity we have projected on to a screen of inanimate objects. "The sea teaches," a poet might say, but literally and scientifically we know that the ocean lacks that power. But it is up to human beings to decide how to use the term "to teach." In this case, the poet is worth listening to. There is no scientific evidence against the sea teaching. The question is simply whether in this way of speaking the human race is using a confused grammar or whether it is recognizing a continuity of life on earth.

Wittgenstein notes that we cannot say "a machine has a toothache"; the grammar of "machine games" does not allow the sentence.[31] Similarly, in reference to sea games, the imposition of an entire range of human emotions can become confusing anthropomorphism. But "to teach" is a controlled reference to an encounter between the ocean and a teachable being.

What has been said about the sea can be said of the other great forces of nature: mountains, forests, deserts, sunsets, snowstorms. Each can teach and has taught powerful lessons to those who encounter these forces. In Gary Snyder's book on wilderness, he writes, "For those who would seek directly by entering the primary temple, the wilderness can be a ferocious teaching, rapidly stripping down the inexperienced or the careless."[32] Even miniature forces can teach those who are willing to respond: the snowflake, the seashell, the pebble, the flower. Jacob Needleman, in exploring religious traditions up through the Middle Ages, found it to be a constant principle that "the universe" teaches.[33]

It is true that we would not use "to teach" of the sea or the mountain if we did not know it from human exchanges. That is true of every term we apply to inanimate objects; some terms are an anthropomorphic stretch. To say "the volcano is angry" is taken as only a figure of speech by modern people. But to say "the mountain taught a lesson to the mountain climber" is to describe a precise interaction. The mountain climber learned something in response to being shown something by the mountain. Presumably the mountain did not have in mind setting out to teach a lesson.

The idea of everything in the universe teaching may seem dependent on a religious interpretation. Is the real meaning of "the sea teaches" the belief that "God teaches us through the sea"? Listening to the sea for wisdom and meaning may imply what is called a "religious" outlook. However, it does not imply a Christian interpretation; in fact, being taught by the sea or the mountain, and especially the forest, was frowned on by the Christian Church and survived despite its suspicion. I am not interested in turning the sea into an instrument of teaching, a kind of audiovisual aid for divine instruction. I am interested in the human-nonhuman interplay and the most comprehensive context for teaching.

Later, I will celebrate consciousness, intention, and the power to speak. I do not wish to reduce all teaching to the way it is done by sea or mountain. However magnificent the things of nature are, they do sometimes need a human voice to speak on their behalf. But sea and mountain provide an instructive element for understanding teach-learn in the world of human beings. Most of the teaching done by humans is – like that of sea and mountain – unintentional and nonverbal.

Nonhuman Animals as Teaching

One of the helpful developments of the past century has been the renewed interest in studying (nonhuman) animals. The Middle Ages often argued from analogy with the animal world. The idea was not so crazy as the seventeenth and eighteenth centuries, with their radical split of "man and beast," assumed. Some bad mistakes in the Middle Ages came not from the study of animals but from mixing facts and myths. Conclusions about human life were often based on mistaken information.

In the past century it can sometimes seem almost the reverse. Our detailed knowledge of the animal or insect world can be used as an exhaustive measure of the human world. Whatever the excesses, however, the study of nonhuman animals can be very helpful in understanding such human phenomena as sexuality, aggression, and fear.

The fact of continuity between human and nonhuman animals has been widely recognized during the past century. Few people would now resist the application of the verb "to learn" to many animals. There is debate about the learning of specific animals. But that animals take in a kind of knowledge and retain it for future use seems clear.

Animals learn, but are they taught? In the language of this tradition of teaching, the answer is yes. Nonhuman animals teach their own kind. In addition, some animals that have close contact with humans are taught by them and in turn teach their human caretakers.

Does the mother bird teach the small bird to fly? Does one deer teach another how to get food? Does a dominant tiger teach a lesson to a would-be replacement? The grammar of animal games can easily bear this way of speaking.[17] The *how* of

30

teaching is restricted by the given structure of teacher and student. *What* can be taught is highly limited. The mother robin cannot teach her young to build a Lear jet. The human world is tempted to look down snobbishly on the restrictions built into one animal teaching another animal. But there may be lessons humans could learn from animals.

Animals perpetuate practices that are life-preserving without going into explanations. The mature animal performs the physical activity and at some point the young one can continue the same act. The first thing a cat does after eating is clean itself. Mother cats know that the best chance for cleaning a kitten is while it is eating. Throughout its life afterward, the cat will associate eating and cleaning. That is presumably not a lesson the mother cat intended but it is a lesson the kitten learned from the teacher. Life, health, and safety tips are passed down from one generation to another.

Animals can teach important lessons to humans. For example, the place of ritual in intra-species conflict is a lesson that humans have yet to learn from their animal next of kin. It is unusual for animals to kill one of their own species. They have ways of signaling that one party has had enough. Humans are the only species that wages warfare which can kill millions of people and now could destroy all life on earth. Humans need to learn rituals that can de-hostilize an enemy and reduce violence.[34]

There are relations between humans and nonhuman animals when humans wish to be the teachers. Humans assume that they are smarter than any other animals and have a right to teach those animals how to behave. Sometimes the human attitude is acceptable but only if humans pay attention to an animal's nature. If humans move a species to a completely new environment, they risk upsetting the environmental balance which they do not completely understand.

31

In the case of animals that humans wish to "domesticate," there is a definite need to teach the animal to behave in certain ways. The term "house broken" is indicative of the way humans look at this process. For becoming a friend with a human, the animal must have limits set on some of its natural inclinations. There are possible advantages for the animal. A cat will live longer when taken care of by humans, but it must trade in its instincts for hunting.

A novel written from the perspective of cats refers to human beings as "the can openers." Still, a regular dish of tuna has advantages over hunting for one's food. A litter box is hardly what cats are looking for, but they eventually settle for it. On many counts, however, cats resist human teaching. Cats are notoriously unreliable for experimentation. They are smart enough to repeat an action when shown what to do; they just think that the demand for their repeating the act makes no sense. A cat that is never let outside an apartment will sleep most of the day out of boredom. When you call a dog, it comes but. when you call a cat it says leave a message and I will get back to you.

Dogs are more responsive than cats to human teaching but only within their nature. Dogs at the least put on a better show of being the friend to a human being. They are willing to sit still and listen to human beings tell them their troubles. A psychiatrist suggested that some people are more helped by their dogs than by a psychiatrist. Dogs become dependent on humans for cleaning, eating, and picking up their excretions.

Every day I meet dozens of dogs out for their daily exercise. Most of them are straining at the leash, an instrument that became necessary in cities. What the dog would obviously like to do is run; that part of its nature is not snuffed out by domestication. At the end of her book on the life of dogs,

32

anthropologist Elizabeth Marshall asks: What do dogs really want? She answers: Other dogs.[35]

With variations according to an animal's nature, humans can teach many animals; the proof of the teaching is that the animal learns. Some people reject the word teaching here and say it is training not teaching. But training is part of teaching – for all animals including human animals. Teaching begins by showing the animal, including a human, how to do something. If the animal is receptive to the teaching it will be willing to do the action and to repeat it until the action is its own. There is little or no explaining at the beginning of teaching; there is movement of the body according to instructions about that movement.

The teaching of animals that is exclusively for human entertainment tends to degenerate into training that does not appeal to the animal's natural inclination to learn. Horses were long thought in need of being "broken in" by a trainer. In recent decades it has been shown that horses are better taught by a human being who respects the animal by physically caring for and talking to it. People who truly care for a horse, rather than for the economic potential of the horse, have a sympathy for the horse and find the sympathy returned by the horse.

Many animals have been taught to do tricks for a circus or a zoo. It is shameful what has often been done to elephants, seals, chimps, and other animals. The animal has learned the trick but at the expense of an abuse of its nature. Fortunately, circuses have been disappearing and some zoos are improved. But the human abuse of its next of kin is one of the human race's greatest shames. The continuing abuse in the meat industry would require a separate treatise. It is likely than in just a few decades people will look back with disbelief at a world that was comfortable with burgers, bacon and chicken breasts.

Reflection on animals teaching other animals and humans teaching animals is important for reminding humans that they too are animals. Whatever humans try to teach, in a specifically human fashion, they can never get away from their animality. With very young children, the relation is most evident; the way to teach is to show the child how to physically do something and then repeat the action many times. The process becomes modified, but it is not retracted when the pupil is six, sixteen, forty-six, or seventy-six years old.

The reciprocity of teaching and learning means that the infant can take on the role of teacher. Every attentive parent can attest to this reversal of roles. Eugene Daley suggested that we need a new verb: "to child." The verb "to parent" was a helpful invention to capture the variety of ways that a mother and a father teach their children. Likewise, as Daley suggests, "there is a variety of ways to child one's parent."[36]

Human Example

Human beings can transcend the limitations of other animals, but the humans cannot with impunity leave behind the physical basis of all teaching-learning. Every mammal mother, including every human mother, knows how teaching begins: place the nipple before the newborn's mouth and the learner sucks.

In the next chapter, I will describe how humans try to improve on what nature gives them for teaching. Especially through various kinds of speech, the human environment can be redesigned. Before getting to that step, there is an intermediate stage between a mother suckling her young and a professor explaining black holes in the universe.

This kind of teaching arises in the human community and has distinct human qualities, but for the most part the teaching is not verbal. Insofar as the actors are human, the patterns may have a degree of consciousness and intention connected to them. Nevertheless, this kind of teaching occurs without any one individual intending to teach. In the acknowledgment at the beginning of his book, *How We Die*, Sherwin Nuland writes, "Even when I had no idea I was learning from one or another of the vast number of men and women whose lives have entered mine, they were nevertheless teaching me, usually with equal unawareness of the gift they were bestowing."[37]

This teaching is not simply a deficient form of *real* teaching. On the contrary, all human teaching rests on two pillars: the bodily organism and silence. Speech arises in the middle of the body's relation to silence. Very often in human teaching, speech will clinch the case, but not without a silent bodily presence as a precondition. Occasionally, speech is a distraction from the power of silent example. We teach by showing people how to live and how to die. At the beginning of life, words are unnecessary, at the end words are inadequae.

Nonverbal teaching can be examined in two ways: a cross-section of the present gives us teaching by example. The flow of learning between generations gives us teaching by tradition.

Teaching by example is simultaneously praised and dismissed in treatises on teaching. John Locke seems more positive than most writers in asserting, "But of all the Ways whereby children are to be instructed, and their Manners formed, the plainest, easiest and most efficacious is, to set before their Eyes the *Examples* of those things you would have them do or avoid." A close reading of this text, however, shows that Locke is starting with the question, "How does an adult instruct a child?" His answer is that examples are the best instrument of instruction. Although there is great value in using examples in several forms of verbal instruction, Locke's language actually undermines a richer meaning of "teaching by example."[38]

The most effective teachers do not begin by setting out examples but by being examples; they may or may not be instructors of anything. Their lives include examples of what to do, although the multiplicity is usually rooted in a single example: this is the way to live and to die. For such a person, "to set out examples," even when the example is from one's own life, or especially from one's own life, is far too directive of other people.

Here is one of the great paradoxes of human life: not only is instruction not the essence of teaching, but some of the most important teaching can only occur when it is not intended. The wise, talented, disciplined, and accomplished person is likely to be aware that other people will be inspired by his or her life. But what any individual on any occasion may be inspired to do is not up to the teacher to determine.

An athlete is always being asked: Do you think you are a role model? The athlete is usually confused or embarrassed by the question. If he or she says yes, it sounds arrogant; if he or she says no, it sounds like a shirking of responsibility. When Charles Barkley was a star basketball player, he said: "I am not a role model. I am not paid to be a role model. I am paid to wreak havoc on the basketball court." Not surprisingly, people lined up to support or to denounce Barkley's statement.

A celebrated person from any profession can provide an inspiring example of how to discipline personal talent and achieve brilliant results. The problem is with the stilted phrase, "role model." Barkley finished his statement by saying "Parents should be role models." It is true that a parent can model the role of parent for his or her children. But that is not an encompassing statement of parental teaching. Children need good examples from adults, including celebrities in sports or the arts. More of it should come from parents, schoolteachers, politicians, police officers, and other adults that the child regularly encounters.

If one wishes to appreciate teaching by example, then neither "role" nor "model" is particularly helpful. "Role" is too narrow for what is taught; "model" is too rigid for how to teach. If a social scientist wishes to talk about role models, it may make sense in some contexts. Or a college baseball player may find a helpful model in the performance of a professional shortstop. But most teaching-learning is not about role models.

We all depend on human teaching every day by people who inspire us to believe that there is goodness in the world, that one can say yes to living another day. Most of the time, the smile, the gesture of politeness or care, is more powerful as teaching because it is not intended as teaching. There is no moral dilemma here; the learner is free to take whatever he or she wishes to take from the available e x a m p l e s.

Consider this example of teaching from Malcolm X's autobiography. He was in Jedda on the way to Mecca in 1964. In the crowded conditions of the city, a government official gave up his own room so that Malcolm could sleep. Malcolm, reflecting later upon the incident, writes, "That white man ... related to Arabia's ruler, to whom he was a close adviser, truly an international man, with nothing in the world to gain, had given up his suite for me, for my transient comfort. That morning was when I first began to reappraise the white man."[39] Malcolm X's life was profoundly changed by the new situation he was in, by the physical, historical, and social influences around him. But he nonetheless pinpoints the connection between a simple act of kindness and the beginning transformation of his thinking on race.

Writers in education get tangled up in their own language when they refer to this simple, but all-important phenomenon of teaching by example. It does not fit their definition of teaching. Unfortunately, however, that does not lead them to question if their definition is adequate. For example, Page Smith, in *Killing the Spirit* writes that the "true person" must have love: "None of us is worthy of it, and yet all of us must have it to live. *It can't be taught.*" Two sentences later in the same paragraph, Smith writes, "Teachers who love their students are of course by that very fact teaching their students the nature of love, although the course may in fact be chemistry or computer science."[40]

If Smith decided by the end of the paragraph that "of course" love can be taught, I think he should have gone back two sentences and changed the flat assertion that "it can't be taught." The contradiction may seem minor, but it is in a chapter entitled "Teaching" in a book that caustically attacks the lack of critical-minded thinking in the university. If one writes a chapter on teaching, there ought to be some consistency in the meaning of "to teach."

The same confusion regularly shows up in essays with the title "Can Virtue Be Taught?" Nearly always the answer is no, with appeals made to thinkers from Socrates onward. And yet if one begins by not unduly limiting the meaning of "to teach," the obvious answer is yes. People do learn to be virtuous; they do so having been taught to be virtuous. How does that happen? Aristotle supplies the simple, clear answer: the way to become virtuous is to grow up in a virtuous community. Virtue is what is taught all day long by virtuous members of the community.[41]

Aristotle's answer is one of those circular-sounding statements that can be ridiculed if it is taken out of its matrix of related assumptions about community, teaching, virtue, and causality. Aristotle is drawing upon a wisdom that goes back millennia. His philosophical formulation is based on principles that were practically self-evident for Jewish, Christian, Buddhist, Muslim, and other religious groups. The way to get good people is by providing good example. Good example does not guarantee good learners, but the absence of good example will assuredly guarantee a deficiency of virtuous learners.

I emphasize once more that this principle does not mean "to set out good examples." That procedure comes later. Teaching-learning by example means first and mainly living with people who show how to live within a way of life. It is amazing that, despite the vast differences among religions, they are in nearly perfect agreement on this point: the way people learn goodness or virtue is by the presence of good, virtuous people.

Teaching by Tradition

The term tradition does not have good standing in educational writing. Indeed, since the late eighteenth century, education has often been posed as the opposite of tradition. "To teach" often means to free people from tradition, which is assumed to be a collection of myths, superstitions, and prejudices. Some kinder words have been said about tradition in recent decades. Overall, however, tradition is still taken to be the stone that rational explanation must dislodge.

A tradition is simply a community's way of doing things. It is composed of practices, rituals and beliefs that hold the community together. Tradition can be the enemy of progress; nevertheless, all enduring progress is built on what tradition provides. The fact that tradition does teach follows from the meaning of "to teach" as "to show someone how to live and how to die." Fortunately, for all of us, tradition has continued to supply us with wisdom about living and dying so that each generation does not have to rely solely on its own insights.

39

The principle of teaching by tradition and community example is perhaps clearest in the case of a small child learning to speak his or her native language. The infant is thrown into the middle of human conversation and from the first moments of life struggles to join in. Almost miraculously, an infant puts words together into phrases and sentences.

Hannah Pitkin recounts a story about a three-year old child that could probably be duplicated by most parents.[42] The child come out for breakfast while carrying her security blanket. The mother says: "Put your blanket back on the bed." The child replies, "But mother I simply can't function in the morning without my blanket." Adults laugh at what they assume is a repetition of what she has heard from the mother, but the child's statement is more amazing than that. If you were to ask the child the meaning of "function," she would not have any idea what the question means. But she has learned the game of language that she and her mother play all the time. She did not simply mimic what the mother has previously said, which most likely referred to a cup of coffee. The child has understood the mother's statement within a particular situation; she recognizes her own situation as similar and has precisely replaced "coffee" with "blanket."

The mother did not use a special language with the child, and she had not been intending to teach any lesson about coffee or blankets. But the mother did teach in the way that she does most of her teaching. And the child had learned about the world by means of the mother's actions and the complex structure of language. Once the pattern is in place, the child becomes a voracious namer with an explosion of the question: "What's the name for that?"

What could be more obvious: the way to speak English is to grow up in an English-speaking community. The practice of English by its users is an invitation to speak English. The child for survival's sake accepts the invitation.

Even with good examples in the environment, an individual for a myriad of reasons might not learn well. These learning problems are issues to be explored. For the moment, however, it should be clear that the way *not* to teach language is by sitting in a room and being given lists of words and rules of grammar to memorize. Language teachers in schools have a very important job of *improving* spoken and written language, but classrooms are poor places for starting to learn how to speak a language.

At the most physical level of teaching, there is usually neither moral confusion nor moral rebellion. The child's body is receptive to learning physical skills; the way to teach the child is to tune into the rhythms of the child's movements. Teaching a child to use eating utensils includes putting the food on a spoon and raising it to the child's mouth and developing a ritual for the practice. So long as no violence is done to a child, each little piece of physical learning is a plus.

The usual evidence that the child wishes to learn a physical skill is the presentation of a receptive organism. The child says, "Teach me to ride the bicycle." The teacher complies not by explaining bicycles in the living room but by running up and down the street. The child's desire to learn is shown by getting up and trying again after falling off the bicycle. The teacher's teaching is mainly to provide a temporary balance by physically holding the bicycle and occasionally saying "push," "stop," or "tip to the right."

A community is a small group of people getting on with life: birth, eating, thinking, talking, planning, aging, dying. The child learns to live by doing what the community does. Throughout life the individual continues to learn by doing what many overlapping communities do. Groups of people and their work get taken up into institutions that also become powerful teachers. Large

41

institutions are very suspect in our day, as well they might be. Simple flight from them, however, does not make them go away or lessen their teaching influence. Institutions need continual reform or else their teaching goes sour.

Our concentration on personal relations tends to isolate teach-learn with the question of individual teacher and (ideally) one student. An awareness of group process only gets us one step beyond the tutorial image. But teaching goes on every day insofar as communities live and institutions function. And although communities can become introverted and institutions can become corrupt, the learning of the human race is nevertheless passed down over the centuries by its being embodied in communal rituals and institutional arrangements. Most of this story is for the next chapter in which we consider.

Chapter Three: Teaching by Design

The teaching described in the previous chapter was not directly intended. This chapter moves on to cases where human beings intend to accomplish a particular result with potential learners. The teaching is still mainly by physical movement, but speech is used for directive purposes.

Every being, including and especially each human being, has a built-in design or pattern to its existence and its activities. Humans come with a certain height, weight, physical strength, hands, feet, sexual organs, senses. There is also a pattern to the inner life of a person that is not available to the outside spectator.

The Human Design

The intention to teach someone something means an attempt to change some pattern of activity in the learner. A question about the learner's freedom immediately arises and it is important to be attentive to signs that the potential learner is freely receptive to a particular teaching. The teacher has a pattern in mind but because the learner already has a pattern of activity the teacher must adjust to what is possible. That means every attempt to impose a design is actually the proposal of a redesign.

The beginning point for teaching by design is a human being in action. The action may be poorly designed for its purpose or the action may be adequate. But practically always, an activity can be done better. The teacher by design studies the present design and proposes a redesign. Teachers are sometimes attacked with the cynical statement that "those who can, do; those who can't, teach." There is a truth hidden under the cynicism: A good teacher need not be an expert at practicing the design; what he or she needs to be able to do is to understand the current design of the potential learner and propose a realistic redesign for that learner.

43

The term design has a double meaning. To teach by design can refer to the conscious intention to show someone how to do something. To teach by design can also refer to the design or designs that the teacher uses. Such a design is often a graphic drawing with accompanying words of instruction. The blueprints for a building are a design for the construction crew; the score of a symphony is a design for the musicians.

My design in this chapter is to present some relevant distinctions of language that deal with the matter of "imposing some design." I will cite some authors and the metaphors they use for describing what a person does who wishes to help others by teaching them. The chapter provides examples of people who teach others by design and what some of the designs are.

The material I have to work with in this chapter, and throughout the book, is words. I design, or rather redesign, language in the hope of evoking within the reader images and understanding. Words are fragile material for the design of meaning. When Wittgenstein chose examples of the design of meaning, he often turned for help to architectural blueprints or Western movies.[1] This chapter does not have accompanying blueprints or videotape. I am working only with the design of sentences to convey the process of teaching by design.

As an analysis of teaching shifts from mostly physical movement to mostly human speech, the gap between intention and effect becomes more evident. That is, the more specifically human the teaching is, the less assurance the teacher has that his or her movements deserve the name "teaching." Thus, at one end of the spectrum, the gestures of a mother with a newborn infant are very likely to be effective teaching; the mother does things similar to, but one step removed from, what other mammals do with their young.

The case is similar for all teaching in which physical action predominates. The teacher of bicycle riding has a feeling of achievement when the child succeeds; surely, the teacher thinks, I had a part in that success. The case is different, however, when someone tries to teach by relying almost exclusively on words. In that situation, the connection between the movement of the teacher's mouth and the learning of a student is, at best, tenuous.

Even the best of teachers cannot fill this gap. Indeed, the best teachers do not try to fill the gap; they know when to stop. The insecure teacher wishes to be certain that his or her efforts produce results. "I will teach this; you will learn this; and we will leave no place for error, daydreaming, or surprise." Few things in life are sadder to watch than a well-intentioned, hard-working, totally dedicated schoolteacher who does not have a glimmer of the paradox that the teacher's effort is not what brings about the student's learning.

This principle is connected to a central strand in Eastern religion, which both exalts the place of the "teacher" and simultaneously warns any would-be teacher to be humble in trying to play the part. There is a recognition here of mystery in the midst of the most common, everyday activities. The paradox of trying to be a teacher does not apply only to classroom instructors or religious gurus. Every human being is regularly in the position of trying to be a teacher, while a big obstacle to succeeding as a teacher is the "trying to be."

This paradox is what leads some people to avoid the word teaching. But the abandonment of "teaching" leaves us with "learning" alone, usually meaning the reduction of educational discussions to psychological categories. In contrast, insisting on the relation of teach-learn presses us to attend to the relation of organism and environment, and to the political, economic, and institutional forces that influence the structure of teach-learn.

In Eastern religious literature the paradox is sometimes pushed too much in the opposite direction; that is, learning collapses into teaching. Psychological theories of learning would be a helpful restraint to placing all the attention on the teaching end. If the issue is only looked at from the teaching side, the political, economic, and institutional contexts tend to fade.

The paradox in the guru-disciple relation is that the learner is encouraged to trust, to identify with, to practically become the teacher. For his part, the teacher is supposed to want nothing from the student not even that he or she learn. When Trunga Rinpoche was asked how a person can have the ultimate experience of "no-self," he responded, "It could only come about through admiration for one's teacher. You have to become one with the teacher and mix your mind with the teacher's mind."[2] The outsider can see here a situation ripe for exploitation. What if the teacher is power-hungry or sexually disturbed? The answer to that query is: He is not a *real* teacher. True enough, which raises a further question of how the real teachers are discovered and "licensed" to teach.

In Western educational systems, we generally have a series of bureaucratic controls to weed out the bad prospects for schoolteacher. We do not expend as much effort in trying to find the best teachers, those who might find it difficult to work within the limits of our educational institutions.

Traditional religions of the East relied on an apprentice system and on the test of time to identify true teachers. The most striking quality of these "real" teachers is an ironic sense of humor. The guru has disciples solemnly trying to mix their minds with the teacher, but the guru has a playful twinkle in his eye. Imitate me if you must, he seems to be saying, but I am not really the teacher at all.

With this description, we come around again to Socrates, who surely believed in teaching but professed that he did not possess the wisdom to be a teacher. That disclaimer may raise suspicions. When famous, successful, and powerful people say that they really don't have much power, we suspect fraud. If they do not manifest some sense of ironic humor, we have reason to suspect that the delicate paradox of teaching is not being maintained.

Take, for example, the writings of Krishnamurti, a well-known guru of the twentieth century. He was relentless in his attacks on teachers. Teachers are not to be trusted; they are power-hungry and egotistical, seeking only to control their disciples. What Krishnamurti may have conveyed in person I do not know, but his books are long, humorless sermons that can only call attention to his opinions, while attacking dependency on all (other?) teachers.[3]

The best of educational reformers through the centuries did not reject teaching, even though they have been severe critics of teachers and the systems around these teachers. The test of educational reform is to offer a redesign of the process of teach-learn, in which the potential teacher finds a better way to work within the process. Such a redesign takes patience, skill, and cooperation with others. The last of those qualities may be the most difficult for many reformers. If someone is trying to radically reform education, he or she must teach other teachers how this new process works.

Design by Some Good Teachers

Here are four examples of modern reformers who have struggled with teaching by design. The examples are from Russia, Italy, New Zealand, and Brazil; the teachers are Leo Tolstoy, Maria Montessori, Sylvia Ashton-Warner, and Paulo

47

Freire. Each of them expresses great ambivalence about "teachers" while being fascinated with teaching.

Leo Tolstoy is probably the most impatient of this group. Tolstoy did many things in life; writing *War and Peace* was no doubt more important than any theory of teaching he devised. However, he did get intensely interested in school reform for a short period of his life.[4] He founded his own experimental school and tried his hand at teaching children. He is still quoted by reformers who are inclined to remove restrictions on the child's learning.

In the small body of educational writing that he left, Tolstoy says extremely radical things. For example, he writes, "There is only one criteria of pedagogy – freedom." More important, however, he attends with a novelist's eye to the details of adult-child interaction. He writes with a sophistication that includes knowledge of several European languages but also with an appreciation of Russian peasant simplicity.

Tolstoy was not so naive as to think that there is no design to what teachers should do with students. But he was truly shocked when he discovered that the children are sometimes the teachers. A passage that describes his work with one child in "Should We Teach Children or They Teach Us?" captures the theme of Tolstoy's discovery:

"As soon as I gave him complete freedom and stopped teaching him, he wrote a poetical work which had no equal in Russian literature. And therefore it is my conviction that we must not teach writing and composition in particular, to children in general and to peasant children especially. All that we can do is to teach them how to set about composition."[5]

The last sentence might seem surprising, a seeming reversal of what precedes. Tolstoy says that as soon as I "stopped teaching him," the child produced a work unequaled in Russian literature (perhaps some poetic license in that description). Tolstoy goes on to generalize that "we must not teach writing and composition," artistic composition being the worst subject and peasant children being the worst group to be violated with teaching. And yet, in the end, Tolstoy says we must teach: "Teach them how to set about composition." His distinction between "teach composition" and "teach them how to set about composition" suggests further reflection, which Tolstoy dues not offer.

A second famous educational reformer came from a time just after Tolstoy and is cited by many of the same people who cite him. Maria Montessori stayed with the work of changing education. Her reforms continue to exist in a large network of schools and in her educational writing. Like Tolstoy, Montessori appeals to a kind of peasant simplicity, especially among women. At the same time, there is need for exquisite design of the environment.

Montessori developed a method, the control of which, after Montessori's death, led to some strong infighting. Is this a true Montessori school with a real Montessori teacher? But why cannot anyone, having read Montessori's books, set up his or her own school on the same principles? Montessorians argue that the method cannot be entirely conveyed through the written word. The master of the method must show teachers how to design the environment and work with the design.

The success of Montessori schools in the United States might have surprised Montessori. She was skeptical of "teachers," by which she usually meant professional schoolteachers. She often contrasted the Italian peasant women who were receptive to her method and the professionally trained teachers in the United States who knew too much of the wrong things: "In America experiments never succeeded because they looked for the best teachers, and a good teacher meant one who has studied all the things that do not help the child and was full of ideas which were opposed to the child's freedom. The imposition of the teacher on the child can only hinder him."[6]

Montessori writes with irony here, but it still raises troubling questions. "The good teacher" or "the best teachers" are obviously not people opposed to the child's freedom. But if a good teacher is one who has "studied all the things that do not help the child," should a teacher simply stop studying? Should she be a bad teacher? In other words, does one abandon the terms "teacher" and "teaching" or study all the ways we might better describe the relation of teaching-learning?

The third example is a woman who is associated with Maria Montessori in educational writing but who had a different approach to classroom design and who wrote in a different style. Sylvia Ashton-Warner was a New Zealander who taught Maori children. One of her best-known books is a novel; the central character describes her successes and failures at teaching in "the infant room."

There is more emphasis on speech than in Montessori, who concentrates on physical design until the "explosion of literacy." Ashton-Warner's teacher keeps probing for the most emotionally charged words (which she discovers in her situation to be "ghost" and "kiss") that will lead to the sound of "erupting creativity."

The meaning of "teacher" remains puzzling for the woman in the novel called teacher. The word does not take on the negative connotations it often has in the hands of other educational reformers. Ashton-Warner's teacher treasures the vocation, but she is constantly puzzled as to how to carry out the vocation. She looks for a "light enough touch" so that "the teacher is at last with the stream and not against it; the stream of children's inexorable creativeness." [7]

Ashton-Warner constantly goes back to the world "locked inside." Like Tolstoy and Montessori, she wishes to avoid "plastering on." The ultimate trust is in the children's creativity. Nevertheless, the term that is never far from her lips is "design." She looks at the volcanic eruptions of her infant room and sees: "What wonderful movement and mood. What lovely behavior of silksack clouds! An organic design. A growing, loving, changing design. The normal and healthful design. Unsentimental and merciless and shockingly beautiful."[8]

Paulo Freire, who worked mainly in Brazil, provides a grown-up version of the three previous pictures. Most of Freire's work was in adult literacy. The basis of the work is like the other three theorists: trust in the simple, peasant-like qualities of the learners and unleash their creative possibilities through careful design or redesign of the environment. Like Ashton-Warner, Freire sought out the most powerful words (political as well as emotional) for a group of learners. Like Montessori, he found an explosion of literacy once that power center had been located.

Like the three previous writers, Freire had a certain ambivalence about "teachers." In a world survey of adult education, John Lowe says of Freire's work: "This identification is to be brought about by a free dialogue between a coordinator (obviously the designation 'teacher' is inappropriate) and a group designed to unravel the social significance of key words germane to the learners' everyday lives."[9] Lowe's parenthetical reference to the inappropriateness of "teacher" is not obvious in Freire's writings. Instead, Freire speaks of the need to create a teacher-student and student-teacher. Like Socrates or Tolstoy, Freire attacked one idea of teacher, but he was intent on the precise design of a teaching-learning situation. A term such as "coordinator" may sometimes be useful but it is not a substitute for the teacher who designs the environment.

Freire has been an inspiring genius of educational revolution. Probably his best-known distinction is between banking and dialogue forms of education.[10] The contrast expresses a stark choice in repressive situations. Unfortunately, the contrast is easily turned into a cliché in cultures where talk is "free" and dialogue about "problem solving" is comfortably acceptable. "Dialogue" is one of the ultimate terms for a fully human life and for the best education. But it needs plenty of support in physical forms of teaching and several forms of discourse that the term "dialogue" might not capture.

Dialogue can suggest an equality that is usually lacking in the teaching situation. The teacher is not the same as the student and should not pretend to be. Equality of power may be what teaching leads toward, but it is not where teaching starts. The one who is playing teacher has the responsibility for designing the environment to make dialogue more possible. Freire knows the paradox: the learner identifies with the teacher's learning while the teacher must break the link of dependence on the teacher.

The four great reformers cited here had a sense of the gap between the teacher's intention and the student's learning. The recognition that the teacher can neither take credit for success nor be burdened with guilt by failure can have opposite effects. Either the teacher is liberated to do the best that he or she knows, without having to worry about the results. Or else the teacher becomes depressed, lazy, and in search of a new job. What is the point of working hard if there is no connection between my movements and the learning that results? There is no simple answer to this question, which must be pondered by all teachers, not just schoolteachers.

Teaching Design and Redesign

The teacher cannot fill the gap between his or her intention to teach and the learning that occurs in the student. In the most physical kinds of teaching, the gap might be indiscernible. Teacher and learner succeed together or fail together in riding a bike, swimming, tying a knot, or catching a ball. The teacher "lays on hands" and the teaching seems to flow from body to body.

Although I have insisted that these cases of teach-learn are fruitful for understanding all teaching, I think that the wrong lesson could be drawn from them. It is true that words can be shaped just as bodies are shaped. But as the teacher's words take on more importance in teaching, one must be careful of what one attempts to shape with the words. The mind of the student cannot be shaped in the way that the child's hand can be physically shaped in teaching him or her to catch a ball.

The term "to shape" can be helpful to discussions of teaching. From Comenius and Locke down to B.F. Skinner, this metaphor of shaping has had a privileged position. The most common images embodying "to shape" have been the shaping of water, wax, clay or slate. When the image is crudely used, it implies that the mind of the child is completely pliable material on which knowledge can be stamped or written. Skinner often uses "shape up," which conveys the most direct behavioral control of the student. Pigeons and people are shaped up to behave.[11]

Most writers on education have allowed some give-and-take with the image of shape. For example, in George Dennison's *Lives of Children,* a book celebrating the freedom of the child, the author writes, "The work of the teacher is like that of the artist; it is the shaping of something that is 'given.'" That statement could be taken as Skinnerian except that Dennison adds, "And no serious artist would say in advance that he knows what will be given."[12]

The implication here is that the lives of the children may have some similarity to wax or water, but human life is a much more complicated material to work in. The lives of even very young children already have a complex design woven into their histories and their makeup. All attempts to shape human life turn out to be a reshaping of past b e h a v i o r s.

When the learner willingly presents his or her body for reshaping, no moral dilemma is evident. For example, suppose that a forty-year old man goes into a health spa and says, "I want to shape up by losing twenty pounds and getting rid of this flab around the middle." The shaping up is a matter of learning some exercise techniques, discipline, and dietary helps. The man is shown how to live according to better standards of health, and after a while he can go on as he has been taught; he is now the teacher of himself.

When a fourteen-year-old boy presents himself in a classroom, he is *not* saying: my mind lacks certain items or qualities; shape up my mind. Two very important differences from the man in the gym need to be noted. First, the child's freedom is always in question. James Herndon said that the only thing you can be sure of when you see a child in a classroom is that he or she prefers that to jail. The statement exaggerates somewhat; most of the time one can presume a little more.

Coming to school for most children does express some degree of interest in learning something. Whether the child really wishes to learn what is taught in the classrooms is another question. Even without compulsory school-attendance laws, the child is under considerable pressure to be at school (from family, friends, the lack of a decent job, or the desire to play football).

Adults also experience social pressures on their freedom, but usually the person attending an adult education class feels a greater sense of choice than do millions of young people in school. Even in the universities of the United States this is the case. Seventy-five years ago, the one in ten young people who attended college usually experienced it as a privilege rather than a restraint of liberty. But the young person in college today cannot be assumed to be there by a completely free exercise of choice. Colleges today have many students who are putting in time to acquire the credential needed for a good job. They would prefer to be somewhere else.

A second and more important difference between a young person in school and the man in the gym is that classroom teaching is directed to the mind. One cannot easily take the image of shaping up the stomach muscles and transfer it to shaping up a mind.

Even if a person were to say that he or she wished to have the mind shaped, the image would still be of doubtful validity. Does anyone know how to shape another's mind? Some people fear that such a process is possible and that, for example, advertisers are using devious techniques to shape peoples' minds. Further out in that direction are religious cults that are thought to be able to stamp beliefs on the mind.

Most acts of intended teaching exist somewhere between the man saying, "Tone the muscle," and the teenage captive of a cult saying, "Take my mind." Human teaching involves an embodied mind or a self-conscious organism. The shaping up of behavior involves mental awareness, response, and a willingness to go with the teaching.

If the man really wants to change the shape of his

mid-section, he will have to change his mental attitude. Conversely, the most highly rational learning involves external bodily movement. Drill, training, and discipline will be either preconditions or integral elements of intellectual accomplishments.

The shaping, therefore, is usually directed to the whole organism in relation to its environment. This relation already has a shape so that one can only proceed by reshaping what is given. The reshaping is within the strict limits of the already shaped material at hand. A dance teacher must work with a body in a setting. The foot of the ballet dancer, the shoe she is wearing, and the surface on which she is dancing constitute a complex relation. With teaching and constant practice, the relation can be changed, though the change can only be within strict limits.

The term "design," attempts to capture both the express intent of the human teacher and the material limits of what can be taught. Design is a more precise image than shape. Impersonal factors in the environment shape the landscape and the living organism, including the human body. A hard rain or a blistering sun may reshape the landscape; factors such as diet, cramped conditions, stress, or accident may change the human shape. All these factors shape the conditions of teaching.

Change by design implies a concerted attempt of a human teacher with a human learner to work with given shapes. The dance teacher must work with the foot, the shoe, and the floor; but there is also the choreography of the dance. The violin teacher must work with arm, chin, fingers, and musical instrument; but the design of the music incorporates and goes beyond these elements.

The metaphor of design and redesign is therefore more helpful for my purposes than is the metaphor of shaping. Whereas shaping has usually suggested an *object* that is worked upon, design and redesign have to do with an *activity*. The potential learner is doing something; to teach is to change what the learner is doing.

A baseball player, who might be among the best hitters will nevertheless have batting slumps. The coach, who might not have been a great hitter but has studied the design of the batter's swings, says, "You are turning your left shoulder a split second too early." The batter tries the new stance and finds out whether it feels right. People who are very good at what they do are usually not averse to learning how to do it better.

Notice the sequence here; it is not teacher gives and student receives. Instead, the pattern is, first, the student acts; second, the teacher studies the design; third, the teacher proposes a redesign; fourth, the student tries the redesign. This sequence can be repeated indefinitely. The student may be skeptical, probably should be skeptical, that the redesign will work. The proposed redesign may not fit this student in this place at this time. But if the new way of acting has a reasonable chance to succeed, the only way to proceed is to try it out.

All teaching-learning is by doing. What exactly is done varies according to the kind of learning at issue. The doing does not always involve a lot of bodily movement, but human action on the part of the learner is the condition of the learning. I quoted Aristotle that there is only one activity in teaching, and it is in the learner. Across the whole range of human learning, Aristotle sees a continuity of principle: "Men become builders by building and lyre players by playing the lyre; so too we become just by doing just acts, and brave by doing brave acts."[13] How this principle applies to forms of teaching in which speech is the main material will be discussed in the chapters that follow. The intimation of a solution lies here in instances where speech still functions as choreographing the body.

We learn to build by building, starting with the blocks in the infant crib. Later, the child may construct a toy house from pieces of plastic brought in a store or from branches of a tree for a secret tree house. There is design to such activities; it may be conveyed by instructions for a store-bought house or by a friend's advice on building tree houses. If the toy or machine comes with printed "instructions," the teaching is very limited. If a living teacher provides "instruction," then the teaching has more opportunity for successful redesign.

The term "instruction" has a central place in the history of teaching. Its directedness worries those who are concerned for the freedom of the learner. However, simply moving away from clarity, precision, and directedness is not the way to liberation. Those who wish to learn usually need some instruction. If the instruction is precisely directed at the element of the skill involved, no limitation of freedom is implied. A vague choreography is not the way to teach dance; a musical score that does not indicate each part's notes is not the way to teach music.

As a person masters a skill, he or she will find ways to go beyond the instruction or to work variations within the instruction. Instruction, nevertheless, remains a highly directive act. The words of instruction are not "What would you like to do here?" but "Turn at this spot," or "Hit an A sharp."

Instruction is not equivalent to teaching. Some cases of "showing how" by human and nonhuman teachers are wordless but for trying to teach a design of human activity, words of instruction are needed. Later, I will discuss uses of speech in teaching that are not bodily instruction; but even in these cases there is instruction of another kind.

58

Trust is indispensable in human acts of teaching. The one who commands, "Turn now," must be trusted. This relation of trust is a precondition of the act of teaching rather than an element of the teaching act itself. At the moment of instruction, there is usually no time to think, Do I trust this person?[14] Within a context of trust, the learner can concentrate on following the instructions in careful detail. The teacher's concentration is on speaking clearly and simply, with the instruction directed to that precise point at which the design of the situation becomes a redesign.

Bodily instruction is where human learners are closest to nonhuman learners ("sit ... bark ... good dog"). Instruction within a rich human context is not demeaning; the choreographed instruction for the body will lead into other uses of speech. With very young children, crisp, clear instruction is a necessity. Even though the commands to a two-year-old sound like animal training ("sit ... watch out... good boy"), the meaning of instruction is within a context of human dialogue.

Take the case of a child learning to walk. Who teaches the child to do that? A plausible answer is that the entire human race does so. Walking on two legs is an extraordinary act, as every nonhuman animal knows. It is not quite natural, and the human's lower back often agrees with the other animals. A young child comes to this strange activity because other humans have designed the environment that way. If you wish to run with the humans, you first must learn to walk.

Most parents have a vivid memory of the exact moment when the infant's ontogeny recapitulated thousands of years of human phylogeny, that is, the child took a first step. A physically safe atmosphere was guaranteed by a trusted parent and perhaps a small, encouraging entourage. The infant, who had been crawling and who has now stood with the aid of furniture, lets go. The only adult instruction may be, "Come to

Mommy." Along with the design of outstretched arms, the words can be a bridge between the fear of falling and the accomplishment of walking. After the child has fallen a few times, a teacher may be able to give it a little more physical or oral instruction. Before there can be that redesign, the child must get up and walk according to the design it responds to, a design that evolution and millions of choices have prepared for today's child.

Some Extended Examples

The appropriate design of this chapter is to finish with some extended examples. I will offer three of my own, after I first call attention to the description of teaching by design, which is found in an essay entitled, "Skiing as a Model of Instruction."[15] The authors break down the complex act of skiing into "microworlds," by which they mean a task that can be performed successfully as a simple version of the whole activity. They identify three elements of a microworld that can be manipulated by the teacher: equipment, physical setting, and task specification.

The teaching of skiing dramatically improved as these elements have been recognized and manipulated. For example, short skis and safety bindings give the novice skier a better chance of succeeding. The instructor must choose snow conditions that are appropriate for each stage of learning. A downhill slope that feeds into an uphill path helps the beginner to learn how to stop. And the skiing coach must be precise in specifying the action.

The authors distinguish between "executable" commands and "observable" commands. The teacher must know exactly what to command as an action. It is useless to tell beginners, "Shift your weight," to the right if they do not yet know where their weight is.

The authors are interested in generalizing from their example to other examples of teaching. They develop a theory of "increasingly complex microworlds" in which the learner faces difficult challenges but also experiences success.

In the examples that follow, I start with experiences that are more universal and less complex than skiing. Despite the increased popularity of skiing, it will probably never be encountered by most people. And I am not interested in developing a technical vocabulary in these examples, but instead keeping the description as close as possible to ordinary speech.

These descriptions must be somewhat extended to convey the flavor of the details. The design exists only with details. Each example has its own unique constellation of detail and requires a separate description. But as a line of T. S. Eliot has it, "Each case is unique; and similar to the others." Each act of teaching requires attention to all the details of the situation. It is in the particularity of human situations that we best glimpse a universal human condition.

The description of teaching by design should include crucial details but not all details. When we watch a great athlete, musician, carpenter, or painter at work, and we ask, "How do you do that?" we are asking for instructional detail. The accomplished person who says, "I don't know, I have never thought about explaining it," is of little help as a teacher.

In contrast, a "reflective practitioner" can pick out some crucial steps. We get impatient with the explanation because we know that there is much more. However, we would not be able to absorb an exhaustive explanation of the process. So perhaps the teacher is providing more than we think he or she is doing in a sketched-out design.[16]

The three examples I have chosen are teaching a person to swim, to cook, and to use a computer. Each of these examples involves bodily movement in a context of human response. The instructive element is clear in each case, the physical movement becomes a lesser element in the learning as we go from the first to the third example.

To highlight the instructional element, I will describe teaching an adult. Children can be and are taught these three things. In the case of the child, the teaching-learning may be so smooth and effortless that the elements of teach-learn are difficult to pick out. With adults, there is likely to have developed an obstacle to the learning. A design is already fixed; the teacher's design to teach requires a careful redesign.

1. *Teaching someone to swim.*

Swimming is a natural movement, at least as natural as walking. An infant who is introduced to a body of water early in life will take to it like a fish. The water does most of the teaching, the arms and legs responding to the relation between body and water. The child does need a little instruction on breathing because a child is, in fact, not a fish. Human beings with the proper equipment can outdo fish at some of their own games. The human's nature is art; they construct such things as motorboats. However, some of the humans in these boats, who can move across the water faster than the fish, have never learned to swim.

Millions of people grow up to adulthood without learning how to swim. Given the near omnipresence of water, it seems likely that most of these people have a block to swimming. The fear of water is a cause of their not swimming while, in turn, the absence of the skill results in still more fear of water. For most adult non-swimmers, there is a clear design in the relation of their bodies to ocean, lake, or pool. When circumstances bring them into contact, the design is a lot of thrashing about without efficiency or satisfaction. Their watching an experienced swimmer teaches nothing, except frustration.

How does a teacher teach an adult non-swimmer to swim? The first step is to reduce (not likely eliminate) the feeling of threat by some careful choices: the location of the water, the absence of spectators, the shallow depth of the water, the relaxed attitude of the teacher. The learning is a simple set of physical exercises, most of which can be found in a book. The learner will never get as far as learning from a book without experiencing some beginning success and getting some feel for the whole process. That is what an effective teacher on the scene must make possible and convey.

The adult non-swimmer is puzzled at the phenomenon of floating. Such an individual, fearful of sinking, will lift his or her head to be sure of not sinking, which is a sure prescription for sinking. The teacher has to say, "Tilt your head back" and "Relax." Often when we tell someone to relax, it has the opposite effect; the person tenses up in an effort to relax. The non-swimmer has never once relaxed in the water. One command to relax will not work, but the presence of a trusted teacher and the accustoming of oneself to an all-water environment can over time bring the beginning of relaxation.

When that point is reached, then floating on one's back or moving under water produces a moment of victory. A voice will for the first time come up out of the center of one's being: The water is not the enemy. From that point onward, instead of fighting the water, the potential swimmer starts to learn from the water and how it interacts with the body.[17]

After running the learner through a sequence of drills, the teacher's job becomes one of watching the design and suggesting small redesigns. The action is all in the learner; the learning is all in the practice. Small things will be discovered in the doing; they may be small, but if relevant to this learner they can be crucial. Two people do not have the same arm movement, kick, or breathing. A good teacher spots some of these particularities and proposes adjustments. The learner is the final judge of whether any redesign is effective.

2. *Teaching someone to cook.*

The act of cooking is perhaps as universal as the act of swimming. Anyone growing up to adulthood, one might expect, would learn to cook reasonably well. One learns to cook by growing up in a cooking community; that seems to apply to just about everyone. Cooking brings us a step beyond our animal capacity to swim. Cooking is a specifically human art that is unknown among other animals.

If a person gets to adulthood without learning even the rudiments of cooking, a block must have developed early in life. Like the non-swimmer shying from water, the non-cook shies from the kitchen as a place of fear and intimidation. In this case, the block to learning has been reinforced by a cultural assumption.

At least until recently, much of the culture conveyed the impression to little boys that they need not cook because someone will cook for them. The culture has shifted rapidly on the point. The present generation of adult men may be an unusual case study in learning to cook. Men who were told a few decades ago that women do the cooking for men now find that this principle does not hold. Tens of millions of men are ill-nourished because they do not cook, and eventually McDonald's and Wendy's blur into a boring chore.

As with the non-swimmer, much of the attention must be directed to overcoming the initial block to cooking. Once the fear is dispelled, then learning to cook is largely a matter of following a few simple directions. If you can read, you can cook. But a lot of people cannot in fact read a cookbook because they have not been initiated into that language. For that initiation, one usually needs a trusted friend or family member who shows the learner exactly what to do, and temporarily acts as translator of the cookbook.

I have said that the attempt to teach by design always leads to a redesign of an existing relation between human organism and environment. Like the non-swimmer, the non-cook may try to avoid the scene of the mysterious power, but he or she still has a thrashing about relation to cooking. The person may not recognize any existing relation but the usual strength to build on is the ability to recognize a well-cooked meal. The person who can do that much is already on the way. In addition, nearly everyone has experiences, at least from childhood, of licking a spoon, watching someone prepare ingredients, or having to scrub a pan.

The person intimidated by the thought of cooking needs to experience some immediate success, like the non-swimmer learning to float. Few people have the talent and the staying power to become great cooks; but everyone has the ability and should get the help to treat food with the appreciative preparation it deserves. For the learner of cooking, someone has to say, "Do this, do this, do this," and the result is a success.

The trick here, as usual, is to contemplate the whole pattern of potential cook, uncooked food, and situation. Reducing the threat level is crucial, perhaps by the barring of spectators; that scene prepares the way for direct commands. Artists of the kitchen, like other artists, are sometimes poor teachers because they cannot state the design in enough detail or are impatient when asked to articulate it. The very good cook may inspire a desire to learn but it is often an inexpert cook who has the feel of what it is like to be bewildered by recipe language and confused by the stove.

The expert cook is liable to end an instruction by saying, Add a small amount of tomato paste, and some parboiled noodles. Make sure the oven is hot. Bake it until it looks done." The not-so-expert cook, who understands teaching, might end the same instruction, "Add a tablespoon (the big one) of tomato paste (the small can, not the sauce); add a cup of noodles that you have put in boiling water for five minutes; bake the mixture (that is, put it in the oven) with the temperature dial turned to 350 degrees; take it out after 45 minutes."

The trust between teacher and student will indicate whether these points would seem either helpful or condescending. In any case, every question by the learner should be allowed without he or she feeling stupid. A cardinal rule of teaching-learning is that no question that is asked in good faith is a stupid question. Once a basic confidence has been gained, the learner does much of the teaching, filling in details of the design, experimenting, and occasionally making mistakes. Tips from friends, the cookbook, and perhaps a television show become one's continuing teachers.

3. *Teaching someone to use a computer.*
The human use of computers carries us far beyond the other animals. The very idea of the computer is a work of human genius, and the construction of computers and their gradual miniaturization has been a marvel to behold. Computers in the home have rapidly spread by the tens of millions.

The principle, once again, is that we learn by growing up in a community where the quality or skill is taught by its practice. The way to learn computers is to grow up in a computing community. For many children, this condition has become a reality. With computers, however, there is human instruction that goes beyond that of swimming or cooking. I am interested in the start of that instruction. For many children the beginning is the "natural" step of playing around with pieces of

66

technology. With just a little coaching, the child can get inside the game and continue to learn from books, friends, and simple trial and error. One can meet three-year-olds working their phones.

The case may be very different for individuals in a present generation of adults. Only a few decades ago, computers and smart phones seemed to have nothing to do with personal life. Then, almost overnight, they inundated the world, much to the terror of many fifty- and sixty-year-olds. The longer the adults wait to confront the machine, the more intimidating it appears. The situation becomes embarrassing when one does not have the language to ask an intelligent question. If one is a university professor, it is humbling to be upstaged by the 17-year-olds in the computer store or one's 8-year-old daughter.

Is it like understanding cookbooks: if you can read, you can text message? Perhaps, although reading in this case is a more complicated affair. Books on computers might be an exuberant playground for those who already know how to use the machine. A manual might contain some simple and effective drills that must be practiced. However, one first needs entrance into this world.

The steps parallel the other two cases, starting with a trusted friend who is often not a computer expert, but someone who knows how to do things with the machine and knows how to break the learning into manageable parts. The environment must be one that reduces the threat level; no spectators are allowed. Every question must be allowed even the most naive. The teacher must "show how," by providing a few crisp, clear commands of what to do first, second, and third. How computers work is material for another time but is a distraction for the person who wants to learn to use the machine.

The beginner wants to know what to do after putting in the

plug. The teacher has to say, "Push this button, hold down this while pressing that, and this is exactly what will appear on the screen." As with swimming and cooking, some experience of immediate success is indispensable even if untold hours of confusion and frustration follow the initial success. The teacher must see that the design has been grasped and that the learner can become the teacher of himself or herself. People on help lines need to be very good teachers who can visualize the learner sitting in front of the computer.

In summary, these three examples, as well as other examples cited earlier, exhibit the same structure. In each case, a human being is acting in a physical environment. To teach that person requires changing the existing design that relates the person's activity and the environment. Much of the effort of both teacher and learner concerns physical behavior that humans share with nonhuman animals. The language in these examples is instruction in physical movement; the words are directly correlated to those movements.

Human beings, however, have learned to use language in ways that increase their ability to learn. Words can be abstracted from the immediate relation to the body. The following three chapters describe other forms of speech used in teaching. But the underlying metaphor of design and redesign should not be forgotten: to teach is to show someone how to do something, that is, the teacher must know how to choreograph the movement of a human body. No matter how abstruse and theoretical teaching becomes, it never severs its roots from this metaphor.

Part Two

Chapter Four: Teaching with the End in View

The next three chapters comprise Part II of this book. These chapters concern the language of teaching when the verbal part of teaching goes beyond the choreographing of bodily movement. In this case, human language can be examined as a movement. Each of these three chapters deals with what I call a "family" of languages that are used in teaching.[1] The teacher is still concerned with choreographing movement but now considers speech as what is designed and what is to be redesigned.

The moral problem of teaching becomes evident at this juncture, where speech emerges from the body and takes on a life of its own. When a child says, "Teach me to swim," the presenting of the body is evidence for receptiveness to the skill. But when a would-be teacher walks into a room and sees a group of people sitting there, the situation does not provide clear evidence of what, if anything, they are prepared, to learn.

Before anyone opens his or her mouth to teach with words, the question must be asked: Why are these people sitting here? Perhaps in some settings the answer may seem obvious. If they are sitting in a movie theater, they wish to see a film; if at a press conference, they expect a government briefing. The question nonetheless needs to be asked on every occasion. A main reason for a moral problem to exist with teaching is that an inappropriate form of speech is used for the occasion. The teacher must ask, what license do I have from these people? What form of speech is therefore appropriate and justified in this setting?

In response to these questions, chapters four and five form a contrasting pair. The contrast is based upon a difference in relation to the end of teaching, that is, whether the teacher has an end in view. The discussion up to this point, has concentrated on situations where intention and its accompanying speech are embedded in bodily movement. As speech takes on a life of its own distinct from the body, the individual can conceive of ends that move beyond immediate physical behavior to future ends. The emergence of such ends, and the language accompanying them, is the great glory of humans. These ends are also the source of humanity's terrible delusions and violent outbursts.

This chapter is about the language of teaching when the end of the teaching is in view. John Dewey uses the phrase "end-in-view" as a human guide for action, an end that can be seen and talked about.[2] The human mind can conceive of a good that it wishes to reach (for example, an increase in salary or improved health) and a teacher can have the task of showing how to get from here to there. A danger ever present is that the end in view can be misconceived as being the ultimate good in life. This danger is offset by the languages in chapter five – teaching when the end is not in view. These two sets of languages can be held together in a healthy tension. When one set acts as corrective to the other, both can be effective and moral acts of teaching. When they are radically split apart, each set is the sign of a human weakness that corrupts teaching.

Since the two sets of languages are so wedded, the case could be made either for the present order of the chapters or the reverse order. Depending on circumstances, for example, the age of the learner, one set may take precedence over the other. In actual practice, over a long period of time, each one succeeds the other.

The languages of chapter five, removing obstacles to achieve an end, might seem to have an obvious priority. Doesn't a person first have to remove obstacles, such as fear or rage, before proceeding toward the end that is seen and desired. In fact, however, people usually discover the obstacles only through their efforts to reach an end in view. I start with the first set both to describe its powerful possibilities and to note its limitations and the need for other languages. In that context, the set of languages described in chapter five has a better chance of being recognized as teaching at all.

Given that there are hundreds of names and dozens of classification systems, any choice of languages is bound to be somewhat arbitrary. The absence of a language being named does not necessarily mean that it is unimportant; it may simply fall within a different way of classifying languages and therefore cut across the names I have chosen. For example, is poetic language a language of teaching? If poetic is the alternative to prosaic, then I would hope for a poetic quality to the examples that follow. If, however, the reference is to poems or poetry, then there are several places in the over-all description where poetry (or a novel, a short story, or a play), can be an example, and I will indicate some of those spots.

Along a different line, someone might note the absence of "political speech." If the alternative is apolitical speech, then most of the languages in this chapter are political. However, if what is meant are the speeches of politicians or the discussions of political science, then these forms could be included in several places. Something similar could be said about aesthetic speech, ethical speech, or religious speech; they are too important to be embodied in just one of the forms that I describe.

A Community Activity

The first family of languages, described in this chapter, arises from a community existence. Every community has a set of beliefs. The languages of the family described here are intended to persuade people to act on those beliefs. The

72

element of command or directive makes this set of languages resemble the choreography of the body. The difference is that the commanding is directed toward the beliefs of the community, rather than toward the body. "We say we believe in the good of children; it follows that we should provide childcare facilities."

This family of languages is intended to persuade the community. The ancient meaning of "rhetorical" captured the intent of this family of languages. Wayne Booth, describing this meaning of "rhetoric," says it "was practiced when the first mother or father went beyond simple caressing or physical restraint and managed to convey, in sound or picture or sign language, 'No, because ... ' with a reason not present to the senses at the moment."[3]

The teacher in this situation steps forward before the community or, better, steps into the center of the community. The person can be elected, appointed, ordained, chosen by lot, licensed by some trusted group, or be biologically responsible. But this temporary assignment of "teacher" should not mean that some people are teachers and the other people are not. A group of people who claim to be a community must consider as an important criterion of community, "Is every member of the group in some way and at some time a teacher of all the rest"? If only a small number of people are recognized as teaching, then the likelihood of a mutuality of persons – the hallmark of community – is greatly diminished.

Most groups, whether political, social, religious or familial, tend to segregate the term teacher for a few people. It then becomes the task of these few to keep turning "to teach" back to the whole community. If other persuasion is to be effective, persuasion as to who are the teachers cannot be overlooked. To teach is to show someone how to live; living as a human being includes the activity of teaching. We know a man for a poet by the fact that he makes us poets. We know a person as a teacher by the fact that he or she makes us teachers.

A teacher in and for the community taps into the memory of the community. The beliefs that are consciously held are a result of a long process of community formation. The process includes forgetting as well as remembering; no set of beliefs can capture the community's most valuable experiences. A teacher with the end in view is someone who can retrieve what underlies community belief, thereby placing the beliefs in a new configuration.

Older people in the community have a special place in this kind of teaching; they are linked by personal memory to the vital force that founds the community and provides continuing cohesion. In one sense, nothing new is added in the teaching. In another sense, everything is made new as the past is brought to consciousness in the present and everything is seen through the prism of well-articulated language.

Embodied in the community's existence is the conviction that the end is known, that is, the good that is to be attained by the group is evident. The teacher does not have the job of discovering the end or proving any scientific hypothesis about it. The teacher's task is to link the past with the end in the future so that the energies of the present are unleashed. The great teacher knows how to touch just those spots of memory so that people are moved to action. This kind of persuasive teacher needs *style*, a distinct personal way of assembling words and delivering them.

It is obvious that reliance on style can be abused. Many political and religious leaders have manipulated masses of people on style alone without substance. That problem arises when community has broken down and left the mass of individuals desperate for a leader. In a genuine community, a teacher cannot rely on a style that would be out of touch with memory, faithfulness, hopes, and convictions. The individual teacher realizes that he or she contributes only a small part in that the words arise from the community and are quickly submerged again. The teacher nonetheless seizes the moment to shape the words for their greatest effect.

The teacher tries to become one with the words that are spoken. There is little space for "critical thinking" that would raise doubts about the truthfulness of the teaching. There will be another time for self-critical reflection, but this first family of languages is concerned with speech in relation to the body's accomplishing an end. The speech is interesting, effective and practical before the question of truth is raised. Alfred North Whitehead said that the first thing to notice about a statement is whether it is interesting; truth add to its interest. Here again one can see the vulnerability of this kind of teaching to manipulators of truth and falsehood.

For the individual, the community's beliefs are prejudgments; the more common term is prejudices. Community teaching precedes the individual and encompasses the individual. An individual does not simply begin searching for knowledge and truth at the "age of reason." The young child has already absorbed a world of beliefs. He or she is a prejudiced person at the dawn of conscious awareness.

The language of the eighteenth century, which we still speak, assumes that prejudices are bad and should be replaced by rational thinking. The aim of education, according to these writers, is to free the child from the prejudices of the father. But if community is to be allowed a place, then it cannot be assumed that all the beliefs of the community are wrong. Some of what has been provided to the child may prove to be true. Every prejudice should be subjected to examination.

Hans-Georg Gadamer distinguished between blind prejudice and justified prejudice.[4] We cannot get rid of blind prejudice until we accept that everyone has prejudices and that we test each of them for truth or falsehood. "The fundamental prejudice of the Enlightenment," writes Gadamer, "was the prejudice against prejudice." This prejudice that each individual should shed all the prejudices that he or she has and invent the world with his or her own reasoning took deep roots in our culture.

Because of this prejudice against prejudice, some comments are needed on whether all the languages in this chapter are for the purpose of "indoctrination." One route of defense for prejudice would be to distinguish two meanings of "indoctrination." What Gadamer does with "prejudice" could be tried with "indoctrination." Leszek Kolokowski is one thinker who endorses indoctrination as educationally defensible. He even writes that indoctrination "is included in the acquisition of language itself....Hence, education without indoctrination is noneducation."[5]

I do not think Kolakowski faces up to the totally negative connotation that the term "indoctrination" has. While there is some foothold for resistance with "prejudice" (and its close relative, "discrimination"), neither history nor contemporary usage offers a realistic basis for what Kolakowski tries to do. I think one must start with a premise opposite to his, namely, education with indoctrination is noneducation. The family of languages that presupposes a community and an end in view is not indoctrination.

Successful indoctrination results in a person so attached to one version of reality that multiple perspectives, ambiguity in language, and the ability to stand at a distance from one's own beliefs have been eliminated. I cannot deny that a use of the first family of languages could lead to indoctrination. The only sure prevention is an effective presence of the other two families of language.

What the parents and community show to a child is a way of life to which the child responds in his or her own way. Since the community's way of life is bounded by definite beliefs, the child's unique response is within definite limits. Someday those limits must be confronted and in one way or another transcended. But first a world with limits of some kind must be absorbed.

Language, which exists in particular and limited form, is a gift that the child appropriates. Being able to speak a language makes possible a human encounter with all reality. Each form of language has its own restrictions and disadvantages. For example, if you wish to speak French in life, you would best be born in France. If you wish to speak English as a second language, it helps to be born in Sweden rather than in Finland. That is just the luck of the draw in every childhood; Finns have their own advantages. Learning any language does not cut off the possibility of multiple perspectives and self-critical distance.

The testing of the community's prejudices takes place over a long period of time and is finally measured by how the small community contributes to the human community. One belief of the community may seem to be irrational, but that single belief may derive its intelligibility from its connection to a complex set of beliefs that has its own human logic. The teacher must be able to comprehend not only the individual beliefs of the community but the connection among them.

The child for its part grasps a pattern or structure of belief. For a child, there must be some kind of world order that provides the security of knowing that someone understands all these confusing pieces and that a benevolent force rules all. The child will fight fiercely for the truth of some propositions because their denial would unravel the fabric of the established world.

The problems of blind prejudice and indoctrination arise when the mind that was proper to a young child resides in an older child or an adult. In this case, the truth is still dependent on the opinion of a powerful person; the adult has not really acquired any beliefs as his or her own. The beliefs have been delivered and accepted. Unless something else happens to the beliefs, they will gradually become more rigid. Paradoxically, they also become more fragile in relation to the external world and therefore in need of greater and greater defense.

The child who is more fortunate is gradually exposed to a plurality of views. There are few places in the world today where plurality is absent. Too much plurality too soon could overwhelm the child and lead to a withdrawal from plurality. Parents and other teachers of the young must gauge the amount of diversity that a child can handle. The child need not be exposed to hundreds of viewpoints on every subject. A good beginning would be two points of view.

For a child beyond age six, or possibly a little younger, the teacher must convey these two viewpoints: the view that what the teacher is providing is true and the acknowledgment that another truthful view is possible. This "other view" may turn out to be a dozen or a hundred. With the help of other teachers. including the learner as teacher, the learner can continually reshape the overall perception that he or she has of the world.

There are crucial moments in the lives of individuals when the mind breaks through to the recognition that to live according to the truth which one knows does not require attacking others who have a different view. Not all teachers, including college professors, have themselves reached this position. A repressive form of teaching might be perpetuated over generations. The fortunate thing is that one need not have been taught only by great teachers. In fact, if a person meets just one or two good teachers in life, that might be enough to break through blind prejudice to receptive listening, respect for others, and an intelligent grasp of complex issues.

It will be helpful to consider three examples of teaching with the end in view: telling stories, delivering a lecture, and preaching a sermon.

Storytelling

The first representative of this rhetorical family is teaching by storytelling. My intention here is to use a term that can encompass all sorts of oral and literary forms that are siblings within this family. Storytelling extends from a   mother telling the tale of "Three Little Pigs Went to Market" to the case of an historian trying to recount the rise and fall of civilizations. What links the many forms of storytelling is a presumed community that has some end in view. Stories at their best do not reduce the end to a simple termination point. The end should be a complex image or metaphor that not only allows but invites a filling in of details.

Storytelling is a universal human trait. It would be difficult to imagine human lives that do not involve the recounting of tales both for entertainment and instruction. As far back as we can investigate, humans have been telling stories. Earlier and simpler cultures show clear evidence of storytelling as a central fact of life. In the contemporary world, people do not sit around a campfire telling stories, but they might sit around the television watching a 'reality" show. Whether this difference shows progress is questionable. But storytelling certainly does exist in the present in hundreds of forms.

The parent's way of communicating with the small child is largely by story. A great fund of children's stories has been

79

built up throughout history. Some of the best stories are the oldest; they have been tested over time. The "end" they offer is not a moralistic message about good behavior but a complex image of good and evil. Often when people try to invent new tales for children the moral is too obvious, and the children see through it. Richly textured stories can be engaged at many levels and allow the listener to take whatever he or she is ready to take, A good children's story is one that adults can also enjoy.

A good story needs little or no explanation; the teaching is in the telling. The Australian historian Manning Clark, while writing of his own work, could also be describing children's stories: "All the great stories of mankind are told without any comment at all. Perhaps that is why they have outlived their generation and said something to men at all times and places."[6] Clark goes on to say of these stories, "They make us explicitly aware of what we had vaguely noticed before of what life is like, of what will happen to us if in our folly or in some mad passion we defy the wisdom of humanity."

Traditional fairytales deal with the great cosmic struggle of good and evil. The storyline often has frightening elements of child kidnapping, vicious stepmothers, threats of murder, and cannibalism. Adults usually wish to protect children from encountering such horrors. However, if something can be told as a story it becomes bearable, and an artistic story well told is educational. The inner fears of the child find expression in a story of what happened in a land far, far away. The story comes to a resolution and the people live happily ever after. This end is, in fact, an invitation to imagine what follows the crisis described in the story.

Starting in childhood and continuing throughout life, people adopt storylines with grand designs of where "my people" came from and what we are going toward. It is not an accident that the term "myth" has a double meaning: a story of foundations and a story that is false.

We know that the great epic myths that tell of the origin of the world, the human race, or the nation involve fanciful details. But at some level below factual accuracy, the great stories of the Book of Genesis, the Iliad, or the Bhagavad Gita provide insight into the human story. Northrop Frye, referring to *Macbeth*, says, "If you wish to know the history of eleventh-century Scotland, look elsewhere; if you wish to know what it means to gain a kingdom and lose one's soul, look here.["7]

The master stories of the human race or the nation do not always get told directly or explicitly. They may be so thoroughly woven into the texture of ordinary life that the lesser stories are constantly reaffirming them. For example, the master story of the United States is America. From the time of its invention in 1507, "America" has been the name of a great myth, the story of the promised land and the chosen people. The artificially constructed nation known as the United States has from the beginning identified itself with the dream, the ideal, or the myth of America.

So successful has the identification been that people throughout the world use "United States" and "America" interchangeably. Even more forceful is the name "American" for U.S. citizens. Almost every other sentence spoken in the United States reaffirms the story of America, the promised land of freedom, justice, and wealth. U.S. people find it nearly impossible to distinguish between their country and a myth about their country.

The United States is not alone in having a myth to hold it together. This country is a dramatic example because its nationhood is so precarious. The modem world with its nationalism practically requires that people have a myth of origins, greatness and unity. Each European nation has a myth about its origin. An old European saying is that "a nation is a group of people united by a common error concerning their ancestry and a shared hostility to their neighbor." A European Union has struggled because everyone knows it was born out of practicality, it is vulnerable to nations deciding that the greatness of their own nationhood takes precedence.

Master stories of religion shape the lives of billions of people. Many of them may not know the story, they may even wish to reject the story, but the stories exist and have overwhelming power. These stories, while inevitable, are not all to the good. Storytelling is often romanticized in uncritical ways. As I have said of this whole family of languages the only protection against their possibly corruptive influence is the presence of other families. Especially needed is academic criticism of the story when it envelops nations or ethnic, religious, and racial groups.

At the everyday level, storytelling takes up much of life. Like Moliere's Monsieur Jourdain, who was unaware he had been speaking prose, we often do not reflect on the narrative character of ordinary conversation.[8] These brief and often fragmented stories are a continuous form of teaching.

For example, consider gossip. Almost no one would be proud of being called a gossip and yet practically everyone deals in it. Gossip should perhaps have a better reputation than it has. When the gossip because malicious, then it needs restraint or criticism. But condemning gossip itself has little effect. As in telling jokes, it is a way of testing out the self in relation to the fabric of community existence.[9]

Among literary forms, consider the mystery or crime story. It is usually not praised as a literary genre It can be a real potboiler where the only point is to get to the end of the story.

It can also be the textured writing of a P. D. James. Reading such stories gives people a sense of order in the universe. One is comforted by the fact that by page 250, the inspector will have solved the mystery and a balance of justice will be restored in the world.

Everyone knows that the world is not so completely ordered, but that does not lessen our need to discover, affirm, or create order in parts of our world. For some people, to be engrossed in light fiction is a guilty pleasure for four hours on a plane or an afternoon on the beach. But light fiction or gossipy conversation is better teaching than sensationalistic television or twitter feeds where the English language is abused.

Those people who are blessed with native talent and a solid education can have their lives sustained by richer, more complex stories. Most of the teachings of great philosophers and religious figures exist in the form of stories. Plato's myth of the cave or Jesus' parable of the Prodigal Son never lose their force for those who are willing to enter the story. In the Jewish tradition, the process of *midrash* goes on today, story about story layered throughout the centuries. Biographies and autobiographies, short stories and novels can become lifelong teachers.

At their best, television and film can be a lively complement to written and oral speech. The evidence of seventy-five years suggests that television is good at two things: soap opera and "live" talk of the day's news, sports, or weather. Television, together with the Internet, is the single greatest potential for educational reform in the present era. Whether that potential is ever realized, and despite the dreary lineup of most evenings on commercial television and the inanity of most twitter feeds, television and the Internet are now the background to most human conversation.

Probably for the first time in human history there is worldwide storytelling, some of it malicious, some of it inspiring. Television and the Internet enable the verbal and nonverbal art of one people to appear in a living room or on a person's phone anywhere in the world. The eighteenth-century's conception of "humanity" is being filled out with something more than a few white men and their romantic notions of what they supposed primitive people to be.

The film industry, especially in the United States, has a profound effect in shaping the culture. Even people who do not go to the movies live in the environment of the world on film and videos. Along with contemporary music, film has become an international language. There is danger in too much of the language coming from one place on the globe which exports fluffy narrative and orgies of violence.

Movies today, just as in the 1930s and 1940s, run the gamut from truly awful to spectacularly good. The same could be said of eighteenth- and nineteenth-century novels. We have a few hundred masterpieces from the thousands of pieces that were read and tossed aside like today's tabloids. Teaching by story involves not just the profound side of human nature, but the mundane side as well.[11]

Perhaps the greatest difference between today's stories and the traditional novel of the nineteenth century is the disappearance of the omniscient narrator. The result is a voice or voices from within the story giving us a fragment of life. There is an absence of trust in someone telling us the whole story and where it all leads. "We trust only the voice of the witness," as William Styron said.

Much of modern fiction, poetry, and drama gives up all instructional tendency and mirrors the confusions and uncertainties of a world in which neither divine nor human intelligence is felt to be in charge. The term "story" has not disappeared. People cling to plot lines even in fragmented form to get them to next year or next week. But more than ever, other forms of language are needed to complement storytelling. Neatly plotted master stories are too rich for many bewildered people. Other languages of teaching need to complement and sometimes precede storytelling.

Lecturing

The second language in the family of rhetorical persuasion is the lecture, a term that means "reading." It usually refers to a kind of reading with an instructive or didactic purpose. A standard approach of authors who teach in universities is to attack the dominance of lecturing and then go right back to using the term for the language of university teaching.[12] A whole set of jokes exists for describing lectures; for example, the lecturer is someone who talks in someone else's sleep; or a lecture is what goes from the teacher's notes to the student's notes without passing through the head of either.

In this section, I wish to take the opposite approach from one that ridicules lecturing as a form and then resignedly accepts its use in the classroom. I think that lecturing is to be affirmed and valued as a form of teaching, but I also think it is unacceptable as a form of classroom instruction. It is a scandal for professors and ex-professors to ridicule lecturing; on the other hand, I think universities cannot examine teaching in their classrooms until they remove "lecture" from center stage.

In a book on university teaching, Kenneth Elbe begins the chapter entitled "Lecturing" by saying, "The best general advice to the teacher who would lecture well is still, 'Don't do it'."[10] Eble does not take his own advice, proceeding to discuss the use of lecturing in the university classroom. On the persistence of the lecture form, Eble says, "As has been pointed out countless times, the lecture was outmoded by the invention of printing and by cheap and easy access to printed works."[11] He then expresses at least partial disagreement with this statement by saying that the book did not sweep out lecturing "for the simple reason that human beings remain responsive to all forms of intercourse with other consenting humans."[14] Although I agree with this conclusion, it does little to match this form of intercourse with the appropriate setting.

When a university installs a person in a chair, the occasion is often marked by an "inaugural lecture." Such a lecture is appropriate so long as it is understood to be an inauguration of the professor to his or her colleagues and not the beginning of the daily work in the classroom.

Lecturing is a highly ritualized act in which a person addresses a community; the end that the lecture has in view is some rational aspect of human affairs. Far from becoming outdated in the seventeenth century, lecturing began to come fully into its own at that time. The spread of books and book learning is the lecture's precondition not its competitor. What has happened in the twentieth and twenty-first centuries is a fragmenting of the cultural assumptions of book learning. Books and lectures have by no means disappeared, but they need complementing in the contemporary diet.

For the lecture to be an appropriate form, a whole set of conditions must come together A person engaged in reading from an easily available book is not a very effective form of teaching. A person reading notes that he or she has taken from easily available books does not make much sense, either. However, an author reading his or her own words, especially if done with dramatic style, can sometimes be effective teaching.

For teaching by lecture, the speaker needs a ritualized setting. The listeners need to be capable of appreciating well-written prose delivered in a forceful style. The author needs to speak words that come from the depth of the self. The aim of a lecture is to change, however imperceptibly, the listener's actions as a human being. A lecture to a three-year-old is pointless; for a seven-year-old, a lecture of one minute might sometimes be called for. Listening to a thirty or a fifty-minute lecture is something most of us are ready for only a few times a year. And most of us are ready to deliver a lecture even less frequently.

Some people have a responsibility to give a lecture on a regular basis. A U.S. president is expected to deliver a State of the Union address each year. Such an occasion should provide an example of careful preparation, clear presentation, and reflective response. It deserves an audience of both Houses of Congress and other important government officials. The speech is delivered in a historic setting. The televising of the event to millions of homes need not interfere with and can enhance the ritualizing of the event. In recent years, the State of the Union lecture has been marred by highly partisan applause after every paragraph. A lecture should usually be heard in thoughtful silence.

Neither a U.S. president nor anyone else can churn out lectures daily, weekly, or even monthly. The practices of the election campaign tend to subvert the idea of the thoughtful speech in a ritual setting. Television often adds to the destruction of lecturing because the presence of the camera becomes the excuse to produce thirty seconds of clever attack. Television becomes both cause and devourer of such speech.

Two examples of teaching by lecture.
On June 4, 1947, George C. Marshall delivered one of the great lectures in United States history at Harvard University. Europe was lying in ruins while the United States and the Soviet Union were entering a forty-year cold war. Some of the military wanted

a quick strike at the enemy; most of the country just wanted to withdraw to its own business.

Marshall went up against both attitudes. In the space of just a few hundred words he profoundly changed the decade that followed. He soberly laid out the picture: "The truth of the matter is that Europe's requirements for the next three or four years of foreign food and other essential products – principally from America – are so much greater than her present ability to pay that she must have additional substantial help or face economic, social, and political deterioration of a very grave character."[12] Marshall was appealing to the United States' own interests while asking for help for Europe. The premise was the good of humanity.

My second example is a speech that Vaclav Havel gave in Washington, D.C., in February 1990.[16] He addressed the Congress of the United States from the well of the House. The politicians, I suspect, were startled by his taking out a yellow pad on which he had written his speech. The lecture had immediate urgency for the several hundred people present. Its appeal, however, was to reasonable men and women everywhere. Havel had spent a good part of his adult life in prison, thanks to Soviet officials. Yet here he was urging Congress to give aid to the former Soviet peoples.

Havel's lecture had all the marks that have been cited for teaching by the form of lecture: the ritual setting, the personal involvement in the message, the carefully crafted words, the appeal to rational order. He was appealing to the self-interest of his hearers, but the ultimate basis of his speech was his own humanism.

The only thing he may have lacked was a sufficiently thoughtful audience. His speech did not succeed in its immediate mission to provide economic aid. On a larger scale of political history, however, the lecture may have given a ray of hope within a depressing world of ordinary wheeling and dealing. Clement Atlee said of Winston Churchill in 1945, "Words at great moments of history are deeds." One could extend that comment and say that great words at any time are deeds. At great moments of history, the deedful quality of careful speech is powerfully demonstrated.[13]

Preaching

Only a thin line divides presenting a lecture and preaching a sermon. In their immediate tasks, the lectures by George Marshall and Vaclav Havel could be called sermons. When politics becomes partisan, when the speech is a rousing call to action directed to the loyal faithful, then politics is more sermon than lecture.

Preaching a sermon is an activity closely identified with the Christian Church, and understandably so. The church developed the sermon into an art form. In the fourth century, John Chrysostom ("golden mouth") complained that the congregation expected a performance in church that was proper to the theater. But Chrysostom himself expected cheering and stamping of feet; "What greater disgrace," he writes, "than to walk from the pulpit with blank silence."[14] In the Middle Ages, some of the great rhetoric of the culture is found in sermons. Meister Eckhart's soaring mystical teaching is found not in his Latin treatises but in his German sermons. We have access to his teaching because nuns in the congregation copied down the sermons.[15]

Lectures are written to be read; the sermon is spoken to be heard. Christianity did not begin as a "religion of the book." It resisted literary language and used the spoken language of the day.[16] In the sixteenth-century Reformation, the call was not to read a book but to hear the word preached. Martin Luther, who wanted the church to be a "mouth house" and not a "pen house," could not have imagined how overwhelming would be the effect of the printing press. The power of the spoken word tended to be eclipsed. During the past century we have been witnessing a resurgence of the spoken word as what tips the balance of power.

In preaching, there is a text that expresses the community's beliefs. A man or woman steps forward, or steps into the center, to comment on the text. The appeal to understand does not neglect emotion and will. The intention is to move people to do something about injustices of the world. Jonathan Edwards was one of the great preachers in North American history. When Edwards preached a sermon, he was often surprised at the emotional outpouring which it sparked. The sermons were learned and intellectual, but deep knowledge, far from being opposed to feeling, is fused with it.[17] The result is that people get up from their seats and engage in political activity.

I have suggested that politicians frequently deal in preaching sermons. They often seem embarrassed by that fact; unfortunately, preachers who are embarrassed to be preachers give terrible sermons. The politician's vocation often calls not only for "discussing issues," but for moving people to action. The focus of belief is narrower than for a lecture; the end sought is more socially oriented. The Gettysburg Address, in Garry Wills's interpretation, was Lincoln's commentary on the Constitution in the light of the need to rethink equality and union. "He came to change the world, to effect an intellectual revolution. No other words could have done it. The miracle is that these words did."[18]

Often it is said that we should not preach to the converted or preach to the choir, but that is exactly the people to be preached to. Preaching to the unconverted can be both ineffective and offensive. Here we have the indoctrination charge: trying to impose a set of practices when the beliefs of a community have not been accepted by the listeners. When black preachers on the left get into politics, they are often assumed to be doing the same thing as fundamentalist preachers on the right. The usual difference is, however, that right-wing preachers preach a "Christian America" while the left wing preaches preach the Bill of Rights. To preach to U.S. people that they should live up to their Declaration and Constitution is fitting; the Americans are already converts. But a major part of the U.S. population is not Christian and does not believe in a Christian America. They should not be preached to as if they did.

Journalists in newspapers or on television are sometimes called upon to be preachers. Newspapers pride themselves for putting only facts on the front page and reporting stories with objectivity. The editorial and op-ed pages admit to opinion; most writers would prefer their essays to be called lectures rather than sermons. Nevertheless, the urge to get one's message across in 750 words often pushes the writer toward a sermon. A television reporter often has the camera's picture as the objective fact and is called to offer commentary. Most of the time the language is a form of storytelling. On occasion, the picture is so emotion-laden – in war, famine, storm, or joyful success – that any commentary becomes a small sermon on the human condition.

Journalists might be horrified by the naming of what they do as sermons. Like politicians, they might preach better if they were not embarrassed to be cast into that position. Their journalistic integrity is not compromised if they touch an emotional chord by letting their own emotions be reached when the situation is profoundly moving. No extra layer is laid upon the facts; instead, one can really grasp the facts within the context of an emotion-filled commentary on the obvious text.

Edward R. Murrow, a figure of mythic proportions in the history of radio and television, was a young reporter in London during the London blitz. His evening reports to the United

States stirred a whole nation. He wrote in a letter to his parents, "I remember you once wanted me to be a preacher, but I had no faith, except in myself. But now I am preaching from a powerful pulpit. Often, I am wrong, but I am trying to talk as I would have talked were I a preacher. One need not wear a reversed collar to be honest."[19]

The preacher can and should presuppose a language that has acquired rich association over years or centuries. Those who sit in front of a preacher give license to him or her to so use the language that the listener will be moved to action.[20] There is necessarily a distinction between the inner language of the community and the language external to it. Community cannot exist without a language of intimacy that is not entirely comprehensible to the outsider. However, the social relation of outsider and insider need not be hostile.

A test for any preacher is to stir the hearts of the community with its intimate language while not insulting or offending outsiders. I recall going to the synagogue one evening, at the invitation of the local rabbi, to hear the great Talmudic scholar Aidan Steinsaltz. I feared that I would not be able to understand his scholarly address, but he spoke in very simple terms of what it means to be a Jew. As the only Gentile in the audience, I could only listen and understand as an outsider. He spoke the intimate language of the Jewish congregation, but he said nothing disparaging of other people. Would that all preaching were so finely tuned.

The main preaching on television is not confined to Sunday mornings. The fifteen-second commercials that blanket commercial television are expensively contrived sermons; they demand that the listener act. If one is not a member of the beer-drinking community, then Bud Lite preaching can be experienced as offensive. The assumption is made by advertisers that the listeners belong to a community that would

92

like to be rich, sexy, and powerful. Their challenge is to show and to say something that will convince the viewer that if I use this toothpaste, I will be sexually irresistible; if I buy this car, I will be judged a success in life; if I eat this cereal, I will live forever. The preaching may be very low key, if the reigning theory is that soft sell works better.

The relentless television advertisements are perhaps a symptom of what happens in a culture when storytelling, lecturing, and political preaching are ineffective. The culture becomes addicted to preaching of the worst kind while thinking it has escaped the preaching of sermons. Because the intellectual leaders do not go to church on Sunday, they believe they are not enmeshed in sermonizing.

"Preaching is not teaching, except in a church," wrote Philip Rieff to his colleagues.[21] I doubt that he really meant preaching is a form of teaching in churches, but that churches only think that preaching is teaching. Rieff's book, *Fellow Teachers*, like many tracts on politics, education, and economics, is a passionate plea that has the qualities of a sermon. Preaching can be a legitimate form of teaching in and out of church; so also preaching can be completely inappropriate in and out of church. When all the conditions are right, a sermon can be among the most powerful forms of teaching. The fact that sermons are often preached when the appropriate conditions are lacking is the reason for the negative connotations of "sermonizing" and "preachiness."

Examples of teaching by preaching:
I finish with examples of preaching from 1963 and 2015. It is not an accident that both sermons were delivered by black men. Preaching in a black church gets a response that is usually absent in white churches. There is a long history of black preaching that goes back to the days of slavery. The white men who preached to the slaves were intent on reinforcing submission. The black preacher was preaching

93

a liberation in this life and the next. The preaching was not confined to the church. There were and are corrupt black preachers who are interested in their own fame and wealth but to the extent preaching is powerful and emotional in this country, it is blacks who provide the model.

At the Washington Monument on August 28, 1963, Martin Luther King Jr. gave one of the most stirring sermons in U.S. history. The speech is almost always referred to as the "I have a dream speech." That name masks the searing indictment of the nation in most of the speech. Without the first part of the speech white people are comfortable with a black man dreaming. That is not what the sermon was. The speaker's life and words fused in a dramatic moment that could not be predicted or completely controlled. No one knew what he was going to say that day, perhaps not even he, but everyone knew that the conditions were right for a nation to be moved.

As any good preacher does, King started with a text that his hearers knew: "When the architects of our republic wrote the magnificent words of the Constitution and the Declaration of Independence, they were signing a promissory note to which every American was to fall heir. It is obvious today that America has defaulted on this promissory note insofar as her citizens of color are concerned."

The task of the preacher, after establishing the text and the failure to live by the text, is to stir the listeners to carry out the implications of what they claim is their belief: "I still have a dream. It is a dream deeply rooted in the American dream that one day this nation will rise up and live out the true meaning of its creed – we hold these truths to be self-evident, that all men are created equal." The cadence and much of the imagery were biblical, but the text was the equality promised in the founding documents of the United States.[22]

94

The second example of preaching is the speech delivered by Barack Obama in Mother Emanuel Church in Charleston, South Carolina on June 25, 2015. The congregation was reeling and in deep sorrow from having suffered a massacre by a crazed gunman a few days before. Obama's text included the Christian scripture and words of Martin Luther King, Jr. which were spoken in the shadow of a horrifying incident fifty years previous. The preacher appealed to the congregation not to give up on the "American dream."

Obama always had some of the cadence of black preaching in his speeches. I never realized why his speeches had that rhythm until this particular sermon. After each of his pauses the congregation added their voice. In most situations, such as the State of the Union Address, the voices of the audience are an interruption and distraction. In Obama's sermon, however, the preacher and his hearers were in complete synch. The words flowed in both directions between preacher and congregants. Toward the end of the speech, Obama broke into song with the hymn *Amazing Grace*. For just a moment, the audience seemed startled but then they joined in the singing. It was a perfectly natural transition and conclusion.

Conclusion

The teaching languages described in this chapter presuppose a precise set of conditions. There must be present a community receptive to the power of language. Someone from the group is prepared to teach and is accepted for the occasion as teacher. The story is told, the lecture is delivered, the sermon is preached. How the teacher uses the language is as important as what is said. Often, no new information is conveyed; the text is likely to be quite familiar. But the individual, as part of the group, gets a firmer grasp on the good to be attained and is inspired to surmount the obstacles to its achievement. To teach in this first instance is to move people to act by appealing to the understanding of the beliefs of their community, one which is representative of the whole human community.

Chapter Five: Teaching to Remove Obstacles

This chapter, starting with the title, is the most paradoxical one in the book. Can we remove obstacles by teaching? Why should we be trying to do so? What obstacles need removing? The answers to such questions involve some strange twists of language and a refusal to accept things as they first appear. The forms of language described in this chapter may seem to have nothing to do with the act of teaching. Nevertheless, these languages in their proper setting are needed to show someone how to live and how to die.

In recent centuries, teaching has been closely connected to the first family of languages described in chapter four. That is, to teach has been identified with "to tell" and "to explain." I described within this family three representative forms: storytelling, lecturing, and preaching. The first and third tend to collapse into the middle. Storytelling is thought to be a helpful softening up for rational analysis, while preaching is anathematized as the opposite of teaching. What remains is lecturing, stripped of its ritual. Teaching becomes telling people the truth backed up by empirical facts and logical reasoning.

For several centuries, the hope existed that the success of the scientific method would eventually solve the problem of teaching. Explanations could be logically arranged in books and lecture notes. A reasonable person, by reading books and lectures, would acquire the knowledge to achieve the aim of education and the aim itself seemed clear: the autonomous individual.

Total confidence in reason and scientific knowledge has been slipping away throughout the past century. From a few artists and philosophers who were skeptical of science's capacity to carry the burden of life's teaching, the attack today is from all sides. The ideal of the "rational man" is charged with being sexist, apolitical, unfeeling, class biased, and more. In response to such criticism, the lecturer may try to incorporate the narrative texture of storytelling or the passion of preaching into the lecture. The real problem, however, is the absence of the clear end to teaching. And yet the dominance of lecturing is so complete that it remains in place even when its purpose no longer seems to exist.

The argument of this chapter is that the explanatory lecture needs help not only from other family members but from another family of languages. Unfortunately, this family has suffered an almost total eclipse in discussions of teaching. Far more than the first family, this collection of languages requires ritual, that is, social patterns that continue from one generation to the next.

Modern times have been hard on the traditional rituals that surround birth, courtship, marriage, family life, religion, and death. Important rituals cannot be reinvented overnight. What we need to look for are rituals of everyday life that have survived even in fragmentary form. These rituals must be nurtured and sustained as we await the slow developments of new rituals.[1]

I will refer to this second family of languages as "therapeutic." They are the languages that calm, soothe, and heal. Therapy is a central need of human life; it should be recognized as central to teaching. This second family has always been the precondition of the first. For example, if someone is distraught with fear or overcome with grief, a lecture, no matter how well ordered, is not going to succeed. Often the need for this therapeutic family becomes evident only as someone tests the limits of the first family. In whichever sequence the two sets of languages emerge, they have a complementary relation.

The perennial need for therapeutic languages has been rather suddenly enlarged. The end of life and the aim of teaching had seemed securely in place. But the scientific ideal that largely replaced classical philosophy and Christian religion was itself undermined. Science was part of its own undoing. It succeeded in getting rid of "final causes." The question now thrust upon increasing numbers of people is, how does one live in a world where no one knows the purpose of things? People still rely on science to bring them wonderful new technological gifts, but they do not accept that science can teach them how to live and how to die.

This feeling of sudden abandonment can lead to skepticism or nihilism. In the flight from all claims to know the truth, therapy can proceed to swallow every other language. People can become addicted to therapy; a whole culture can slide in that direction. In the 1960s, Philip Rieff wrote a book entitled *The Triumph of the Therapeutic*[2] The intervening decades have seemed to move further in the direction he was describing, namely, the reduction of politics, economics, and education to a massaging of the emotions.

As lecturing took over the meaning of "to teach" in the first family, the reaction against lecturing tends to be a single form of therapy: the bull session. In a classroom, the alternative to the lecture is usually assumed to be "group discussion." In these groups, whether or not anything is learned, everyone is supposed to feel better at the end for having expressed his or her opinion. With radio call-ins, television talk shows, and computer chat rooms, the whole country sometimes seems to be a bull session.

Consider once again the literature on "adult education." I noted in chapter one that if teaching is confused with big people telling little people what to think, then to teach an adult is impossible. To try to teach an adult is insulting. The alternative is taken to be adults talking to each other with the aid of a facilitator or group leader.

Adult-education theorizing is enveloped in therapeutic language. It opens with "needs assessment:" Tell me what you need, and I will try to design a program that fits your need. While youngsters are often challenged to think about new things by studying subjects they have never imagined, adults are supposedly only interested in solving problems which they can readily identify. A low-cost group therapy is the result in many adult education classes.[3]

This narrowing of education to "facilitation" is a major problem in today's culture. It is particularly deleterious for disempowered people. A culture intent on making people feel good is a comfortable place for the rich but a hopeless place for the poor and the dispossessed. Parallel to what was said in the previous chapter, the cure for the dominance of a therapeutic language is twofold: the acknowledgment of other languages with a family resemblance and the affirming of other families of languages. There is usually nothing bad about feeling good. It becomes bad only when individuals become so obsessed with feeling good that it undermines their own best selves and obscures the severe injustices that support a feel-good culture.

A Fragmented Community

The therapeutic does not presuppose a well-functioning community. On the contrary, the therapeutic assumes a fragmented community in which the individual is trying to find himself or herself. It is the nature of human communities to be imperfect and to have individuals who feel some disconnectedness. However, recent times have cast the individual into a confusing overlay of communities, with doubt arising as to how any community relates to a universal human community. The feeling of disconnectedness that has increased is likely to include the individual's own sense of the body. The right of people to choose for themselves is more strongly insisted upon, but how their "willing" relates to the bodily organism is not so clear.

One sign of this individual aloneness is talk of "rights." No one is sure of the "common good," but individuals should have the right to engage in their own search. Since the good is unknown beforehand, the individual may have to will it into existence. Immanuel Kant was, if not the inventor, at least the gatekeeper of this way of conceiving ethics and political philosophy.

At the beginning of a book on morality, Kant writes, "Nothing in the world can be conceived of as good, without qualification, except a good will."[4] Kant himself pushed on toward a reunification of "man and nature" but the solitary consciousness trailed in the wake of his work. By the twenty-first century, the feeling of aloneness had spread far and wide. It sometimes manifests itself in outbursts of violence; at other times, the individual withdraws into bouts of apathy and depression. The United States has a shocking drug problem among both rich and poor.

When these problems become severe enough, society calls upon the prison and the mental hospital to stem the tide. The prison uses harsh, repressive language to cure the problem; however, it would be difficult to find anyone who thinks that prisons cure anything. Similarly, well-staffed mental hospitals can help the sick but underfunded hospitals are often only holding areas that return disturbed people to the streets.

Most people are not at these extremes. What most people do need at certain moments of a day, a year, or a lifetime, is the help of restorative language. The needed help is not a complex theory that explains life but ordinary speech that calms and comforts. Speaking is itself a therapeutic process. Violence, terror, anxiety, and depression leave us outside conversation.

The person who is sick must learn to trust in words, using speech to relate to other humans. Part of the strange technique that Freud and others developed is that people should talk about whatever comes into their minds. The point of the conversation is not to reach any conclusion; it is to allow the force of life in the form of the will to reemerge in the context of ordinary life.

The family of therapeutic languages therefore ranges from the most ordinary of expressions to the most paradoxical twists of language. At the surface level, we can be taught something by someone saying "uh-huh:" the bond is holding, it is safe to continue.[5] Below the surface, human beings trap themselves in plans and projects that they can neither execute nor let go. Effective speech here must dart behind and below the obvious; it is, as Buddhists say, speech to destroy speech.

Even if one does not go all the way with Buddhism's search-and-destroy mission, selective strikes on the mind's imprisonment of itself can be helpful. All the main religions have used enigmatic sayings to teach the human mind that it has limits. One needs a technique to stop the mind from chattering on. At the center of speech there must be a profound silence. Forms of therapeutic speech are constituted more by silence than by sound.

In teaching with therapeutic languages, one tries not to "move the will" but to restore the person to willing. However, there is no direct way to accomplish that; the disempowered cannot be directly empowered. Any direct assault ("pull yourself together") will likely drive the problem deeper. Freud rediscovered what most religions know, that what we think of as free will is not free. Human freedom is at a deeper level where a yes or no is given to life. One must be able to act; just as important, one must be able to not act, to stop speech and allow what is nonverbal to lead.

Much of twentieth-century philosophy abandoned the project of explaining reality with a grand theory. Philosophy turned back on itself and was released from its pretension to take up a view that God had before creating the universe. Wittgenstein was most explicit in seeing philosophy as therapy: "The real discovery is the one that makes one capable of stopping philosophy when I want to. We now demonstrate a method, by examples, and the series of examples can be broken off"[6]

In the early Wittgenstein, the silence is found by going up a ladder to the point where speech is surpassed. His contrast was between what could be shown and what could be said.[7] In the later Wittgenstein, the silence is found at the center of speech. Our many games of language show a way, but the greatest philosophy is what stops philosophy and leaves us at what Wittgenstein calls the mystical center of ordinary life.

The frequent mark of therapeutic speech is the double negative. When language is negating life, the solution cannot be more of the same kind of speech. What must be negated is the negation in order that life can flow again. Philosophy or religion can seem negative when it is constantly nay-saying. The question is whether its no is a single or a double negative. Most of the sayings and stories in Buddhism deal in double negatives, which the West has often mistaken for nihilism.

A famous Buddhist saying begins, "Monks, there is a not born, not become, not made, not compounded"; the way is offered to overcome the "born, become, made, compounded." One could miss the point that the negatives are the "born, become, made, compounded." At least, they are negative insofar as each one is a fracture, a split unity. What is presented as alternative is not a simple image of oneness but a language of nonduality That is as far as language can carry us.

Western mystical tradition is also rich in this kind of nondualistic speech. When Maimonides asks if God is alive, his answer is that God is not dead. An image of a living being is still too confining; "not dead" affirms life with no limiting image. Thomas Aquinas says that "God is not a being" because for Aquinas being is a limitation of the act of to be.[8] Of course, simply saying that God is not "a being" could be misconstrued as simple atheism. Thomas Aquinas's last word on God is that God is "not not being." In a similar pattern, many mystics, such as Meister Eckhart, deny that God "exists." To exist is to be one among many, divided from the others.[9] The ultimate healing unity cannot be expressed in speech as a thing isolated from other things. One can only hope for the overcoming of division.

Development

One modern way to speak of teaching when there is no end in view is the term "development." This term began to come into prominence in the economics of the late eighteenth century and part of its meaning is still weighted in that direction. In the late nineteenth century, the meaning of "development" came to overlap that of "progress" and "evolution." By absorbing psychological meaning, "development" came to be more comprehensive than either "evolution" or "progress." For a while, "development" almost became a subset of psychology, but it is not confined there today.

"Development," meaning "to come out of the envelope," is an alternative to having an endpoint that would predetermine movement. Teaching for "human development" would therefore mean removing whatever object is acting as endpoint. Of course, within the process of teaching without end we still need the stimulus of short-range goals. The student submits a paper to receive a grade; the student takes a required number of credits to get a degree. Goals such as these, which are static objects that can be possessed, have the danger of becoming the end of education.

"Development" in educational circles arose in reaction to a form of teaching in which adults had tried to force-feed children and fit children into a preexisting mold. An etymology of education as "to lead out" does not of itself avoid authoritarianism. A teacher leading out a student still suggests a highly directive process that goes wherever the teacher wishes it to go. If "development" is really the issue, a teacher must use more indirect means and use a variety of languages, some of which are spelled out below.

The paradox is how to move from knowledge that is in some sense already present to knowledge that is actual and gets discovered by the learner. In the story of Alexander the Great's visit to Diogenes, the famous teacher is asked if he needs anything. Diogenes's reply was, "Only stand out of my light." Some people require a little more help than that, as in Plato's *Republic* where teaching is understood to be the teacher turning the student's mind toward the light.[10]

Comenius, in the introduction to *The Great Didactic,* says, "While the seeds of knowledge, of virtue, and of piety are naturally implanted in us, the actual knowledge, virtue and piety are not so given. These must be acquired by prayer, education and by action."[11] I prefer to use "education" in a broader sense that can include prayer and action. Education includes people being instructed by story, lecture, or sermon. Education also includes both social-political action and stillness at the contemplative center of life.

Wittgenstein lists "asking, thanking, cursing, greeting, and praying" as languages associated with ritual.[12] Although his statement is a major inspiration for this chapter, I do not think he was trying to make a complete enumeration of this cluster of languages. I do not feel compelled to follow his lead in naming this set.

I do not name "praying" as a language because it can cut across several that I do name. Similarly, "asking" seems to me not a distinct language but a grammatical form that shows up in many forms of teaching. "Cursing" is an interesting case, although I prefer a different term for some of its meaning. His other two examples, thanking and greeting, I address directly. Wittgenstein's great contribution is his recognition of the many languages in life and in teaching. Especially important is his calling attention to this ritual cluster of therapeutic languages that are crucial to teaching.

When these languages are neglected, they tend to collapse at the threshold of the professional psychotherapist, much like explanatory teaching is handed over to the professional schoolteacher. In both cases, the burden on the professionals is too great. To receive therapy becomes equivalent to putting yourself in the hands of one person who is presumed to possess a skill of curing. People who really are sick may not have the means for this kind of treatment; those who do have the means to get treatment may be misled about the nature of healing, helping, and therapy. As James Hillman insisted, the analyst is not the one who heals; he or she can at best mediate the healing forces within the person and between people.[13]

The professional therapist as teacher engages in teaching with the strangest of languages. A therapist saying, "Yes, that's interesting, continue," may not sound like he or she is doing much. However, most of us cannot be still enough to allow the conflicting elements of another's personality to be brought forth and healed.

In Albert Camus's novel, *The Plague,* one of the characters says that he is certain only "that there are victims and there is the plague, and as far as possible I do not wish to be on the side of the plague."[14] This stark contrast is softened by another passage where it is suggested that there may be some people who are healers. The rest of us should take notice of those people who seem to ameliorate the effects of plague.

As in much of tribal religion, we seem to be returning to the figure of the teacher as healer; not the one who lays claim to the title of healer but the one whose effect on a community is healing. There may come a time when great visionaries arise who can point the way out of the desert night. For the present, we can only help people "to stand fast, with their souls in readiness, until the dawn breaks and a path becomes visible where none suspected it."[15]

I wish to illustrate this cluster of languages with three paired terms, plus a pair that is presupposed by them. The three pairs are: welcome/thank, confess/forgive, mourn/comfort. I precede these three examples with a discussion of praise and condemn. The format of pairing is not strictly necessary, but it calls attention to the therapeutic as a constant giving and receiving. The person who is teaching can be on either side of the pair, and the teacher and the learner can easily reverse positions. Giving can be understood as a form of receiving and receiving as a form of giving. The healing occurs because of this flowing back and forth.[16]

This characteristic of the therapeutic cluster contrasts with the operation of the first set of languages. In storytelling, lecturing, and preaching, the teacher is much more clearly on one side. A lecturer might learn something from an audience, but it is nearly impossible for the teaching to flow smoothly in both directions. In the name of democracy some church congregations have tried "dialogue sermons." But without other changes in physical setting, clerical role, and congregational size, such dialogue tends to be awkward.

When the educational setting invites stories, lectures, or sermons, there is nothing wrong with the teacher using these forms. But in the forms described in what follows, the teacher is never entirely in control of which language and which side of the language is operating.

Praise and Condemn:
This first pair of languages is both precondition and continuing theme for the other pairs which follow. Praise and condemn should not be personalized, at least not too quickly. Preachers tend to condemn people, which is not what I have in mind. And even praise is not to be easily assigned to individual people. As *teaching* languages, praise and condemn start from an impersonal or nonpersonal basis. Most of the therapeutic languages have a strongly interpersonal character, but praise and condemn begin with an attitude toward the universe.

At stake in all the therapeutic languages is a freeing of the individual from its egocentric predicament. So long as a man or woman is striving to control the world, the self is not receptive to what the universe is offering. The cosmos is ready to teach, but the individual must let go in order to learn. Aristotle believed that philosophy begins in wonder, in being awestruck by the miracle of existence. There are technical problems that people must solve but why bother unless there is a sense of wonder about it all.

Praise is the language that is evoked by wonder and awe.[17] Praise is often given in the form of poetry or song; one sings a "hymn of praise." Religious people may imagine a definite object to the praise ("the creator of the universe"). However, in the soul of every man and woman lies a song of praise waiting to be brought forth. The praise is directed toward all that is, the universe and every marvelous element within it. Why praise? It has no end, no function, no good to be attained. It simply is the special response of the human being to being human within a universe of surprise, beauty, and invitation.

Praise is thus concerned with both natural environment and human accomplishment. It is related to people's actions more than to people themselves. It is often unclear who should get "credit" for the good results of an action. With communal activity, an individual can take some pride in being integral to the praiseworthy actions. But the motivation for the individual's action ought not to be the receiving of praise.

Especially with children, praise should be used sparingly. The child must learn that the reward for doing good is the good not the praise that may or may not follow. A child who is dependent on praise is vulnerable to a confusion of self-identity when the praise is absent. More important, the child who is doing his or her very best may not be able to accomplish much of what is praiseworthy. That may not be the child's fault; various social and environmental conditions may interfere with the child's efforts at successful actions.[18]

The term that I have paired with praise is "to condemn." Good teachers do not condemn people, but they sometimes are outraged by situations that ought not to be tolerated. The capacity to feel joy that is expressed in praise implies the capacity to feel anger, outrage, and disgust. The two capacities do not have equal shares in life. What is to be condemned should be condemned directly and quickly; what is praiseworthy should be praised at length. The emotions connected to condemnation have to be carefully budgeted. In one direction, they can overrun an individual's life; in the other direction, they can be unworthily exhausted on trivial situations.

Despite the dangers in the act of condemning, there are times when a person must say, "This is an intolerable situation that needs to be condemned." If young people are destroying their lives with drugs, if the poor are homeless in the streets, if the rivers and seas are being polluted, then a parent or a politician, a schoolteacher or a social worker, an economist or an environmentalist ought to get angry. Who exactly is to blame is of less importance than marshaling whatever forces are available for changing the situation?

There will be need for technical solutions to technical problems. But the motivation for such actions cannot only be reasonable calculation. David Hume thought that the basis for human ethics is "sympathy."[19] He thought that reason needs the drive of a powerful emotion. His point is well taken, so long as sympathy embraces more than the interpersonal. One must sympathize with the suffering earth and sea, as well as with individual human beings.

No human being can offer ultimate condemnation of another human being. Here again the child is the dramatic case in point. Whatever correcting of a child's behavior may be needed, the child is never worthy of condemnation. Even when the situation into which the child has been born is indeed deserving of condemnation, the child remains a being of illimitable potential. Human possibilities deserve to be praised at length. A realistic assessment of human failure must be distinguished from a mean-spirited perception that does not let itself praise.

One of the most famous intellectual battles of the last century pitted Reinhold Niebuhr against John Dewey. Niebuhr saw himself as the "realist," acutely aware of the arrogance and self-delusion that can corrupt the loftiest human projects. Dewey, however, wished to know why Niebuhr had "to believe that every man is born a sonofabitch even before he acts like one, and regardless of why and how he became one."[20] Niebuhr's attitude was based on the Christian doctrine of "original sin." That doctrine ought to be understood as a statement about the social conditions into which people are born rather than the imputation of a fault to the individual. If

Christians want to cope with original sin, let them feed the hungry, clothe the naked, and provide shelter for the homeless.

To condemn situations that breed poverty, suffering, and shame says nothing against people having to "take responsibility" for their own actions. Condemning a situation is never the whole story; but it is the initial step in intolerable cases, a release from a cramped rational calculation. If condemnation is genuinely experienced, the next step can be vigorous action to relieve the intolerable situation.

Welcome/Thank

Unlike praise/condemn, welcome and thank are not opposites Rather, they are reciprocal and interlocking expressions. One leads to the other and then back again so that one could say thank/welcome or welcome/thank. The sequence is to some degree arbitrary, although I think that welcome/ thank brings out the relation a little better.

Like praise and condemn, welcome/thank can be directed to the universe as a whole and all manner of natural and human greatness. But unlike praise and condemn, welcome/thank deserves to be brought directly and fully to interpersonal exchanges. Welcome/thank exists not primarily in the song of a poet but in the rituals of daily, hourly life. Civilized life could not exist without these fragile arrangements that structure the delicate give-and-take of human life. The other animals can rely on their built-in rituals of instinct while the humans must maintain rituals of politeness, formalities that some people dismiss as silly and unnecessary.

Teaching by welcome/thank begins from a welcoming receptivity to the universe and all its surprises. The person who welcomes life, taking it in as it reveals itself, is freed from having to try to invent it every day. The human being remains human, not absorbed into the rest of nature, but moving with the rhythms of nature.

If welcoming is a basic attitude to life, then expressions of welcome to other human beings generally follow with ease. For friends, welcome is expressed in highly individual expressions; for strangers we need formulas that convey respect, lack of hostility, and a readiness to be helpful. The formulas must be simple and clear, though they are bound to cultural particularity.

For an outsider to the culture, expressions of welcome may seem forced or silly. Being met at an airport by a stranger who lays some kind of necklace on you may not be your brand of welcome. Nonetheless, one can appreciate the significance of the gesture, and even the words in a language which is foreign to you.

The reciprocal character of welcome and thank is neatly captured in the U.S. custom of replying to "Thank you" with "You're welcome." However, for many speakers of British English this U.S. custom seems a bit ridiculous. Perhaps the phrase, "You're welcome," comes across with an ironic or cynical twist. Or perhaps it has the effect of abruptly ending an exchange in which one person has just extended a word of gratitude. A neat closure is one way of looking at "you're welcome" but it is also the breaking of dialogue. As for the objection of cynicism in the phrase, that problem depends on the tone of the person using it. When some people say, "You're welcome," they convey welcome; other people suggest that they wish you had not bothered them.

In the cause of international understanding, I offer the following reflection. Perhaps the two parts are right but would make more sense if they were reversed. If the one person offered "You're welcome" before there was thanks, the cynical twist would largely be eliminated. The "thanks" is directed toward the experience of being welcomed. The first moment is welcome, the second is gratitude, the third is further welcome. Since the movement is a reciprocal and continuing one, the U.S. practice was not all wrong. Welcome is a kind of thanking and thanking is a form of welcome. Whichever action comes first is less important than the recognition that we are thoroughly dependent on the kindness of strangers.

I do not expect U.S. custom to change in the direction I have proposed. However, a change has been occurring in recent decades. "You're welcome" seems to be on the wane. Other phrases are sometimes substituted, such as the jaunty "No problem." More often, the word "Thanks" is being met with "Thanks." This development can cause confusion among people who expect closure to the exchange. The nervous interaction sometimes runs, "Thank you. Thank *you. No,* thank you." Although there may be no clear logic in both parties saying, "Thank you," the wish to acknowledge mutual exchange is clear enough. And the scattering of "Thank you" in all directions is probably bringing U.S. and British English closer together.

As another example, take the phrase, "Have a nice day." When it arrived rather suddenly and aggressively on the scene, many guardians of the language reacted with horror and ridicule. But the phrase proved to have staying power. The main objection to the phrase was that it seemed to be an order. It replaced polite acknowledgment of gratitude with a command to feel a certain way; the word "nice" was especially grating. However, as the phrase blended into ordinary speech, the well-intentioned meaning has become easier to accept and "nice" is often replaced: "Have a good day." The meaning is "(I wish that you) have a good day." A phrase such as "good-bye" probably once sounded a bit pushy: "[I wish that] good be with you as you go." Such expressions are the rituals of speech that carry good will, kindness, and willingness to care.

To the extent that someone feels welcome in the universe and the recipient of miraculous gifts, expressions of gratitude are called forth. In Wittgenstein's statement cited above, thanking follows asking and leads to greeting and praying. In any genuine form of religion, praying is more about thanking than asking. Thanking is a human necessity a response to being in the universe.

As in the case of praise, religious people say "thanks" to God. For many people, the sudden removal of God from the map of life creates a vacuum. In *The Brothers Karamazov,* what worried Alyosha about the possibility that there was no God was "whom shall we thank, to whom shall we sing our song?" He goes on to ridicule the idea that "humanity" can simply step in as replacement.[21] And the past century supplies considerable evidence that our abstract idea of "humanity" cannot bear all the burden of religious devotion. The human race would have to go through a long process of concretizing gratitude in rituals that mutually relate men and women, humans and nonhumans.

The sequence and the precise formulas are not most crucial here. The therapy is in the interaction. We should welcome/thank with bodily presence and with whatever words best convey our attitude. Whenever our offer is reciprocated, then we heal, and we are healed in the exchange. The language can be as simple as "yes" (or "uh-huh") said at a moment when affirmation is called for. With rituals of welcome and thank, the human world goes on to the next day without interruption.

Confess/Forgive

The next pair of languages confess/forgive, become necessary when human life does not flow smoothly. Human beings exist in the context of promises about the future. We all make agreements about how we will act. On occasion, we all fail to keep our promises. Sometimes the culpability is clear when we are guilty of breaking a promise because of fear, laziness, or avarice. Sometimes other factors intervene that prevent us living up to the agreement. But very often we are in a gray area where we are not sure of our own guilt. Perhaps we could have kept the promise; or perhaps that was too much to expect.

Whether or not we are guilty, humans need a ritual of confession to remove the burden of feeling guilt. Hannah Arendt notes that only bad people have good consciences; that is, they live behind a veil of culpable ignorance that hides them from guilt. The rest of us have at least a partial sense of our failings. Unless we can deal with that feeling, it threatens to become dead weight in all our actions.[22]

Confessing, like other therapeutic languages, is as wide in scope as the whole universe and as narrow as an individual saying, "Excuse me," for blocking an aisle. The premise of confession is that there has been a rupture in the life of a community. A balance needs to be restored and the individual needs to be brought back into the community. Traditional religions had elaborate rituals for this restoration, such as the scapegoat carrying away the faults, or the Catholic Church's sacrament of penance. Even though the confession was directed to God, the community that suffered the disruption also had to heal its split.

In Jewish history, the symbol that carries the community's promise is "covenant." The people are related to God in being related to each other. One commentator on the story of Moses at Sinai says that there were 503,500 covenants, the supposed

115

number of adult males at Sinai; no, says another commentator, there were 503,500 x 503,500 because the covenant is also between the people. The idea of covenant carries the element of covenant renewal, when the people recall their past failings and promise to do better. Confession of faults is made externally and verbally to the community or its representatives.[23]

The modem era secularized the idea of covenant and came up with the symbol of "social contract." The individual has an implicit agreement to live according to the laws of society. The law court becomes our confessional box and place of exoneration. If an individual throws himself or herself on the mercy of the court ("I plead guilty"), the penance is likely to be lessened. However, our courts are very limited in the kind of behavior they can judge. There is no confession/forgiveness for the daily failings in the interpersonal world. If there are no other rituals for confess/forgive, the professional psychotherapist will soon be needed to heal the splits within family, between friends, and on the job.

The ability to promise is at the heart of human life. Other animals do not make promises; only the humans can contemplate the future and place their lives in a promise. A handshake or a statement on a piece of paper is the foundation for many human ventures. Because we cannot know the future and because we do not fully know ourselves, we are bound to fail sometimes in living up to promises. Our stories, lectures, and sermons often include promises. Praise and thanks also imply a world of promise. The restoration of what has been broken needs to be shown by a teacher if other teaching languages are to be effective.

Human trust is fragile; it depends on the trustworthiness of a person's words. A person who regularly tells lies undermines the whole social structure. The United States was founded on covenant or contract. Every new immigrant must swear allegiance to that agreement. In this context, lying is considered an especially grievous failing. People are often put in jail for perjury about their crimes, rather than for the original crimes. The only thing worse than telling a lie in this country is denying the lie when found out.

Richard Nixon probably could have saved his political career in 1973-74 if he had just said, "I'm sorry. I told a lie." Donald Trump is also notorious for an inability to say "I am sorry" or to ask to be forgiven. Numerous other people in public life could also have saved their souls, if not their powerful positions, by saying, "I'm sorry." And in the intimate exchanges of private life, love often requires *(pace* the line from *Love Story)* the simple statement, "I'm sorry."

The healing effect of confessing depends on its reception in the act of forgiving. The one who has been wronged is the one who is best able to do the forgiving. Forgiveness is indeed a power, one of the most powerful forces in the world. Hannah Arendt argued that it is one of the few activities that can effectively change the future of the world. But it is a philosophical idea that has been of almost no interest to philosophers.

Forgiveness is an activity that is needed within families, between friends or colleagues, within nations, and between nations. There are very few families in which longstanding feuds or slights do not exist in the relations between parent and child or between siblings or with other relatives. It is often difficult to get the problem out in the open. Ideally, there is an apology that is answered with forgiveness but often it is not clear who is the one at fault. If the parties cannot agree on who is at fault, then the healing may have to start with forgiveness rather than apology. The act of forgiving recreates the world. It "is the only reaction which does not merely react but acts anew and unexpectedly, unconditioned by the act which provoked it and therefore freeing from its consequences both the one who forgives and the one who is forgiven."[24]

What about between peoples or nations? The possibilities for confession and forgiveness become cloudy, especially when a long passage of time is involved. Can a religious group confess its fault in the persecution of another group many centuries ago? Who exactly is doing the confessing and what exactly is being confessed? Should the European invaders of North America or Australia confess their guilt to the remnant of the native peoples? Perhaps in some cases a ritual asking of forgiveness is a good idea if coupled with specific helps for the surviving population. The legal complications are often staggering.

Should German leaders ask Jews for forgiveness for the Holocaust? Perhaps a ritual of confession shortly after World War II would have helped to overcome the horror. At this point, with most Germans having been born since World War II, a national confession is not as meaningful as efforts to see that any similar horror never occurs again. On the Jewish side, survivors of the Holocaust must consider their personal feelings of forgiveness toward individual people. The collective Jewish people is not in a position to issue generalized forgiveness.

The standard cliché is, "Forgive and forget," a strangely illogical phrase. If we were to forget, there would be no need to forgive. We forgive what we remember. Our hope lies in "remembering," which mean a gathering together of members, to forge a new unity. The memories are good and bad; both must be preserved in the remembering. Where we have failed, confession is called for; where others have failed, forgiving is called for. The readiness to forgive is an acknowledgment that we are vulnerable to failure. The one who teaches by forgiving knows that in another place on another day he or she will have to teach by confessing

118

Mourn/Comfort

The final pair of therapeutic languages is directly related to the final experience of life: dying. Unless we can talk about dying, then all our other talk becomes veiled in illusion. Plato conceived of philosophy as a meditation on death. Traditional religions were centrally concerned with funeral rituals. Modern philosophy has been, in large part, a flight from death, a distancing of the self from remembrance of mortality. Since the most fundamental meaning of teaching is to show someone how to live and how to die, the flight from death is also a flight from teaching. Conversely, the languages of teaching must include the language of mourning and its correlative, the language of comforting.[25]

Nothing is more certain about human life than mortality. "They give birth astride a grave, the light gleams an instant, then it's night once more."[26] As to the fact of death, the humans "die like all the animals"; as for its meaning, however, the humans alone can foresee death and can retain death both in memory and in outward results. "The gorilla, the chimpanzee, the orang-outing and their kind, must look upon man as a feeble and infirm animal, whose strange custom it is to store up his dead."[27]

We mourn the death of someone we love; we also mourn our own deaths in anticipatory ways. A teenager mourns the death of childhood; a middle-aged man mourns the passing of youth.[28] In these and other instances throughout life, what seems dark and destructive is new life trying to break through.

The feeling of grief and loss needs outward expression lest it turn against the griever in the form of violence or depression. "Give sorrow words; the grief that does not speak whispers the o'er fraught heart, and bids it break." Paradoxically, the absence of joy is the sign of our inability to mourn. Turned in on our own grief

119

we cannot rejoice in life or turn our attention to the hurts of others. Thus, the language of mourning is crucial to all the other languages of teaching.

Even more than the other therapeutic languages, mourning requires a ritual. An era impatient with ritual has been especially hard on the language of mourning. Geoffrey Gorer's study of grief in the 1960s found an almost total absence of ritual for mourning. He compared mourning in the twentieth century to sex in the nineteenth: no one admits to it in public.[29] In the years since then, there has been some change; in fact, on the surface there has been a lot of talk about death.

The books of Elisabeth Kübler-Ross and the historical studies of Philippe Aries, followed by Sherwin Nuland's *How We Die*, were welcome.[30] Courses on "thanatology" became part of some school curricula. At the national level the Vietnam Memorial in Washington, D.C., in stark contrast to the thrusting swords and guns of the other war memorials, is a place of genuine, ritualized mourning. It is unclear, however, how much has changed in the lives of individuals and groups concerning their rituals of mourning.

Mourning is mostly waiting. At the most elementary level it consists of a "no to death" followed by a "yes to death and no to life," and then a "yes to life inclusive of death." All of that takes time. "Every cell of the body must be informed of what has been lost." The middle of mourning is a period of withdrawal in which the acceptance of death is symbolized by not taking part in ordinary life. Each of the religions specified a definite length of time for mourning and detailed prescriptions of dress, food, responsibility of friends, and so forth.

The funeral rite in the past often mixed the living and the dead in ways bewildering to the modem consciousness. Describing nineteenth-century Irish wakes, S. J. Connolly writes, "To outsiders the results may have appeared incongruous and shocking; but they may also have relieved those who took part from some of the burdens of anxiety and guilt with which more modern modes of reacting to death have made us familiar."[31]

The modem cemetery, which dates from the mid-nineteenth century, was conceived as a way of hiding death. So also is the practice of embalming and much else in the funeral industry. Religious rituals of death that look so strange to the outsider had the effect of holding together the community while the individual was temporarily cut off from public life. When all such rituals disappear, we are returned to the couch of the professional psychotherapist. For teaching to be effective, the remaining rituals of dying need preserving and new developments (for example, in relation to hospital technology) need careful shaping.

Comfort is what the ritual of mourning should bring. The ritual itself in supporting the mourner brings comfort. The words spoken by relations and friends are also comforting. "To comfort" means to bring strength. Death, which is our point of greatest vulnerability, can also be a source of strength. Usually, those who can best comfort are those who have learned to mourn. The comforter can sympathize with the mourner, which is itself strengthening.

The therapeutic languages tend to be fragmentary, indirect, and illogical. Often at funerals, the first thing said is, "I am sorry," which sounds like a confusion of comforting and confession. The point is to express some solidarity with the mourner. We reach for formulas because few people can come up with original and spontaneous statements.

The Book of Job is one of the world's masterpieces on grief and mourning. Harold Kushner says that Job's friends did two things right: they showed up and they listened. But the mistake they made was in assuming that when Job asked, "Why?" they should answer by explaining.[32] There are many right ways to comfort; there are a few wrong ways. One wrong way is to explain why the loss is for the best; another is to tell people not to feel bad. Both mistakes are often made with children.

Comforting is a simple process that greets us as one of the first things in life and, if we are fortunate, it accompanies us in the end. We begin and end life in silence. Comfort is what breaks the silence for the infant; the difficult transition from uterine to extrauterine life is managed with physical embrace and the language of lullaby. Similarly, at the end of life, there may be little to say, except "We are still here," or "I love you." The dying person who cannot converse may still be responsive to physical touch and to song.

Between birth and death we all need comforting for the hurts and crises that constitute the little deaths within life. When the first child goes to school or the last child leaves home, when a career falters or a marriage dissolves, when the body or the mind begins to weaken, then comforting the mourner is called for. A gesture and a few words give the grieving person a chance to heal. The saying, "Time heals all wounds," is not necessarily true but time is an ingredient in whatever healing is possible.

"You're on earth and there is no cure for that" can be a depressing thought if no word is spoken in comfort.[33] But for those who can mourn, it becomes the passage to new life. The young man in Edmund Wallant's *Children at the Gate* experiences the death and mourns the loss of his friend. At novel's end, "a blade twitched into his heart, beginning that slow, massive bleeding he would never be able to stop, no matter what else he might be able to accomplish. He was surprised and puzzled as he walked with that mortal wound in him, for it occurred to him that, although the wound would be the death of him, it would be the life of him too."[34]

Chapter Six: Teaching the Conversation

The title of this chapter can suggest an activity that encompasses the whole of teaching. Insofar as teaching refers to the human community, teaching is always a form of conversation. To be taught as a human being is simply to enter the human conversation. As one learns virtue by growing up in a virtuous community and one learns building by growing up in a building community, one learns to converse by growing up in a conversing community. Or, put more simply, one learns conversation by joining the human race.

This chapter, however, is about a more specific kind of teaching. I have been examining the languages that can be sorted out within teaching situations. The two previous chapters have dealt with contrasting families of languages: the one where the community has a goal in view and helps the individual to move toward that goal; the other where the community is fragmented and the individual needs healing. The third family, to be discussed in this chapter, presupposes the other two languages. If they are imagined as horizontally parallel, this third cuts across them vertically. In the other two cases, the teaching is in words, but the words are still contiguous with the body; in this third case, the words are on their own.

I have argued that choreography is a helpful image to describe the place of speech in teaching. At first, speech has the function of directing bodily action. However, speech itself can be taken as an action; therefore, one can imagine the choreographing of speech. The teaching in this chapter is speech about speech; language is examined in relation to itself.

This kind of teaching, not surprisingly, can be utterly vacuous. Nonetheless, it is the most specifically human form of teaching and potentially the most powerful. Richard Rorty notes that there

123

are three ways for changing a person's beliefs: a change of perception, a change of inference, and a change of metaphor.[1] Only the third brings about radical change in people. This chapter is about changes of metaphor, an examination of the language of the languages of teaching.

At first. sight, the discussion may seem headed for high-level abstraction. Terms such as "second-order language" or "meta-language" are sometimes interjected here. But my aim is not to construct an artificial language above ordinary language. With language, as Hannah Pitkin says, we are sailors out at sea who can never put into port to fix our boats.[2] Everyday speech is what is available for examining everyday speech. As the words are forced back on themselves, the result is not to abstract from the words but to go deeper down into the words. The search is for the controlling assumptions in any use of words. What is the meaning of a word and how far can the meaning change?

I said that this third family of teaching languages presupposes the other two. The first family of languages – storytelling, lecturing, and preaching – involves a body of beliefs. The third family of languages does not reject those beliefs but neither does it accept them as true. Instead, the main question is what these beliefs mean. The point is obvious that you must have beliefs before you can criticize them. Nevertheless, much of modem criticism has not abided by that principle and simply rejects beliefs. Objecting to that approach, Peter Elbow says that "mental housecleaning by doubt" is futile.[3] He suggests as an alternative that we "sleep around" with a wide range of ideas if only to find out what is in our minds. Then we can ask critical questions about keeping or throwing out one of our beliefs.

The second family of languages, the therapeutic, also needs to have been experienced before we can ask questions about the meaning of the pattern. These languages free us from trying to reach the end of speech and they return us to the giving and receiving found in ordinary life. If we are obsessed with the realization of some future project, we do not have the mental space to attend to the present. The second family of languages is needed for the individual's healing of a fragmented self. The future is not denied; it is simply bracketed for the time being. What are the deeper implications of this stance? Can we live without an end? Nietzsche warned that "a man would rather will nothingness than not will."[4] The world's inhabitants cannot live on willing alone; neither can they live on not willing. This chapter reflects back on the relation between the first two families, one of willing and one of not willing. It asks about the meaning of their relation to each other.

While this third family draws its material from the first two, the relation is not entirely one way. The analysis of this chapter reverberates back on the previous two. Like therapeutic languages, this third family has no end beyond itself, but by penetrating further below the surface it can unlock more healing power in language. It breaks the chain of language that can interfere with the use of therapeutic languages. This third family is also like the first in being concerned with reaching understanding. The mind is called into play in its most intense way. In the first family, the question is, what is the meaning of this text for our lives together? In this third family, the question is, what does it mean to ask the meaning of texts? Not this text's meaning or that text's meaning, but the meaning of the search for meaning.

A new kind of advocacy emerges here, which does not look to the changing of social structures. The advocacy is linguistic: how to speak so that greater understanding is possible. Hegel writes, "One word more about giving instruction as to what the world ought to be. Philosophy in any case always comes on the scene too late to give it.... When philosophy paints its grey in grey, then has a shape of life grown old. By philosophy's grey in grey, it cannot be rejuvenated but only understood."[5]

Hegel's contrast in this passage led to a more famous statement by Karl Marx: "Up to now philosophers have only tried to understand the world, the point is to change it."[6] Marx's opposition of understanding and change is a scandalous one from the point of view of teaching the conversation. It is true that the understanding is not in the business of "giving instruction as to what the world ought to be." Nonetheless, understanding, with a concomitant change of language, is not the alternative to change but a powerful force of change. "Wittgenstein's remark about philosophy – that it leaves everything as it is – is often quoted. But it is less often realized that, in seeking to change nothing about the way we look at things, Wittgenstein was attempting to change *everything.*"[7]

Understanding of this kind may require privileged spaces where other kinds of change are kept at bay. Many people grow impatient with an artificial segregation of disinterested speech, that is, inquiry that temporarily suspends political and social engagement. Some eras become more insistent than others that all speech, in order to be genuine human speech, must be rhetoric persuasive of political and social change. Language is pressed into the service of one overriding purpose.

Consider this comment by Stanley Fish: "In these contexts, the context of ordinary life, you go to the trouble of asserting that "x is y" only because you suspect that people are asserting that "x is z" or that "x doesn't exist."[8]

I have described in the previous chapter the "ordinary life" where a range of languages exist that are not arguments or explanations. Fish's ordinary life sounds exhausting in its contentiousness. Where is the praise, thanks, confessing, or mourning that is not asserted against anyone's assertion that *"x is z"?* The only point of "good morning" is to be pleasant. Most of ordinary life contains speech that celebrates life with its shared sorrows and joys.

Fish's statement that "everything we say impinges on the world in ways indistinguishable from the effects of physical action" is particularly directed at sanctuaries of "free speech." He wants writers and professors to "take responsibility for our verbal performances," which is an admirable aim. However, the argument that everything said has effects *indistinguishable* from those of physical action seems wildly overstated. The statement lacks precisely those careful distinctions that a reflection on speech – perhaps in a sanctuary of free inquiry – might provide.

Truth and Meaning

One way to elucidate this issue is with the distinction between truth and meaning. The assertion that "x is y" is a true statement can be held in suspension while we examine the meaning of "x." In an algebraic context, x is the name of one clear-cut reality; it either is or is not the equivalent of "y." However, in ordinary life the meaning of "love," "free speech," "equal opportunity," or "right to life" raises unsettling questions. Are we certain we know what we mean when we defend or attack free speech? Would we know what it meant to get equal opportunity? Could the right to life include a right to die?

As soon as such questions are asked, they reverberate across a web of related meanings. A term does not have its meaning in isolation. Words have their meanings in context; to understand the word is to be able to place it in a context. The context or contexts spread out indefinitely to more and more participants in the conversation. If two people are speaking, the ambiguity in the meaning of any statement can usually be held in check by innumerable factors of history and present environment. The tone of voice and the facial expression are often the key to what is meant by the words. A person saying, "uh huh," can mean at least half a dozen things, but in any instance of utterance the meaning is usually clear.[9]

In a written document, especially one from the distant past, fewer guidelines are available for discerning the meaning, In the seventeenth century Baruch Spinoza introduced the idea of distinguishing truth and meaning in the reading of the Bible. He found himself in a lot of trouble.[10] But an appreciation of the Bible demands an understanding of what the authors were attempting to write in its various books. To read Genesis, Job, and Song of Songs as if all three were the same kind of literature is to distort the meaning of all three books. None of them consists of a series of assertions that "x is y." To read Paul's Letter to the Galatians and his Letter to the Romans without asking in each case who he was writing to, who he was fighting against, where he was writing from, and similar questions, will mislead the reader as to what each letter says.

It is amazing that the Bible has survived its defenders as well as its critics. The interpretive questions applied to that document are now widely used for other literature. Spinoza's distinction between truth and meaning can now be seen not as disrespectful of the text or as a flight from truth, but as the way to a deeper appreciation of the text. Frank Kermode, referring to the Bible and other texts, says: "All modern interpretation that is not merely an attempt at 'recognition' involves some effort to divorce meaning and truth. This accounts for both the splendors and the miseries of the art."[11]

The distinction between truth and meaning allows for a playfulness with language.   Truth is not to be toyed with; the opposite of truth is falsehood which should not be entertained. However, *meaning* invites the play of imagination and the testing out of alternatives. To be sure, meaninglessness is no friend, but it is a threat only when we cannot live in the house

128

of single sense and yet cannot imagine an alternative. We assign "play" to children and it is indeed their métier. However, the ability to play is also the mark of a mature attitude.

This third family of languages for teaching cannot be grasped or lightly taken hold of unless the teacher has a sense of humor. To teach in this instance is to suspend asserting that "x is y," preferring instead to investigate playfully the meaning of x. The humans are the risible animals, those that can laugh. A teacher who does not laugh is suspect.

The child consciously enters the human conversation as he or she senses the mysteries, the wonder, the simple fun of human speech. When Wittgenstein proposed the metaphor of "game" for language, some people thought this comparison not serious enough. But many games are very serious, calling forth concentration, dedication, and staying power. One must follow the rules to play the game, but within the rules all kinds of variations can be tried out. A living language always includes the inventing of new words and the bending of the rules as life bubbles up and overflows. The guardians of proper speech sometimes take themselves too seriously, instead of moving with the rhythms of the game.

The child who is just learning to speak tries to flows with the structure of the language, plucking out of the air the words that resonate with the soul and awaken consciousness. There are two ways to understand the relation between thinking and talking. Talking can be understood as thinking out loud. Or, thinking can be understood as talking to oneself. The child regularly talks to himself or herself; adults are usually embarrassed to admit that they do too. Talking out loud on the subway to no one in particular is not to be recommended; it usually indicates that the person's life is empty of people to talk with. But if one has human partners, then conversation with oneself is stimulated.

The child, in any case, is not averse to taking both parts in a conversation. Why does the child do that? To find out what he or she thinks. Thinking, says Plato, is "the conversation that the soul conducts with itself."[12] Contemporary thinkers, including Dewey and Wittgenstein, pick up this same theme. If the child's sense of play is not suppressed, he or she will later be able to look at language from several directions. Words will be material for thoughtful artistic play rather than vessels that encapsulate thought.

Knowledge begins not with an isolated consciousness but a conversation. Both Martin Buber's, "In the beginning is relation"[13] and the New Testament's "In the beginning was the word" refer to the Book of Genesis where God creates by speaking. Who was God talking to? He was apparently talking to himself, although when he gets to creating humans, one interpretation of his saying "let us make man in our image" is that God was speaking to the other animals.

Dramatic Performance

One of the ways that language is played with in adult life is in dramatic performances. Indeed, the staging of drama is sometimes called a "play." The actors' step into roles and pretend to be characters who create a whole world within our everyday world.

Some plays fall within the first two families of languages. Some plays resemble the first family in having a directly instructive purpose; they intend to convey a message. There is nothing wrong with plays that are instructions. But most plays that moralize by dictating simple solutions to life's heartbreaks do not usually last long.

130

Other plays seem to fit with the therapeutic family of languages. These dramas are concerned with life's little foibles and how we cope with them. Such plays give us release, let us laugh at ourselves or rejoice in life's triumphs. No struggle toward life's goals is at issue. A comedy of manners by Moliére, Chekhov, or Noel Coward provides us with delight, which is of no small importance in life and in teaching

Most important are the plays that involve the third family of languages, concerned with a kind of message, but they are about life's complexities. Plays that are great tragedies, *Oedipus, King Lear,* or *Hamlet,* imply some purpose or end to human existence. They warn against destructive obsessions without telling us how we should live our particular lives.

The play best lends itself to this third family of languages, concerned with teaching human conversation. In fact, the structure of drama is itself designed to fit this form of teaching. The play has the possibility of transcending story or therapy by being a reflection on language itself. One can perform that reflection in a novel, a short story, or a poem, but in those cases, one must twist the form beyond its shape. Within a play, the play of language is already in place with the adoption of the format. The characters exist in a play; so that it is not surprising when there is a play inside a play.

Much of modern drama has been fascinated by the structure of the play and its relation to "reality." What happens when the actors on stage break down the wall that creates an audience and the audience becomes part of the play? Or, what happens when the characters in the play start reflecting on what it means to be characters in a play?

Such situations are sometimes called Pirandellian (after one playwright who explored these possibilities), but the tendency is found in much of modern drama.[14] Shakespeare has his plays inside of plays; in Hamlet, "the play's the thing wherein we shall catch the conscience of the king."

In the twentieth century, Tom Stoppard lifted Rosencrantz and Guildenstern out of *Hamlet*; they then have their own play, within which is Hamlet. Confusion is everywhere, not only for the characters in the play, but in the minds of the audience. We are left with Stoppard's dazzling word play. A typical Stoppard play is a physical romp, together with philosophical ruminations on language. Concerning one of his plays, Stoppard writes, "The first idea I had was I'd like to write a play in which the first scene turned out to have been written by a character in the second scene. That was all I started with."[15] Plays do not necessarily tell a story; they often reflect on storytelling and other forms of speech.

A favorite form of play in the past century has been the comedy routine between a couple of characters who continually misunderstand each other. Puns calls attention to the ambiguities in language. Good routines by Laurel and Hardy or the Marx Brothers work with children and adults, work in the 1930s or the 2010s.

The Marx Brothers deserve a linguistic study of their own.[16] Each of the brothers takes a different approach to the undermining of ordinary speech. Harpo reminds us that silence is part of speech, Chico regularly mangles the language, Groucho has the puns that endlessly delight. The worldwide collapse of Marxism suggests that Groucho was ultimately more subversive than Karl. And any course on the analysis of language could use Abbott and Costello's "Who's on first, What's on second, I Dunno's on third."

Perhaps the most revolutionary play of the past century is *Waiting for Godot*. At one level it is a comedy routine in the manner of Abbott and Costello; the play is often acted by comedians. It is filled with outrageous puns and continual misunderstandings between the two clowns and between them and their visitors. The play goes nowhere in that the setting at the beginning and the end of both acts has the characters in the same place.

This play and others by Samuel Beckett are pure conversation; the characters exist because they are held in by the play of voices. Sometimes it is unclear whether the voices belong to one person or a plurality of persons. The ambiguity is not a failure of the playwright. The characters themselves are unsure if the voices in their heads are coming from outside. A recording device plays a prominent part in several plays. Is the voice on the recording another person or the same person at another time in life? Is that even a meaningful question?

Perhaps the purest form of Beckett's plays is reached in *Endgame.* The text can be read as a conversation within one person's head (the set design of the play appears as a head with the two main characters as eyes). Or the play is a conversation between two people who cannot separate. The content of the play is play, with the two characters commenting on the play they are in. The human race seems to have disappeared. "Why do I stay with you?" asks the character Hamm. "For the conversation," is the answer. Or as Estragon says in Godot, we are "incapable of keeping silent."

The plays of Beckett and Ionesco in the 1950s were sometimes called "theater of the absurd." In fact, however, they are very rationally constructed plays that force us to reflect on the nature of conversation.[17] Note that the play does not consist of only the dialogue written by the playwright. The stage directions and the set design become part of the conversation, too. The whole performance is what is choreographed. Beckett was almost fanatical in his demand that directors abide by his directions for the set, lighting, and movement.

In a play's performance, the teacher is not an individual but the interaction of the actors. The conversation also reaches out to include the audience who are a necessary element in the play. The actors in Broadway and Off-Broadway plays perform up to eight times a week. To an outsider it might seem boring to repeat the same lines hundreds of times. Good actors say that every performance is a new performance because the audience is different. The actors respond to how the audience is responding to a performance.

An illustration of this principle is provided by the producer Garson Kanin about his wife, the actress Ruth Gordon. Kanin went backstage after a Wednesday matinee of *The Matchmaker*. Gordon had recently set a record for the number of times she had performed in that play. When Kanin asked her what she was doing, she replied that she was studying her lines for that evening's performance.

Dialectical Discussion

For the second language within the family of conversation, I use the somewhat technical term, dialectical. My intention is to use a term that can include philosophical thinking but one that can also embrace ordinary discussions that bend back on the meaning of the terms in use. In the middle of a conversation between friends. the question might be raised, "What do you mean by that?" If it is not a hostile question, it is likely to engage the speakers in a dialectical discourse.

Eric Havelock says that dialectic arose when a speaker in Greece was asked to repeat himself. The very act of repetition sets up a dialectical exchange within the speaker and disturbs the single strand of speech.[18] Dialectical refers to their being two voices and a movement from one to the other. In that sense, dialectical discussion is just another name for dialogue. I use

134

"dialectical," however, to indicate a more reflective use of language and a concerted effort to find the meaning of the words in the dialogue.

One might also speak here of debate or argument so long as we are still referring to a quest for meaning rather than the scoring of points against an opponent. In philosophy, as in the rest of life, questions and their answers are sometimes a cover -up or a tool for polemical purposes. When Michel Foucault was asked why he avoided polemics – issuing harsh judgments on other people and their views – his admirable response was, "Questions and answers depend on a game – a game that is at once pleasant and difficult in which each of the two partners takes pain to use only the rights given him by the other and by the accepted form of the dialogue."[19]

The term "dialectical" is probably best known through its prominence in Marxism. For Marx, dialectical refers not to peaceful discussion but to the conflicts of class warfare. Marx borrowed the term from Hegel, who had posited a movement of history through the dialectical synthesis of opposites. Since Marx claimed to turn Hegel upside down (from philosophy standing on its head to standing on its feet), the relation between the two thinkers is itself dialectical. Thus, Marxism is part of a dialectical discussion about the meaning of "dialectical"; and other disciples and opponents of Hegel (for example, Kierkegaard) also become part of the dialectic.

Many people trace the idea of dialectical back to Socrates (or to a slightly earlier era; Aristotle traces it to Zeno the Eleatic). Socrates engaged people in intense discussions that open into a larger philosophical conversation. Socrates did not have much time for protecting reputations, although he also did not engage in *ad hominem* attacks. Aristotle carried forward the process in more orderly fashion by arranging the views of previous thinkers on particular topics.

135

Dialectic became the mode of argument in the Middle Ages, starting with Abelard's *Sic et Non* (Yes and No), which showed that the church fathers had contrasting views on many topics. The scholastic method at its best, for example, in Thomas Aquinas's *Summa,* was a conversation that encompassed the centuries. Each question in Thomas' *Summa* begins with a set of objections to the position he is about to take. After stating his view, he then responds to each of the objections. One of the rules of debate was that you had to state your adversary's position, to his satisfaction, before giving your own.[20] This rule would still be helpful to contemporary debates. One would be forced to see the world from the other's perspective; the debate would likely be more thoughtful.

Political life at its best has some of the qualities that are associated with philosophical inquiry. The first responsibility of the political assembly is not passing laws or making speeches. Rather, it is to be a forum that asks about the meaning of our lives together. In contrast, a politics that is based solely on polls and consumer goods is in danger of being swallowed by therapeutic speech, while surrounded by ineffective lectures and sermons.

A political official cannot just be out to satisfy the people's needs. What constitutes real need can only surface in reflective discussions. "Human subjects have no privileged access to their own identity and purposes. It is through rational dialogue, and especially political dialogue, that we clarify, even to ourselves, who we are and what we want."[21] Harsh polemics ought not to be the heart of political dialogue but there is plenty of room for disagreement. A culture is not so much a place of common values as a place that has the means to allow disagreements that do not destroy political life.

Dialectical discussion proceeds by oral exchange and by reading that is respectful of the otherness of the text. Learning to read so that one learns from one's opponents is a skill necessary to the survival of a living tradition. In a dialogue, an author's voice may have been silenced by death but his or her text still has power to speak. That power is in turn dependent on the willingness of someone to listen. The reader must be gracious and receptive to the text. If the written statements seem absurd to us, perhaps we have not yet understood them in context. Sometimes we will find that letting in a strange voice from the historical record will awaken a strange voice within ourselves.

Dialectical discussion is the immediate preparation for academic criticism. By reading books or by listening to a discussion, a student can observe a play of conflicting ideas. One of the worst things about "textbooks" is that most of them have no texts, that is, original pieces of writing by thoughtful individuals. In what are called textbooks, the differing thoughts of reflective people have been boiled down into a thin soup. Most textbooks are veiled sermons rather than dialectical discussions. They give little sense of minds struggling to get a ray of light on complex matters that may not have solutions.

What the student should find in genuine texts and in oral debate is the play of ideas, the fact that people of fine intelligence and good will imagine different worlds. John Stuart Mill writes, "What Cicero practiced as the means of forensic success requires to be imitated by all who study any subject in order to arrive at the truth. He who knows only his side of the case, knows little of that."[22] Sometimes in a political debate two individuals simply represent their party's orthodoxies. The result is more a sermon than dialectical discussion. The same can happen in discussions between economists, psychologists, or social theorists. The listener, who is trying to learn, is simply asked to choose sides and then he or she will have the truth.

Even when this partisan attitude underlies a debate, there may be moments when a breakthrough occurs. If each party is interested in truth, then the play of ambiguous meaning is liable to peek out. Can a person on one side imagine what it would be like to view the world from the other's point of view? If so, the debate will include dialectical moments, the granting of some truth to a position different from the speaker's convictions.

Paradoxically, this recognition is often easier to get when the two parties have very different positions. A Freudian and a Jungian may be able to recognize that they start from differing assumptions, while spokespersons for two Freudian schools may find it more difficult to grant their opponent's legitimacy. Many Christians find it easier to acknowledge Buddhism's different truth than to grant Judaism's right to a distinct existence. Protestant and Catholic Christians have at times killed each other over doctrinal differences that to the outsider can look slight.

Academic Criticism

The third language in this last family of languages is academic criticism. As the very last language, it can incorporate aspects of all the previous ones, which gives it its potential. As the furthest example in a process of turning language back on itself, academic criticism can be the most vacuous of languages. This characteristic is reflected in the frequent reference to something as "merely academic." For much of the population, academic matters are trivial or unreal. However, it can also be the case that public figures dismiss academic matters as trivial so that they will not have to be challenged by academic criticism. My intention in this section is to show how academic criticism can be among the most powerful of teaching languages.

As is true of the other languages in the third family, academic criticism presupposes the other two families. Without stories,

138

lectures, and sermons, academic criticism would have nothing to work on. And without a sense of the therapeutic, academic criticism could not achieve the distancing it needs, the suspension of both belief and disbelief in stories, lectures, and sermons.

Academic criticism shares with dramatic performance and dialectical discussion the calling into question of language itself. It may have some drama about it, but it is not cast into separate roles for several players. It shares with dialectical discussion the conversation with great minds of the human race. But whereas in dialectical discussion the student is a spectator to Nietzsche discussing Kant, or to Heidegger's writing on Nietzsche, in academic criticism the student is a main participant. His or her own words are the focus of the criticism.

Compared to dialectical discussion, academic criticism is in one sense more personal, in another sense more impersonal. By becoming a participant in the conversation, the student is more personally involved. However, a distance is still allowed by the fact that it is not the student but rather the student's written and spoken words that are the direct object of concern. Criticism ought not to be personalized; the student should be able to get out of the way.

In ordinary speech, the term "criticism" usually has negative connotations. When someone offers "constructive criticism," the adjective must be insisted upon to indicate that the intent is not destructive. This reputation for the negative is not without foundation. Although the ultimate hope is for a positive effect, to criticize is to call into question part of the established world. What up to this time was simple fact or assumed truth has its foundation undermined. The presumed fact or truth in question may survive this challenge but it can never be accepted again in the same way.

Criticism therefore has its dangers both for what is criticized and for the critics. People who criticize should not be surprised to find themselves on the receiving end of criticism, one that is not necessarily restrained by an academic intention. "Let us admit the case of the conservative," writes John Dewey. "If we once start thinking, no one can guarantee what will be the outcome, except that many objects, ends and institutions will be surely doomed. Every thinker puts some portion of an apparently stable world in peril, and no one can wholly predict what will emerge in its place."[23]

Dewey's contrast here between "conservative" and "thinking" is not fair. The act of criticizing may indeed come from the liberal side, but the material for criticism must come from a conserving of the past. Or another way to make the point is that we cannot live on criticism alone. Michael Oakeshott writes that *"ceaseless* criticism never did anyone or anything any good; it unnerves the individual and distracts the institution."[24]

One way forward out of conservative-liberal stalemates is to tie criticism to the words of a particular text. One must engage the texts before criticizing them. And after criticism, texts do not disappear; they often flower in meaning. "Liberal" need not mean rejection of the past in favor of a yet to be invented future. The impression has sometimes been given that the enemy of a liberal approach to learning is tradition and traditional beliefs. "Liberal" would then mean coming up with new *thoughts*. However, if one attends not to thoughts but *words*, then "the new does not emerge through rejection or annihilation of the old but through its metamorphosis or reshaping."[25]

Academic criticism, like every other language of teaching, presupposes a community. The phrase "academic community" is tossed about as casually as those other "communities" that

140

clamor for public support. The phrase "academic community" is both an assertion of positive cohesion and an opposition to the give-and-take of most areas of life where academic criticism would be dismissed.

The cohesiveness of a particular group of scholars or the whole world of scholarship is quite fragile. The practice of academic criticism presupposes knowledge, discipline, and care for one's colleagues. When there is no sense of community, then criticism quickly turns cynical and self-serving. It becomes a sharp knife that does harm in *ad hominem* attacks.

As is true of most communities, "academic community" is raised in opposition to the wider society. Those who practice its academic language often feel like a beleaguered few. Outside of some guarded preserves, the language of academic criticism is not often found. But although the larger society may sometimes seem the enemy, society's political and economic arrangements are what provide those guarded preserves of academic life. An all-out attack on society is neither fair nor gracious. No area of society is exempt from criticism, but the criticism ought to be measured, focused, and fair. It should be a radical questioning of specific policies and institutional arrangements.

The ironic question is the mark of academic criticism. The teacher wishes the listeners to hear his or her own questions and bend back on the ambiguities in the words. If a teacher asks a straightforward question, it is likely to draw forth information as *the* answer. If the question is a bit shocking and forces the listener to consider whether the teacher is really serious, then the question forces deeper questioning.

Consider the case of a famous speech by Philipp Jenniger on the occasion of the fiftieth anniversary of *Kristallnacht*, the beginning of the Holocaust. Jenniger was at that time speaker

141

of the West German parliament. The audience, I imagine, was ready for therapy in the form of confession and mourning, combined with a bit of sermonizing. Jenniger did those things at the beginning and end of his remarks, but in the middle of his speech he tried some academic criticism, a move with disastrous consequences.

His remarks caused a worldwide uproar. The headline in Italy was "Anti-Semitism in the German Parliament"; in the Netherlands, "Hitler Worship Causes Mayhem in the Bundestag." His well-intentioned speech turned out to be disastrous because the conditions were not there for academic speech. In proper academic form, Jenniger asked a series of ironic questions that included: "And as for the Jews, hadn't they in the past sought a position that was not their place? Mustn't they now accept a bit of curbing? Hadn't they, in fact, earned being put in their place?"[26] The members of the audience that evening were not ready to be academic students. Jenniger's failure "had been to misjudge the occasion, which called for a memorial, not a sober historical speech. "[27]

Academic dialogue is between teacher and students. This dialogue can happen in other places, but the classroom is the established place for this language. Conversely, other languages show up in the classroom, but academic criticism should be the centerpiece of classroom instruction. Most often, classroom speech cannot sustain two hours or even fifty minutes of academic criticism. A variety of languages provides for relief. But a classroom without academic criticism is not functioning as a classroom.

In academic criticism, the main point of reference is the student's own words. Of course, the exchange will be the more valuable if students are in touch with a variety of sources for the topic at hand. In educational discussions, phrases such as "experiential learning," "student-centered learning," or "self-

142

directed learning" can be slogans for avoiding the hard work of finding out what the human race has said about science, politics, religion, love, family life, literary theory, gardening, diet, animal breeding, or any other topic.

In eras of rebellion against the formality of education, and especially against academic knowledge, teachers are supposed to avoid demanding that students actually know something about the topic being discussed. Great hope is placed in the sharing of uninformed opinion.

A teacher cannot offer academic criticism unless the student does the work of bringing knowledge to the arena of criticism. The student who has read books or essays, has listened to stories, lectures, and sermons, will have formed particular views on the subject at hand. The teacher in this setting – the critic – invites the student to bring forth his or her words. "Put your words on the table between us" is the explicit or implicit request of the teacher.

Very likely, the student will initially resist; no one likes to have his or her views exposed to withering attack. The academic teacher must show in practice and over time that he or she is trustworthy. The teacher, while offering pointed criticism, will treat the student's words with respect. The teacher's challenge does not go beyond the words on the table. The student's thought world is not directly accessible to the teacher or, for that matter, to the student either. What is out in the open for criticism are the student's words.

The academic teacher's job is to propose a redesign of the words. As always, the sequence is not teacher gives and student receives. Instead, student acts, teacher studies design, teacher proposes redesign, student tries out the new design. The teacher's design should not be in generalities or hesitant suggestions. The teacher says, "I know what I am talking about.

143

Try this out and you will find it an improved design of your speaking or writing."

When teaching undergraduate students, I became concerned that many students came to class with the attitude of "I did my job of showing up. Now it is your job to perform." As the way to convey to them what game we were playing, I required them as the first exercise in class before I said a word was to write a response to a question about the day's assigned reading. Each day I returned their previous day's work with my comments but not a grade. I criticized in the most positive way I could what they had written. At the end of the course they had a stack of papers with their own writing and my proposed redesigns. I extended this practice to graduate students who seemed to appreciate that someone paid attention to their words.

The academic teacher does not begin with the premise that "I am knowledgeable, and you are ignorant." The premise is, "We both have knowledge and we both are limited in our expression of the truth. But I have a better way of speaking and writing than you do. I am not necessarily a better person and there are other areas where you would be the teacher and I would be the student. Nevertheless, on this academic topic I have spent years learning the language. Where I am convinced you are wrong, I will not let it go by. Where you are right, I will propose distinctions to enrich the meaning of your statements." When two informed people strongly disagree, the issue is not usually truth against falsehood. One side is richer in meaning because the metaphors assumed on that side allow more comprehensive and consistent meaning.

The search is to understand the words between us and to distinguish meanings in a way that leads to greater understanding. The teacher does not try to change the student or the student's thinking, only the student's words. Why should the student be convinced? For two reasons: the history of the words and their geography. The two sources are not entirely separable; history asks how the meaning has changed throughout the past and geography asks how the meaning changes from one group to another in the present.

For example, to understand "nature" one must know how the term has shifted in meaning over the centuries and what are its various meanings today. There are things the student can say of nature that are simply false; there are other things that might be true but are not revealing. And there are other ways of speaking that have been common but are misleading and unhelpful (for example, continuing to use "nature" as synonymous with the nonhuman world). The teacher's job is to show that some ways of speaking about nature open new understanding and lead to practical conclusions.

The academic teacher thus is an advocate of certain ways of speaking. In the academic world, a common way to classify speech is to label it as either description or prescription. The only choice offered in this contrast is between a neutral statement of fact and a statement of how things ought to be. The metaphor of description/prescription is borrowed from the medical profession. In this language, a person has a problem and goes to a physician. The patient delivers a description of the facts, or even better, a machine measures the problem. The physician then writes out a prescription that gets filled by the pharmacist.

In contrast, teaching as linguistic advocacy borrows its metaphor from the legal profession. Within this language, the teacher as advocate of language *neither* describes nor prescribes. Human language will already have cast the issue into language that is not neutral or merely factual. The teacher's job is not to prescribe a solution; most times there is no solution. The teacher can only advocate a way of speaking, plead a case before the judge or jury. In advocacy, if one approach does not work, another can be tried. At the end, some of the jury may remain unconvinced. Those who are willing to

145

try the position advocated may find their lives slightly bettered; they are the ultimate judges.

Two last claims must be noted about this process of academic criticism, one concerning age, the other gender. To turn the words back on the words and poke about for underlying metaphors may sound like a teaching strategy fit only for esoteric courses in the university. However, my intention is to describe academic work with any students of any age. Indeed, six-year olds may be better at this game than some twenty-six-year olds. Children are still in touch with the sound and feel of the words; human conversation is still an interesting new discovery. In contrast, the twenty-something graduate student (or fifty-year-old professor) may have become immunized against the excitement of words, their connotations and ambiguities.

People described as "intellectuals" are sometimes good at manipulating ideas but lack attentiveness to the words. If such people teach in schools – whether primary, secondary, or tertiary – their classrooms become places of prescribed ideas. University students find ways to cope with this problem (by changing courses, being absent, or daydreaming in class). Six-year olds have less protection; they may be forced to listen to one person all day. It is therefore more imperative for second graders than for university students that classroom teaching be restricted to examining the words that the student willingly brings forth.

My other point concerns a possible gender bias in the invitation to "put your words on the table between us." Is that a typically male invitation? If the words were separated from personal investment and feeling, perhaps that would be so. My description of academic advocacy allows for varying degrees of emotional investment in the words. I think there may be gender bias in the assumption that "to teach is to explain" or "to teach is to give reasons for." Not that women teachers or women students are incapable of participating in such a process. However, women have historically embodied a wider and richer meaning of "to teach" than the simple equation of "to teach is to explain."

Whatever are the difference between genders, advocacy of linguistic change is at least as important today for women as it is for men. Changes in language have been indispensable to the women's movement. Numerous feminist studies are about women finding "voice," and women having full participation in ethical, political, and academic discussions.[28] The invitation in a classroom to bring forth words may not find equal response in a group of boys and girls. Schools have a responsibility to study this issue. Schoolteachers have been discovering biases in the educational system that discouraged girls from having equal voice with boys in the classroom.

Three examples of academic criticism:

I finish this chapter with three examples appropriately drawn from previous chapters. Since academic criticism presupposes the other two families of languages and the siblings within this third family, my examples are a return to previous examples with attentiveness to the ambiguity of the words. The examples are "America" from the first family, "development" from the second family and "to teach" from all three families.

As one form of storytelling, I cited the myth of America.[29] Practically everyone who grows up in the United States is enveloped in this story, even people who have little share in the freedom and wealth which are recounted in the story. The story conveys a message of hope, particularly to a young person or to a newly arrived immigrant. Most public schools begin the day with the religious ritual of saluting the flag. The history, social science, and literature texts are saturated with talk about "America."

There is nothing generally wrong with this story. It holds together hundreds of millions of people who have little else in common. As a unifying religion, it can soften the conflicts that come from religious and ethnic diversity. The story turns bad only when intellectual leaders exercise no academic criticism and unthinkingly interchange "United States" and America." Academic criticism should be aware of the history and geography of terms. Obviously, America and United States are not co-extensive. In length of existence, "America" is two and a half times the age of the United States; in geographical meaning (North, South, Central), America is two and a half times as large as the United States. The history of the idea of America may be about peace and justice; unfortunately, the history of the United States includes a good amount of violence and injustice.

Academic writing or university teaching that does not regularly distinguish between the United States and America is enveloped in myth. The myth has been a destructive one for Latin America and for other countries as well. The scandalous fact is that the distinction is very seldom acknowledged in scholarly writing. The failure of the left-wing critics is far more shocking than their right-wing opponents. A stream of books attacking America goes nowhere. Unless one criticizes specific policies of the United States and its government, what we have is not academic criticism but preaching.

The second example from the therapeutic language family is "development." It is a way for people to talk about almost any kind of advancement. It is not only a modern term; it helps to define what modernity means. We live in what we conceive to be a developed world because we assume that things progress or, advance. Development has become a backdrop of hope that everything will be fine if we let things take their course.

I do not think that development is a bad idea. We probably

148

cannot manage without some metaphor of hope that things will get better. But the idea easily degenerates into mindless ideology unless it is subjected to academic criticism. What is badly needed is to understand the development of "development." The history of the term's rise since the eighteenth century needs to be traced. And its geography includes two fields of usage that almost never intersect: economics and psychology. Academic criticism ought to investigate how these two uses are related. The failure to explore the relation between economic development and psychological development leaves both uses vulnerable to illusion. Is it possible that economic development is a psychological blind spot? Is it possible that psychological development is a rich person's way of looking at things?

The third example, "to teach," comes from this chapter and from the book as a whole. The most detailed example I have of academic criticism is what I have done with "to teach." I have tried to break open a too narrow conventional meaning of "to teach." My route has been both history and geography.

Historically, I have brought in voices on teaching from Greek philosophy and ancient religions. I adverted to the etymology of the term and a thousand years of ordinary usage. I have tried to show a narrower meaning that has dominated since the eighteenth century. I have referred to philosophers in the past century who are allies in my attempt to retrieve the alternate tradition for the meaning of "to teach."

The geography of teaching is the other main source for examining "to teach.". I pointed out the great variety of instances of teaching. The universe and all its life forms teach those who are ready to learn. Animals teach each other to behave in certain ways and can offer some lessons to humans. The human community is always teaching, mostly in ways that are not directly intended. Even when the human individual intends to teach, much of the teaching, for better or worse, is outside the intended effect. Human teaching usually includes a verbal element, although initially the words have the function of directly commanding bodily behavior. Up to that point, there is seldom a moral problem with teaching. The learner signals bodily what he or she is ready to learn; the teacher shows how to do what the learner wishes to do.

These three chapters, comprising part two of this book, have examined language when it takes on a specifically human character of being separated from bodies. The teacher now must choreograph not a movement of the body but a movement of language. And the crucial moral decision is to get the appropriate language or languages for the occasion of teaching. The learner provides the license, often signaled through an institutional arrangement.

Depending on whether I walk into a chapel, a classroom, or a counselor's office (all three might be in the same school building), I indicate what kind of language I am ready to hear. If I go into a therapist's office, I give permission for questions that intrude on my privacy, a permission that I do not give by crossing the threshold of a classroom. We would recognize a moral problem if a therapist were regularly to say, "That's terrible; don't do that." We less easily recognize the corruption of teaching when it is taken over by preachers of "feeling good." Or we do not grasp the moral problem of professors telling students what to think about the. world.

The third family of languages is a step removed from bodily life. Its first concern is with intellectual understanding, not physical activity. It advocates ways of speaking that would let loose better forms of life. Its positions are not demonstrably correct, but neither are they merely idiosyncratic. They arise out of conversation with humanity. With no one in principle excluded, the conversation is with whatever part of humanity

150

is available. This form of teaching can never replace the other forms, but with their help it can transform the world.

Languages of Teaching

Rhetorical	Therapeutic	Conversational
Storytelling	Welcome/Thank	Dramatic Performance
Lecturing	Confess/Forgive	Dialectical Discussion
Preaching	Comfort/Mourn	Academic Criticism

Part Three

Chapter Seven: Educational Forms of Teaching

In this chapter I address a theme that up to this point I have put aside, namely, the meaning of "education." My procedure may seem backwards in that most writing on teaching shows up within what is taken to be the main question: education. It is assumed that if the nature and purpose of education are clear, the meaning of teaching follows. I do not think there is anything necessarily wrong in proceeding from education to teaching; the two meanings are intertwined. Unfortunately, however, writing on education has not led to a richly textured meaning of teaching but has implied one narrow meaning of teaching.

I have been describing teaching separate from institutional assumptions about education. A richer meaning of teaching might provide a novel perspective on the ambiguities of "education." If one were to say that I have assumed a meaning of education from the beginning of this book, I would agree. But that implied meaning of education can now be articulated better with the help of a comprehensive meaning of teaching.

Jacques Barzun, introducing a collection of his essays, writes: "Forget education. Education is a result, a slow growth and hard to judge. Let us rather talk about teaching and learning."[1] I can almost agree with his first sentence, except that he does not follow his own advice in the second sentence. Instead of saying, "Forget [for a while] education. Let us talk about teaching and learning," he cannot resist saying in the middle sentence what education is. And the two references he makes, "slow growth" and "result" mirror the confusion of so much writing on education. The two images do not go together and each of them represents a misleading way to describe education.

In the first half of this chapter, I propose a comprehensive and consistent meaning of "education." I argue that education is an interaction of forms of life. This set of relations is the most

153

adequate way to understand education in the past and to address the needs of today. In the second half of the chapter, I name the most important forms of education and describe the pattern of a lifelong and life wide education.

Meanings of Education

There is no single "true meaning" of education. Like "teaching," and any other important word in the language, the most adequate meaning is found in its use. One must trace the usage both historically and geographically.

Historically, the perspective must include etymology and the shifts in meaning throughout the ages. Geographically, one must examine the meaning of education assumed by various groups today. The groups that most control the definition of the term may be excluding voices that should be heard. While definitions of "education" are all too plentiful, they tend to leave out what makes "education" a fighting word and a word worth fighting about.

Throughout the world "education" remains a word of almost magical power. No politician makes speeches against education. There appears to be unanimity that education is supremely important.[2] Yet this seeming agreement is accompanied by intense frustration and disappointment. At least since the nineteenth century, education has been the great hope that never seems to fulfill its promise.

During the last century and a half, education has been closely identified with schools for children. Writers on education often use the terms "education" and "school" interchangeably, although if they were challenged, they would acknowledge a difference. It is assumed that while education can be acquired elsewhere, school is the place that is deliberately and intentionally set up for education.

154

The "professional   educator," therefore, tends to talk of education as what you get in school, or at least what is supposed to be available from school. It is said that school is a mere means; education is the result. Or, for other writers, education is the process of learning which the school should serve.

One common distinction in the twentieth century, which seems to acknowledge the difference between school and education, is "formal" and "informal" education. But "formal education" tends to be a fancy name for school; every other aspect of education is left formless or amorphous. The school retains all the power by reason of appropriating "formal"; nothing else is given an educational name, except otherness to the one form that is school.

Religion   provides   an   instructive   comparison   here.   The religions of the world are not adequately described by naming one's own (form of) religion and then waving in the direction of otherness. There can only be dialogue between different forms of religion, not between form and informality. The world of religion is not adequately described as "Catholic and non-Catholic," "Jewish and Gentile," or "Christian faith and world religions." Caught up in our own language, we might not realize that "non-Catholic" is a Catholic word, or that "Gentiles" exist only for Jews, or that Christians would have to join the world's religions before speaking with any one of them.

The world of education, like religion, does not consist of one form and amorphous otherness; instead, there is a multiplicity of forms. The language of formal and informal education cannot lead to serious educational conversation. The distinction between formal and informal tells us little about how people have been educated.

David Elkind writes: "The idea that there are many different forms of education is one of the most important insights we can glean from the observation of young children." I could not agree more. But his very next sentence is bewildering: "The children described so dramatically by Maria Montessori were engaged in *informal education*, an education in which the materials are self-didactic." Maria Montessori was almost obsessively attentive to form. The children are taught by the (carefully arranged) things in the environment; the form is the most critical element. Elkind is puzzled that people do not see the importance of informal education, that they think "all education is formal education."[3]

Perhaps people think that "all education is formal education" because the term "education" necessarily connotes formalities: forms of time, place, materials, and the relation of organism and environment. I share Elkind's objection to the idea that education means a classroom with an adult at the front explaining things to children. We need other rooms, other languages, other age groupings, other material than that image conveys.

Before the rise of modern education and the assignment of children to school, education had no single form or clearly defined age range. It usually did refer to an immature being that needs guidance toward maturity. The age of the learners was not limited to six – to sixteen-year olds. At the beginning of *Emile*, Rousseau cites the poet Varro for the two Latin words that give us "education" "*Educit obstetrix, educat nutrix*." The midwife begins the leading out (*educere*) the nurse continues by nurturing (*educare*).[4] Both of those things happen before the child is of "school age."

Schools have not always existed. When they have existed, they usually served only a minority of the population. Schools have always been only one of the institutions involved in education. In its early usage the word "education" was not restricted to human

156

life; an animal or a plant could also be educated.[5] Education had to do with forms of life and the relation between those forms.

Education in premodern times operated mainly family patterns, religious rituals, and apprenticeship for one's station in life. With the rise of the modern sciences and an accompanying criticism of religion, educational reform was needed. The (school)teacher as a trained expert came to the foreground. What the emerging world looked for was explanations based on laws discernible by reason. For the founders of Western Enlightenment, the school was the new temple. Where religion had failed in the areas of personal knowledge, good behavior, and social order, success would come through the school.

In the North American colonies, universal schooling was already an ideal by the middle of the seventeenth century. Every town of fifty families was to establish a school to teach pupils to read.[6] The ideal would take several centuries to fulfill because a full-time occupation of children in school could only be afforded by the rich. Both Rousseau and Locke, with their new educational theories chose as the typical student a boy of the upper classes; they were not describing classrooms for the masses.[7] Nevertheless, their meanings of teacher and teaching were assimilated by the modem school.

In modem usage, the teacher is an adult who has studied books; the student is a child who, sent to school for the purpose of absorbing the knowledge available in books, sits before the schoolmaster. The actions of the schoolteacher constitute teaching: to teach is to explain, to teach is to give reasons, to teach is to convince little boys to learn their letters.

Whether a certain form of education fixed the meaning of teaching or whether a single meaning of teaching led to a collapsing of education into one form, the fit between this teaching and this education is obvious. Other forms of education with their own

157

embodiment of teaching did not immediately disappear, indeed they have never disappeared. In the seventeenth-century British American colonies, even as the school was being affirmed as necessary, the main business of education was still being carried out by family, church, and apprenticeship. But in the last century and a half it became more difficult for other forms of education to be accepted as serious partners with the classroom.

When John Dewey began his educational writing at the end of the nineteenth century, he looked back nostalgically to a time when home, church, and apprenticeship were partners with the school. Dewey concluded – fatefully and prematurely – that these other institutions were now all but impotent.[8] The school was faced with the task of picking up the slack and carrying the whole burden of education, which included socializing the child, challenging the child's intellect with scientific knowledge, and preparing the child for a job in the technological world. The overwhelming task required religious zeal and supreme confidence.[9]

The narrowing of education into schools for children was already in process before Dewey. His writing, however, towered above other literature on educational reform. He was a man of great ideas that could be used to support the growth of the school business. Of course, there were protests from the beginning of the school system's ascendancy.

One potentially fruitful criticism came from the "adult education" movement first in Denmark and England, and later in the United States.[10] I have noted that the adult education movement grasped the inadequacy of equating education with the schooling of the child. The early leaders of the movement foresaw twentieth-century educational centers where people of any age would learn from a wide range of experiences.

Throughout the twentieth century it sometimes seemed that we were on the verge of this new educational world, but our language badly trailed behind. The very existence of the adjective "adult" (or various replacements such as "continuing") was symptomatic of the problem. There was and still is (real) education and adult education, instead of a use of "education," which if unqualified would include all ages. In towns across the country, no one confuses the educational budget with the cost of adult education. On university campuses, the school of education sits next to the school of continuing education; no one ever suggests that adult education is part of "higher education."

The tragic flaw in the adult education movement was its assigning "to teach" to the one form in which an adult explains things to a child. Instead of fighting to diversify the forms of teaching, the literature of adult education quixotically attacked teaching. The result is that "adult education" took on an image just as narrow as (children's) education. Adults do continue to get educated but most of them do not do so by participating in the industry called "adult education." There is nothing wrong with discussions lasting six or eight weeks on every conceivable topic so long as such programs do not lay claim to overseeing the education of adults.

An educational pattern that would truly be lifelong would begin by naming those forms of life in which people are taught how to live. This first step is not inventing something new but retrieving what has clearly existed in the past and has continued to be present during the past century and a half, even if shunted to the periphery in the discussions of professional educators.

Education in premodern times involved several forms of life and the relations between them. If "education" is contracted into the single institution of school, then education becomes an "it," mainly if not exclusively available in one institution. If someone tries to broaden this "it," either education stays put in its one clear setting, or else "education" becomes increasingly vague as it is assigned to numerous agencies besides the school. When "education" does not mean the "it" available in school, its meaning loses concreteness and practicality. Yes, there is "informal education," but most books on education address the one clear thing that everyone agrees upon, namely, the school.

One author who tried valiantly to break through this dilemma was Lawrence Cremin. In the early 1960s, Cremin wrote several fine historical studies of the school. He assumed that the school was the center – if not the whole story – in the history of education. Then he read a monograph by Bernard Bailyn entitled *Education in the Forming of American Society* and underwent a conversion.[11] As a result, Cremin tried to write a history of education that would be much broader than the story of the school. The project became more and more unwieldy as Cremin found the need to keep adding pieces and players to the story.[12]

Although Bernard Bailyn's study of seventeenth-century education is a stimulating book about the *agents of education,* it does not spend much time on the *meaning of education.* Cremin took over the configuration of educational agents that Bailyn described without an accompanying change in the meaning of education itself. What Bailyn offered was a picture of education broader than what he calls "formal pedagogy." More exactly, he added church, family, and apprenticeship. The procedure seems logical: if school is not the only institution, add the others. But the reasoning is flawed. The school in taking over the meaning of education ceases to be a "form of education" and becomes an institution that houses education. Adding other houses ("agents of transfer") does not reinstate an interaction of forms. In trying to broaden the meaning of education, the one thing that seems certain is school. This one thing that seems clear is where the confusion lies.

160

The modern school is not a form of education; it is an institution that contains several forms of education, such as classroom instruction, community experience, and artistic performance. Of course, some of those educational forms exist outside school. As a result, one cannot discuss the interaction of educational forms by naming the school and then adding other forms. The task is to name the main forms that shape human existence by a *lifelong* and *life wide* interaction. The modern school can be a place where some of this interaction occurs.

Neither Bailyn nor Cremin could resolve this issue. Bailyn's meaning of education goes toward vague generality; Cremin's meaning remains tethered to the school. At the beginning of his historical inquiry, Bailyn says that education is "the entire process by which a culture transmits itself across the generations."[13] That definition may seem comprehensive, but lacking any indication of what constitutes the teaching-learning process, the term "education" has little meaning distinguishable from culture.

Cremin, in contrast, had a precise definition, which he regularly used and which he had his students memorize. Education is "the deliberate, systematic and sustained effort to transmit, evoke or acquire knowledge, attitudes, values, skills, or sensibilities, as well as any outcomes of that effort."[14] Despite all the qualifiers, the one word that controls the definition is *effort*. "Education is ... effort ... as well as any outcomes of that effort." The standpoint seems to be that of the individual human teacher: education is the effort a teacher makes and the hope for outcomes from the effort. With education as effort, Cremin had set himself an impossible task to write the history of education.

I suggest that the key word for beginning a description of education is *interaction*.[15] How is the organism transformed as it interacts with the environment? How do various forms of life

161

interact with and transform each other? The human efforts amid these interactions can sometimes alter the forms, but if human effort is to be worthwhile, one cannot lose sight of the overall context; one must gauge precisely how human influence can be exercised.

Education connotes interactions that are not random or mindless. Education has an "end" in the sense of purpose, design, or meaning. This end is not always obvious nor is it always imposed by a living human individual. The family as such a form shapes life; it can include generations of design and redesign. And whatever the contribution of persons and groups today, the process continues. As a result, education has no "end" in the sense of a termination point; it is both lifelong and history long.

Education's interactions can therefore have several ends internal to the process but no external thing to be acquired that would bring the movement to a conclusion. Education is always "with end and without end." The difficulty of education is in maintaining a tension between these two meanings of "end," that is, education must have direction and accomplishment but it should never reach a final product.

Forms of Education

If education is the interaction of forms of life with end (meaning) and without end (termination), then what remains to be done is to describe the major forms that are lifelong and life wide. The curriculum of education consists of those social forms with which a person interacts in his or her journey from conception to death. The individual life is transformed by these encounters. The forms themselves are also changed although their transformation is usually a very gradual one over the course of centuries.

There are innumerable social forms that human life takes. I will concentrate on four of these forms that cut across the lifespan and influence the individual's entire life. Every child starts out being cared for and taught in some family pattern. Children then receive instruction for living in their society; this form of education evolved into the classroom. Every society expects its healthy adults to perform tasks for maintaining and enhancing life. Every society allows its older members to step back from the most laborious jobs to take part in what we now call leisure activity. Thus, family, classroom, job, and leisure can be viewed as a lifelong sequence, the simplest basis for a theory of education.

A more developed educational theory will see these four forms as interacting at every stage of personal life. For education at any age, each of the four forms is either at the center or at the periphery; none of the forms entirely disappears at any age. For example, when a child goes to school, the family's teaching recedes, but it remains a partner with classroom teaching. The family may later reemerge as central to education, at least until the last child leaves home. Finally, being a grandparent at fifty or sixty may bring familial teaching to the center once more.

The point of so describing the family in education is not to fit each individual's life into a preset pattern but to recognize that a person's life is educationally shaped by familial relations, with variations depending on age, gender, marital status, parental responsibility, housing arrangements, and many other factors.

What is true of the family can also be said of the other three forms, that is, they are likely to be at the center during one period of life, but they are of subsidiary importance at other times. Classroom teaching may be especially appropriate for children and youth, but it can be important at any age. Similarly, having a job is the mark of younger and middle-age

163

adults, but each person is taught by the tasks that he or she performs from infancy onward. Leisure activity is most prominent in old age, but it cannot fully blossom there without some cultivation throughout life.

Each of the four social forms is a partial embodiment of some ultimate value that can stand in for the purpose of education. For example, the family partially embodies the value of community. The family educates to the degree that it is truly communal, that is, to the degree that the person and the group, the group and humanity, humanity and the biotic community are mutually enhanced. Even the best of families cannot be more than an imperfect teaching of community.

The familial form of community always must be complemented by nonfamilial but communal expressions of human life: friendship, neighborhood, religious congregation, athletic team, and so forth. As I note in the following chapter, a school ought to be a nonfamilial, communal form of life that teaches community by its procedures, personal interactions, and system of rewards.

Rather than pursue dozens or even hundreds of social forms that teach every person at every age, I will stick to the more manageable task of describing the four major forms of family, classroom, job, and leisure activity. The attempt to be exhaustive here can end in a shapeless profusion of details. However, approaching this question from the perspective of teaching helps to keep the description of major forms of education manageable.

Family

I choose to use "family" here rather than "home." Although "home" in the English language does have rich connotations, it may be too weighted toward architecture and place. Those are

164

elements of the context, but "family" emphasizes the individual's interaction with a human form of life, a social pattern that stamps the individual for the course of his or her lifetime. The term family throughout history has meant parents and children; it also implied other relatives whether or not they lived in the same household. For at least several thousand years, family has clearly deserved to be called a form of education. And for all the bewailing about the collapse of the family and the deficiencies of the contemporary family, there is not even a serious competitor on the horizon.

At least since the time of Plato, there have been proposals for alternate social arrangements to rear children.[16] The proposals and their execution have usually involved violence. These attempts to dismantle the family have often been confused with helpful social experiments that recognize sexual diversity. Many communal ·experiments that exclude children (for example, the Roman Catholic religious order) are not in competition with the family. In fact, the constellation of friends and intimate relations that surrounds the family provides the helpful support system that the family requires.

Other communal relations lift a burden from the family so that it does not have to provide a complete range of communal experience to the child. The right wing's terror of gay and lesbian relations is particularly unfortunate because same-sex marriage and stable homosexual relations would enhance any child's (and adult's) education in friendship, love, and community.

Libraries are full of books on the family, augmented by a daily outpouring of talk in the press and on television. I have no hope of settling all the disputes or eliminating all the myths. This book is on teaching and I restrict my comments to three points: the form of family teaches, parents and children teach each

165

other, and family uses a balanced mixture of the various teaching languages.

First, the use of "to teach" in literature on education regularly obscures the fact that the composition and activity of the family is one of our earliest and most powerful teachers. We are only occasionally forced to face that fact as, for example, in family therapy. Whether with good or bad lessons, the family form is the first great teacher.

The assumption that teaching depends on an individual's intending to teach blinds us to what is taught by the daily interaction of a family. If there are two parents, the child learns much from parental interaction. We should also attend to what is taught when families have only one parent, or when a friend exercises parental influence or when both parents are of the same sex.[17] The reality of a mother working outside the home surely teaches something to her children. The teaching can vary from a terrible lesson of neglect or poverty to a lesson of responsibility and creative talent. But we will not look carefully at what is happening and try to improve the form, if we do not accept the fact that the first teacher in the family is the *form* of family.

The second point to be noted is that parents are teachers of their children and children are teachers of their parents. The first half of that sentence may seem too obvious for stating, but that is precisely what is denied when "teacher" is regularly used for "schoolteacher." Emile Durkheim begins his discussion of education by saying that "education is the influence exerted on children by parents and teachers." The statement excludes parents from the category of "teachers."[18] While educational writing is fond of saying that parents are the child's first teachers, that assertion is denied in every use of the phrase "parents and teachers." The parental teacher and the schoolteacher should be spoken about as cooperating in teaching.[19]

166

Jane Martin, as noted previously, attributed to gender bias the blindness to the fact that mothers teach. No doubt that is interwoven throughout the entire discussion of teaching.[20] But we could still miss the full extent of the problem if it were seen only as bias against women. What men as fathers and grandfathers teach has also not counted as teaching. I agree that what mothers do with infants is especially fruitful for reflection on teaching.[21] But we should not neglect what spouses teach each other, what a parent's interaction with a grandparent teaches a child, and what an 80-year-old has to teach grownup sons and daughters.

Children also teach their parents.[22] The teaching varies according to the age and the situation of the child. A sixteen-year old has different lessons to teach than a six-month-old; a genius child and a child with severe impediments offer challenges different in kind. The modern verb "to parent" (one's child) needs the complementary verb "to child" (one's parents). Once again, it is not a lesson that the child intends to teach; nonetheless, any parent willing to listen will learn lessons from the child's life.[23]

At the 1992 Democratic convention, Elizabeth Glaser gave a moving speech on her own HIV affliction and the AIDS death of her child: "My daughter lived seven years. And in her last year when she couldn't walk or talk, her wisdom shone through. She taught me to love when all I wanted to do was hate. She taught me to help others, when all I wanted to do was help myself. She taught me to be brave, when all I felt was fear." [24] Glaser's situation was extreme, but every caring parent knows that the repetition of the verb "to teach" in reference to a child who could not walk or speak was no mere rhetorical flourish.

167

The third point is to notice the family as unusually rich in its variety of teaching languages. All three families of language show up in ordinary family life. From the first family, storytelling, lecturing, and preaching are there, with storytelling being very prominent in the family. The preaching and lecturing, one would hope, appear only intermittently.

Similarly, with therapeutic languages, the family is the main place where people learn to show gratitude, to forgive failure, to comfort hurts. Each of these teaching languages is embodied in the rituals of daily family life.

From the third family on teaching the conversation is prominent in family life. For example, children early acquire an attitude to reading, reflective thought, and understanding a wide range of people. Parents (and grandparents) often succeed in conveying a positive attitude to these practices even if they are not "academically trained." The adult's taste for learning and an excitement with ideas are usually more important than academic credentials. Many immigrants who never had the chance to get beyond primary school have taught their children to value ideas, knowledge, and the pursuit of academic skills.

Classroom

The classroom represents a form of learning that should continue throughout life but is especially prominent in a young person's life. In the modem school, several other kinds of activity take place in addition to classroom teaching.. The school can house preparation for a job and actual experience of paid or unpaid work. The school is also a place for artistic and athletic performances that are integral to one's education but have never fit comfortably within the walls of the classroom.

I will be brief about classroom learning here because the next chapter goes into detail on this issue. I simply wish to name this form of learning and to place it within the constellation of the four forms of education. It achieves its power by having a distinct time and place, but it can effectively use that power only in interaction with the other three forms. During one period of life the classroom is likely to take center stage; at other times, it recedes to satellite status. However, for some individuals it can have either a more permanent or a recurring centrality. Some people in the modem world have jobs that involve constant study. Many people at ages fifty, sixty or seventy-five are discovering that they are finally ready to hit the books.

I will make three points here about the classroom that parallel to what was said of the family,

First, the existence of classrooms and the arrangement of a particular classroom teach. The form sets stringent limits on what can effectively be carried out in the name of education. But if the appropriate things are happening in this setting, the classroom as teacher can be a powerful element in education. "In our schools," wrote Maria Montessori, "the environment itself teaches the children."[25]

Second, most classrooms have only one person called "the teacher." In fortunate circumstances, there may be two such people. If the two work well together, the effect is not to double the amount of teaching, but to change the dynamics of teaching. Two people start a conversation and others ("the pupils") can be drawn in. The person or persons called "teacher" is obviously expected to teach, but one of the tests of good teaching is that sometimes the person called teacher becomes the learner.

One need not imagine an obliteration of roles or a complete equality of participation in the teacher and learner roles but there is always reciprocity in the relation teach-learn.[26] Like the family, the slow student and the very bright student teach different lessons to the instructor. A six-year old and a sixty-year old have different things to teach the person who is called the teacher.

Third, the classroom is a deliberately invented setting for one kind of learning. It is reflection on information that is now available in books, television, newspapers, and computers. Unlike the family with its balanced mix of teaching languages, the classroom concentrates on the third linguistic family: teaching the conversation. And within that group, academic criticism has a privileged place.

Although the *school* has a range of educational languages as wide as the family's, the *class*room must be focused on one language. In practice, every classroom instructor must deal with deficiencies in the backgrounds of a group of students. But if there is little academic criticism occurring in the classroom, the students are not getting the education that the school promises. ·

Job

As in the previous two cases, the form of education called "job" is a partial embodiment of the educational value at stake. In this case the value is "work" referring to an individual's contribution to the betterment of society. Almost everyone has a job, if we extend the word beyond salaried employment to the tasks people must accomplish. Sometimes the jobs we are required to do have little or no educational value; they are not real work. If people have such jobs in order "to make a living," then they must find meaningful work at other times.

Most jobs can be reformed in the direction of their being meaningful work, although some aspects of maintaining human life involve drudgery. Machinery has reduced or could reduce

170

some of the laborious aspects of work. However, the dream of completely eliminating such labor is probably a dangerous dream for bodily creatures.

In this context, Maria Montessori's method places great emphasis on the child learning to work and learning by work. She realistically relates work to discipline but she tends to reduce work to labor. Doing so, she undervalues the connection of work to play. "I have to defend my method from those who say it is a method of play. Such people do not understand that work is natural to man Man's true name should be *homo laborans* rather than *homo sapiens.*"[27]

Montessori was reacting here against followers of Friedrich Froebel who believed that the child's highest activity is play. Froebel had a kind of mystical sense of the divine presence in children's play.[28] Montessori took all the talk about children's play as evidence of adult control and the trivializing of the child's activity. These two theorists were perhaps not so far apart as their language suggests. If the child's work *is play*, then one does not have to reject the one in affirming the other.

Maria Montessori would not have liked that formula. She believed that affirming *homo laborans* was the way to overcome the split between working-class laborers and the new professional class. I agree that many professionals could use some labor experience (for example, in the work of caring for the home or children), but unfortunately that will not do much for the laboring class. The laborers need, among other things, the availability of better classroom instruction and, to whatever extent possible, more play in their work.

"Apprenticeship" is a common term in educational history. Its standard use was for the kind of teaching provided by a master workman to a young person learning a trade. It fits well the root meaning of "to show someone how to live." Occasionally,

171

writers use the term not only for learning a job but for all kinds of learning that involve an expert showing by example how to do something. This meaning is a helpful one to have. But the meaning of apprenticeship needs a wider context.

The assumption in former times was that a master instructed an apprentice who having learned the job in his teenage years was set for life. The more common pattern today is training for the job, training on the job, retraining for a new job. The job has become a more important teacher today, with each job teaching lessons to a student who is willing to learn.[29]

Many parents today struggle to combine work outside the home and work within the home. The former neat division of men doing public work and women doing "housework" (which often was not classified as work at all) has undergone what is probably a permanent downfall. We do not yet have a healthy, fair, and efficient system. Ideally, no one should be forced into somebody else's idea of the correct system of dividing work. Whatever is the pattern of individual lives, nearly everyone is taught by the tasks which they must perform. And for most people that requires including more than one job in a balanced life.

The job in educational interaction with the classroom is a relation that does get some attention these days. The job is also related to family life and leisure activity. For several decades of a person's life, his or her job may hold center stage. But even then, the striving for money, prestige, power, and status must be balanced both with other kinds of work and other forms of education.

One way that young people can acquire balance and insight is by experiencing work that provides a needed service to people. The work is done not for pay but because it is worth doing. This "pro bono work" can begin in childhood and continue throughout life. Such work can include helping friends with schoolwork, minding younger brothers and sisters, helping in a nursing home, and volunteering to serve poor people with one's skills as a nurse or a lawyer.[30] The school is a chief agency for organizing service work, especially when youngsters are in junior or senior high school.

The *meaning* of work is most likely to be found by the young person in donating time and energy to help the very young, the very old, the poor, the disabled, or the stranger in distress. A criterion of the educational value of work is that the work is experienced as worth doing.

Business corporations can have a role in education. Corporations can provide money to schools as well as a realistic experience of work for young people. The job that a person goes to throughout his or her life provides a continuing education for good or ill. A worker learns a discipline of life in the daily routines of a job.

As to the forms of language that are found in the job and work world, it is difficult to draw generalizations. Each line of work has its own mix and its own emphasis. If one is a law student or lawyer, then dramatic performance and dialectical discussion of the third family have a permanent place. If one is a counseling psychologist, the second family of therapeutic languages predominates. If one is a clergyman, the preaching in the first family may be central. There is no one formula for even these well-defined jobs.

Each job has an occupational hazard, which is that a language central to the job can take over one's life. The clergyperson might always sound preachy. The psychotherapist is in danger of always talking therapeutically. The lawyer might be ready to debate everyone. The only protection from this hazard is the interaction of several forms that provides a complementarity of languages.

Some jobs, I have acknowledged, are such laborious drudgery that we should try to replace them with machines; until that happens, those jobs ought to be distributed equitably.[31] For example, the aspects of caring for the home that are bothersome labor should be divided equally among family members. The fairness of the split as much as the execution of the job becomes the teacher. An equal sharing of the laborious jobs makes it possible for everyone to have a share in the creative work of the family.

Professional work is of such a nature that it should not be laborious drudgery. If professional people are bored with their work and careless in its performance, we have a shocking situation. The work is not teaching, perhaps because the professional is not ready to learn. Donald Schön describes what he calls a researcher-in-practice who is continuously taught and therefore finds joy and relaxation in the work itself. "When practice is a repetitive administration of technique to the same kind of problems, the practitioner will look to leisure as a source of relief, or to early retirement; but when the professional worker functions as a researcher-in-practice, the practice itself is a source of renewal."[32]

Leisure Activity

This fourth and last form of education shows up most strikingly in old age but must be present throughout life. Schön's reference above to "early retirement" is to suggest that if someone thinks that early retirement is the solution to being bored with work, disappointment is likely to follow. Schön uses "leisure" in the way it is commonly used today; leisure is taken to be time off the job. I have combined "leisure" with "activity" to resist this modern bias that classifies leisure as nonactivity. The modern era has reversed what earlier peoples assumed; it takes business (busy-ness) as activity and leisure as emptiness. I am positing an activity called leisure that expresses a deep human experience of completeness.

This attitude finds expression in a multitude of ways, ranging from utter stillness to exuberant play.

A drastic shift in the meaning of leisure occurred in the nineteenth century. In the classical and medieval periods, leisure was related to the high value placed on the contemplation of eternal truth.[33] Leisure was the soul's best attitude and the culture's calm center. For Aristotle, leisure was a way to describe the purpose and end of education. The fact that the Greek word we translate as leisure *(scholia)* is the word that gave us "school" indicates that a discussion of leisure belongs within the meaning of education.[34]

It is unlikely that "leisure" can be restored to its pre-nineteenth-century meaning. Too much has happened in the interim, especially in the industrialization of our world. But as one era of machinery made a new meaning of leisure (time off the job) increasingly attractive, so a new era of postindustrial technology is now reshaping our idea of leisure. We could just fill "spare time" with another job or with endless tweeting, texting and television viewing. But it is possible that an increasing number of people will have the chance to engage in pursuits that are enjoyable and educational, personally fulfilling, and socially valuable.[35]

The older part of the population is the chief place to look for how leisure is doing. People, on the average, are living longer lives with better health. Those who are finding no great fulfillment in their jobs and can manage to retire at an early age often seize the opportunity. The question, then, is what to do with several more decades of healthy life. I am not suggesting older people must create a busy schedule of daily events. Having many hours to be present with one's grandchildren is a worthy retirement activity. Getting one's hands dirty in the garden is an activity attractive to many people who have lived their young adulthood separated from the soil. Both grandchildren and gardens can be great teachers.

All the talk about leisure in old age can sound obscene to people who are overwhelmed by poverty or sickness. No doubt there are signs of a dangerous selfishness among well-off older people. "I want my comfortable life; I deserve it. I don't care about anyone else's problems." That is one of the reasons why one must resist the trivialization of "leisure" by travel agencies and other commercial interests. Leisure must be related to profoundly human activity that links the generations.

Older people do deserve much of the economic benefit that has come their way in recent decades. They have the right to step back from the production and management jobs that are burdensome. But for their own happiness as well as society's well-being, leisure activity must have human depth.

Education among the elderly need not mean classroom discussion – although that should be available, and many older people love it. Education in old age concerns the pattern of activity appropriate for the age, health, and talents of the individual.

As was true of the other three forms of education, leisure activity predominates in one part of life (the last part) but it should also be an educational satellite at each stage of life. If one has not been educated in leisure in one's early life its meaning and practice are not likely to emerge at age sixty-five or seventy. Leisure must be cultivated daily, weekly, annually.

Religious rituals were once a help here and for some people they still are. For other people opera, baseball, or ballroom dancing has taken that place. One steps out of ordinary time and place to be immersed in a rich pageant of human emotions. From the standpoint of rational productivity, such leisure activity may seem to be a terrible waste of time. For the individual participant, it can be a glorious and transformative experience. The whole culture would be the poorer without such leisure activity.

The child is taught leisure both by times when "nothing is happening" and by times of sheer enjoyment of any activity. The very young can probably best learn leisure from the very old; the two are co-conspirators in a world where everyone else is rushing to get things done. A child sitting quietly with its grandmother on a park bench may be learning a rich lesson in life. When the child must settle into work at school and at a job, the relaxation, play, and joy may have to recede, but they should not disappear.

Schools, as I shall describe them in the next chapter, are places for the teaching of leisure activity. Arts and sports do not fit the classroom curriculum, but they are part of the school curriculum. One way that the classroom can contribute to leisure is by teaching intelligent spectatorship. Being a spectator may not be as satisfying as being a performer but, especially later in life, it can be a valuable part of leisure activity.

Chapter Eight: Teaching in School

The question of school reform has generated a library full of books. Proposals for change have been constant since the founding of the public school system in the 1840s. This chapter does not attempt to compete with proposals that offer a detailed blueprint of how public schools should operate. Much of the economic, political, social, and racial complexity is beyond my scope here. However, I do think that this chapter might contribute to the discussion by offering several clear distinctions about teaching.

Clarity can sometimes simplify. Behind all the details of complex proposals to improve schools is someone's assumptions about what constitutes a school and what are its proper activities. I have approached the question of school by asking, What is the meaning of "to teach"? That journey led up to the previous chapter, which set teaching within four major forms of lifelong and life wide education.

Classroom teaching is one of those four forms. The form of classroom teaching exists in relation to forms of teaching outside the school. In addition, classroom teaching is related to other forms of teaching *within* the school. That is, the task of this chapter is not to describe school teaching," but to describe the configuration of teaching forms that a typical school can house.

Many of the books on school reform have thoughtful, exciting, and detailed proposals. But what usually does not get asked is the nature of teaching. In most of these books, the reader is not likely to find a page, let alone a chapter, asking the question, "What does it mean to teach someone something?" The question and the answer are, of course, implied. I can understand that documents which are largely political and institutional in nature need not always ask philosophical

178

questions. Nonetheless, teaching is at the center of the school; in addition, teaching is an act that is regularly obscured in educational discussions. If we come to the question of school reform with some clarity about the nature of teaching, we might be able to have a clearer outline of the school. Debate about school reform would be based on a firmer understanding of the limits of a school and what kinds of activity do and do not belong within those limits.

What a School is

Any vision of a reformed school needs to be grounded in what "school" has been in the past and what it could realistically be in the near future. Reform books are often cast either in utopian programs of progress or in apocalyptic announcements that time is running out. People who work in schools often feel battered by what they perceive to be the latest fad – a new piece of machinery, a new management technique, or a new testing procedure. The great new reform is often accompanied by a slogan or an acronym.

At the back of the room, someone is usually muttering "we tried that in 1990 (or 1970). But even the schoolteacher, who just wishes to close the classroom door and get on with the lesson plan for the day, knows that drastic changes are occurring in the world surrounding the school. How much and in what ways should the school be changing in response?

Schools cannot pretend that computers, high-tech industries, and an interlocking world economy do not exist. No modern invention or interest should in principle be excluded from the school. But there is a debatable issue of how to incorporate the school's "relevancy" to the contemporary world without obscuring or destroying the fragile institution of school. If "school" is the name of a single place with a limited time, then reformers must keep in view the simple outline of the school when new things are suggested. If something is being added, what will be subtracted?

179

Herbert Kliebard, in a history of school curriculum, notes that "one major function of life adjustment education was its emphasis on the indefinite expansion of the scope of the curriculum." The intention was for the school to face "real-life problems," but theorists must face the fact that the curriculum cannot indefinitely expand. The attempt to add every social problem to the school curriculum eventually causes the inevitable reaction: Let's get rid of all these frills and go back to the three Rs. Reform movements with too wide a curriculum lead to reform movements that are too narrow in their concern.[1]

The peculiar cry of many educational reformers has been that the school should deal with "real-life problems." That concern is related to the commonly made contrast between the school and the "real world." To say that the school is outside the "real world" is contemptuous of the school and its endeavors. It is shocking to hear schoolteachers accept and use this language. The fact that the contrast is embedded in common speech is not a good reason for participating in self-degradation. Who determines what the real world is? CEOs, generals, lobbyists, advertisers?

The school is a place to step back from many of life's pressing concerns. The school is an extraordinary world but not an unreal world. In fact, the classroom is one of the few places that takes as its concern the entire (real) world. Theodore Sizer noted that the contrast between school and real world allows society to neglect "the real world found inside the school."[2] For young people who are legally required to be there, the school world is undoubtedly real, often painfully so. The students are not going to respect their world if the school's administrators and teachers do not accept the importance or even the "reality" of school life.[3]

180

If school reform starts from the premise that the existing school is outside the real world, it is not surprising that reform proposals go in one of two directions: either make the classroom as painless and entertaining as possible while children are kept segregated from the real world; or else tear down the school walls and put teachers and students to work in reconstructing the world.

One can see these attitudes reflected in two of the most important educational movements in the past century: the "child-centered classroom" and the "social reconstructionist movement." Both movements were credited to, or blamed on, John Dewey. The two movements were most prominent in the first half of the twentieth century, but they continue to resurface with only slight changes in their language.

At the end of the nineteenth century, the school reformers wished to make the classroom a kinder place for the child. More particularly, they thought that the curriculum should serve the child's development. "Child-centered" was a way of saying that the psychologists should direct the child's education. And very quickly educational language was absorbed into psychological language. By 1900, John Dewey was already trying to correct what he thought was a new misplacement of emphasis.

As someone who was identified with the new psychology, Dewey was assumed to be on the side of the child. However, in *The Child and the Curriculum,* he insisted that the center of the school is not the child but the *relation* between child and curriculum.[4] By 1930, Dewey had dissociated himself from the Progressive Education Association's program of child-centered education. In one of his last books on education in 1937, Dewey was still trying to make his point when people were attributing to him whatever was being done in the name of child-centered education.[5]

Dewey never succeeded in extricating himself from the widespread perception that he wished to place the child at the center of the school. An author quotes Dewey as saying that "the child is the starting point, the center, and the end. His development, his growth, is the ideal. It alone furnishes the standard." The author then comments: "In theory, this ideal is unassailable. In practice, it has proved largely unattainable."[6] The words quoted are in fact those of Dewey but they are a description of the theory he was criticizing. It is not that our problem has been failing to put the theory into practice. Dewey's contention was that the theory is wrong.

Why is a position that Dewey was at pains to deny for more than forty years still attributed to him? His express intention was to interrelate "child" and "curriculum," but he could not overcome the limitations of his own language. I think he would have fared much better if he had distinguished among the curriculum of education, the curriculum of the school, and the curriculum of the classroom. In addition, he should not have assumed that "student" and "child" are interchangeable.

John Dewey never developed a theory of teaching. It is amazing that in his major educational treatise, *Democracy and Education,* he seldom uses the verb "to teach." When he does, he nearly always refers to what schoolteachers ("educators") do. Education is assumed to be what children receive in a classroom.[7]

To this day most books on school reform begin by assuming that a classroom is a place for an adult to instruct children or youth. It is understandable that a writer may wish to concentrate on the high school or the elementary school. But even to analyze either of those settings it is not helpful to assume that a classroom is a place in which adults instruct children.

The meaning of teaching is seldom explored when one assumes that the teacher-learner relation is a variation on the adult-child relation. In contrast, the question of the nature of teaching will very likely be raised if the teacher can be the same age or younger than the students.[8]

Within the configuration of educational forms, the classroom has a special, but not exclusive, relation to young people. Classroom learning belongs to every age above five or six. Some reflective and literate knowledge is best learned between the ages of six and sixteen. Many other things are better learned later in life.[9] Our university and community college populations now embody a great diversity of age. Nothing helps a classroom discussion by 18-year-olds like the presence of some forty- or seventy-year-old students. Beyond the university, tens of millions of people in the United States are involved every day in courses, seminars, and workshops.

The phrase "schools and universities" has the effect of keeping schools equated with children. A preferable way of speaking is to include universities within the meaning of school. Students often do experience a big difference when they move from the twelfth to the thirteenth grade, especially in living arrangements. However, the continuity of the classroom experience should not be overlooked.

The United States could profit from a closer relation of primary, secondary, and tertiary schooling. The ones who might learn the most about teaching from this relation would be university professors, who often reflect little on the nature of classroom instruction. They do their research and give their lectures, assuming that is what it means to teach. But teaching in a classroom is a special kind of teaching that a university professor might learn about from watching someone who does it well.

There are places in John Dewey's writings where he suggests that education is not exclusively for children. His test of good education is that it stimulates the desire to get more education. On that basis, education (including classroom teaching) should never cease. Dewey also warns against adults and children being thought as opposites when it comes to matters of dependence, that is, the adult teacher as independent and the child student as dependent. Human beings at any age have their independence in relation to dependence on other human beings and the nonhuman environment.

Dewey also has intriguing comments on teaching by indirection: the teacher influences the student by altering the physical and social environment.[10] But because Dewey has no overall theory of teaching, it is quite possible to read his writings with one's assumption undisturbed that teaching consists in professional educators telling things to children.

The other direction to school reform – social reconstruction – is also traceable to Dewey's writings. This movement reached a high point during the economic hard times of the 1930s. When Dewey broke from the child-centered movement, he aligned himself with the movement to reform the social order. The phrase "social reconstruction" is not heard much these days, but the school is still often asked to solve the problems of society: racism, drugs, suicide, war, traffic deaths, pollution. The school is asked to confront "real-life problems."

In his Pedagogic Creed, Dewey wrote, "I believe that education is the fundamental method of social progress and reform."[11] If by "education" is meant a lifelong and life wide interaction of social forms, then indeed one can look to education, as opposed to violence, for transforming the social order. But if by "education" one means school, and by school one assumes a place for six- to sixteen-year olds, then burdening "education" with the task of reconstructing society is unrealistic. John Dewey did not invent

184

the equating of education with schools for children but neither did he free himself from that assumption.

Dewey's comments on the role of the teacher are especially revealing and unrealistic. He ends his Pedagogic Creed with the statement that "the teacher is the true prophet, the usherer in of the Kingdom of God."[12] If Dewey were referring here to the teacher and not the schoolteacher, the statement would be defensible. The great revolutions of history have been brought on by teachers: Moses and Confucius, Jesus and Socrates, Newton and Einstein, Jefferson and Lincoln. However, Dewey regularly refers to "teacher" when he means "schoolteacher." Asking a schoolteacher of children to lead a social revolution is to lay an unfair burden on both schoolteachers and schoolchildren. Schools, especially those with students of all ages, can make a definite contribution to social progress, but only if schools are protected from being wielded as political instruments.

Dewey's alignment with the social constructionists of the 1930s was short-lived. He was not prepared to go the route of some other reformers in involving the school in social activism. While he regularly refers in *Education and Experience* to "real-life experience," he seems to mean a continuity between in-school and out-of-school experiences. He still appreciated the school as a place set apart for academic study.

The conflict between reformers was brought to a head in a provocative book by George Counts: *Dare the Schools Build a Better Social Order?* The question for Counts was not "Can the schools do it?" but "Are the schoolteachers daring enough to do it?" For Counts, "Progressive Education cannot place its trust in a child-centered school."; instead, it must "become less frightened than it is today at the bogies of *imposi*tion and *indoctrination*."[13] For Dewey, that dismissive attitude to the problem of indoctrination was too much to take. In 1937, he wrote, "It is unrealistic, in my opinion, to suppose that the schools can be a

185

main agency in producing intellectual and moral changes ... which are necessary for the creation of a new social order."[14]

By the end of the 1930s, therefore, school reform had two opposing parties. Both parties claimed lineage to John Dewey, but he had repudiated both. It is almost the trademark of great thinkers that they are misunderstood in opposite directions. Dewey tried to take down the wall separating school and non-school worlds. But in the absence of consistent distinctions between school and education, the result is not a dialogue of educational forms but an engulfment of school by the non-school world. Even more seriously, in the absence of a theory of teaching, the schoolteacher is either told to get out of the way so that children can grow up or else is hectored to tell the school pupils how to live.

Forms of School Teaching

Almost any kind of learning could be housed within the school's borders, but the most likely candidates are those forms of teaching-learning that are valued by the population being served and require the leisure of space and time. Schools throughout the centuries have generally provided two forms of learning: first, knowledge of a scientific or philosophical kind; second, learning how to do the tasks required to sustain the society. This latter form of learning refers to "work" in the full range of its meaning, including labor, art, sport, and religion. The modem school is still a place for these two forms of learning.

The very existence of school, its functioning as a human assembly, is itself a teacher. The community and the physical environment of the school are always teaching. No one intends this teaching, or people usually do not think much about it. Despite the inattention, or possibly because of the inattention, the influence can be profound. It can make the difference between

186

the two main forms of teaching in the school flowing easily or those forms not being understood.

A school need not be one big happy family; it does need some minimum conditions of physical comfort, efficient organization, and a non-hostile body of people. Both the teachers and the students deserve some respect and personal dignity. The school ought to teach decency in being a school.[15]

The metaphor of family should be used sparingly in reference to schools. The school should be a partial embodiment of community, that is, a communal expression that complements the family. Schools need not have father and mother figures, nor obedient children (including grownups who are treated like children). But when schools abandon the family posture they need not switch to modeling a free market of competing individuals.

Schools need to be disciplined communities of people that teach cooperation between students, as well as between the students and school staffs.[16] Everyone in a school has a stake in seeing that the school be a communal experience which keeps bureaucratic procedures at the service of learning. Nothing can guarantee or permanently secure such an atmosphere, but memos, bells, and loudspeakers do not substitute for face-to-face encounters.

The school's influence on behavior, especially on that of young children, is often called "socialization." A lot of discussions concern whether the school should be in the socializing business. A good part of the argument could be eliminated by clearly distinguishing between school and classroom. If socializing means picking up the ways to act in society, then children acquires some of that in school. The fact that schools socialize the young is not really debatable. But that the intention of classroom instruction is to socialize is a different proposition. The effect of classroom teaching might very well be to challenge society's ways not only outside the school but even inside the school.

If we move from the backdrop of community and environment to the kinds of teaching forms designed for schools, there is a single clear-cut division. On one side should be the *classroom* with its distinct form of learning and on the other side should be the *performance area* with its teaching-learning that happens both inside and outside the school. There should not be a chasm between the two school forms; in fact, reaching some harmony and balance, if not integration, should be the heart of school reform.

I identify these two school forms of teaching by place names: the classroom and the performance *area*. Without disparaging the individuals who are trying to teach in these places, I call attention to the environment as teacher. The individual teacher is faced with manipulating the environment to bring about student response.

A distinction between the two physical environments does not necessarily mean their mutual exclusion. A room that is clearly designated as a classroom might have computers along the wall for one kind of performance or a small theatrical stage for another kind of performance. Conversely, the sports complex or the dance studio might have sections for classroom instruction.

There is also continuity in the metaphors that can be used for both areas of teaching in school. Three of the most promising metaphors are apprenticeship, coaching, and instruction.

Apprenticeship. In writing of job-related learning, I said apprenticeship is no longer comprehensive enough in its meaning. It should not be limited to a craftsman training a boy to work in a trade. As a metaphor for describing teaching, it lights up connections between what a teacher does in a classroom and what a teacher does in an art studio. If the root meaning of "to teach" is to show someone how to do something, it is not surprising that the relation of master-apprentice can encompass both the classroom and the performance area.

Alan Tom notes that "apprenticeship is verbal and analytic just as much as it is modeling skilled performance."[17] Or one could vary that formula and say that a classroom teacher must put on a skilled performance with words. When the metaphor is extended this way, the gender bias that has been part of the idea of apprenticeship throughout the centuries is at least lessened. People today are likely to prefer the word "mentor" instead of "master," which was used for the man guiding the boy.

A person mainly learns to write by reading someone who writes well. The response ought not to be slavish imitation but inspiration to exercise one's own talents. The mark of the skilled master /mentor is that the apprentice does not imitate the teacher but discovers his or her own way. Maria Montessori used to say that two things should be done for the children: show them exactly how something is done and destroy the possibility of their imitating that.[18]

The skilled person manifests the skill along with a few tricks of the trade. Someone who knows how to do something very well often finds it difficult to think along the lines of rules. The apprentice will pick up some of these rules, perhaps some that are not consciously known to the master /mentor.[19]

Coaching A second metaphor that helpfully connects the two main forms of teaching in school is "coaching." As apprenticeship comes from the world of work, coaching comes from leisure activity, including art and athletics. Many classroom teachers might take offense at being compared to a football coach. But the metaphor of coaching can transcend sports-crazed coaches

189

and their supporters. Classroom teachers might get new insight into their work by watching how a good teacher in art or athletics operates.[20]

As I described in chapter three, the sequence in teaching is: student acts, teacher contemplates design, teacher proposes redesign, student tries out the new design. A good coach does not have to memorize that sequence; it is the only way he or she could imagine the activity of teaching to be done. Good coaches are not necessarily great players; the advantage of coaching over the mentor/apprentice metaphor is that the coach does not need to be a genius or possess some special talent. The coach, by carefully studying bodily movement and suggesting slight changes, may bring out talent and genius in others.

One author who explored the metaphor of coaching in teaching is Donald Schön. Both *The Reflective Practitioner* and *Educating the Reflective Practitioner* provide detailed examples of how expert teachers coach their students in art, industrial design, city planning, or psychotherapy. It is, therefore, surprising to read the comment of Patricia Graham: "As Schön has observed, professional practice, in this case college teaching is both learnable and coachable, but not teachable."[21] An opposition between teaching and coaching is not at all the point of Schön's books. On the contrary, he is trying to show how a good teacher teaches by using both apprenticeship and coaching.

Instruction. Finally, there is the metaphor of "instruction." In modern educational literature, this term gets identified with the classroom. But as coaching and apprenticeship could illuminate the classroom, instruction could use some fresh air on stage or on the ballfield. What instruction connotes is precise, direct verbal commands. Instruction is a natural part of teaching any bodily skill. It can be thought of as a subordinate element within coaching or apprenticeship, but it

190

is often the most crucial element in those practices. Every teacher of anything must know how to give precise verbal commands that imply analytic understanding of the student and the situation.

The classroom instructor is a choreographer of words. He or she is trying to do with written and spoken language what the dance instructor is doing with arms and legs. If one loses all connection between teaching and bodily movement, one is left with giving direct commands to the mind or the memory. The term "instruction" is sometimes used as synonymous with indoctrination. Any metaphor for classroom teaching must be grounded outside the classroom or else the classroom will be thought of as a place where big people tell little people what to think.

Classroom Teaching

What I have called classroom teaching can and does go on outside the walls of a classroom. However, in this section I wish to draw a portrait of what can and should happen inside the sacred space of classroom walls. What are the conditions under which this strangest form of teaching-learning can occur?

First, the physical setting needs notice, both the bare physical facts and some of the aids that technology provides. Classrooms throughout the centuries have tended to be bare-walled boxes. The modem classroom arose as part of the modem concern for control that is embodied in prisons, asylums, and hospitals.[22]

Several specific reforms of that traditional classroom were needed but its basic form should remain: a place that conveys a quiet sense of order, dedicated to ear more than eye. There should be fresh air and plenty of light, along with a minimum of distraction from outside the room. Nothing helps a classroom more than carpeting. Janitors may not like carpets, and children are prone to dirty them, but a carpet is often the difference between thoughtful conversation and someone straining to be heard amid reverberating sounds. Many classrooms have chairs nailed to the floor in proper order facing forward. Fixed chairs may be useful, but the overwhelming choice must be chairs that can move in all directions.

Traditional classrooms have a chalkboard at the front; it is a human piece of technology not wholly replaceable by power-point and films. Chalkboards are for thinking with and working through long trains of speech. Traditional classrooms, especially in the university, had a platform for the teacher. The idea was not all wrong, but the platform should be a small performance area either within or attached to the classroom. The platform is for students as much as teachers, or more exactly, for the students when they act as teachers.

Classrooms should not be cluttered with machinery. If a television monitor is helpful to a course, the equipment should be readily available and easy to use. If computers are needed, they should surround the main conversation area. Computers are now indispensable to the school's work but they are not necessarily central to the classroom. The clear focus of the classroom ought to remain the spoken word. Classrooms are one of the few places in the world where people might listen carefully to what someone says and as a result change their minds.[23]

Before commenting on the languages of the classroom, I think it is necessary to defend the classroom against the charge that it is merely talk. People who should be sensitive to the issue often pick up a language that denigrates the classroom. To complain, for example, that the classroom is all talk and no action is to accept the modem split between talk and action. If, in contrast, one begins with the premise that action can be verbal or nonverbal, one is more likely to see how classroom action of the verbal kind can change the world.

John Dewey and successive waves of reformers have begun with the principle of "learn by doing," a principle never to be forgotten in teaching. But the peculiar action or doing in the classroom is speaking. Failing to grasp this point, reformers are always trying to shove things into a classroom that do not fit there. The pieces of equipment may belong in school (in the library, performance studios or computer center) but they can obscure the *kinds of speech* appropriate for the classroom.

John Dewey often sets up an unwise dichotomy that undercuts the serious conversation in a classroom, as when he writes in *Democracy and Education:* "That education is not an affair of 'telling' and being told, but an active and constructive process, is a principle almost as generally violated in practice as conceded in theory.... Its enactment into practice requires that the school environment be equipped with agencies for doing, with tools and physical materials, to an extent rarely attained.[24]

Dewey's unfortunate contrast here is between "telling" and "physical materials." The tools and physical materials certainly belong in schools but not usually in the classroom. Dewey fails to name forms of language for the classroom other than "telling." The alternative to telling is not physical equipment but the other teaching languages discussed in chapters four, five and six.

None of those languages of teaching is excluded in principle from the classroom. Over a period of time, a classroom teacher will use almost every imaginable form of speech to spark interest, to probe for understanding, or to clinch an argument. But of the three families of languages, teaching the conversation holds a special place in the classroom.

193

All human life can be imagined as conversation or dialogue. The classroom is a dialogue about dialogue, a reflecting upon the preconditions of conversation, the ambiguities of any genuine human speech, the possibilities of organizing large bodies of information. The classroom is no less than an entrance into the conversation of the human race. The professional schoolteacher's job is to mediate between past writing and present situations.

Here is an appropriate place to reject the assumption that to teach in a classroom is "to lecture." The assumption is perhaps behind Dewey's contrast of "telling" and "using equipment." The rebellion against lectures seldom leads to the naming of alternative languages for teaching. The only term paired with "lecture" is "discussion," which is often conceived to be the application of the lecture. The university is particularly lacking in imagination when it comes to naming the languages of the classroom. I think that the first step in improving university teaching would be a complete moratorium on the use of the term "lecture."

This language of the university filters into secondary and even primary schools. Perhaps it is a fact that what many university professors do is lecture. But elementary or secondary school teachers, who survive and do a respectable job in the classroom, do not use lecturing as a main way of teaching. They use a variety of forms of speech which, if they could better name, might help them to understand better what they are already doing and what are new possibilities in their work.

I defended the form called lecture but also said that lecturing does not belong in a classroom or at least it should not have a prominent place there. Lecturing should not be more common than its close relative, preaching. Every classroom teacher gives occasional sermons; students do not mind so long as the sermons are brief and to the point. Similarly, lecturing can sometimes seem an efficient way to convey necessary information. Students do not mind a little of that, too; in fact, they can easily become addicted to the teacher being a substitute for the library. Student and teacher may end up with a comfortable arrangement of information giving and note taking that does not challenge either student or teacher.

The old saying is truer than ever: any teacher who can be replaced by a machine (or a book) should be. Machinery can be a tremendous aid in enriching the environment by supplying the information that is the precondition, but not the aim of the classroom. When Chris Whittle announced his ambition to revolutionize schools, he said, "It's amazing to me that we don't bring the best lecturers electronically into schools."[25] Television can be a helpful tool in a classroom but televised lecturers are not what we need.

In addition to lecturing and preaching in chapter four, I discussed storytelling. Ideally, students come to class with stories from home, stories out of books, the story of the school, the great stories of the human race. Then the teacher can launch into dramatizing, analyzing, comparing, playing with stories, all with the purpose of having stories better shape our lives. In practice, however, much of classroom time must be spent going over stories for the first time. Students are usually deficient in a knowledge of some important stories that affect their lives;

The second family – the therapeutic languages – must be kept more at bay in the classroom. A school cannot function without them, but a classroom must be carefully distinguished from a place for therapy. Sometimes people should not be in a classroom because they first need to get past some obstacles to learning. There are, however, some therapeutic languages that are appropriate in the classroom: the rituals of politeness, kindness, and respect. If a sense of self-respect and graciousness is not

195

evident, then the hard work of thinking about academic matters is stymied.

The classroom's main languages are those of the third family. This family includes dramatic performance, dialectical discussions, and academic criticism. Each of these can be a way of shaking up usual patterns of speech that confine our minds. Dramatic performance connotes playing with language and role playing. The drama may be one that tells a story, but instead of the story simply being a vehicle for the deliverance of truth, dramatic performance interjects a distance between speaker and story.

A lot of modern writing has dealt with "role playing." As a technique for getting a group of students to reflect on the words they use, such reversals are quite effective. In a class that is dealing with sexual practice, an adolescent playing the role of a parent can change the outlook of a group.

What is less often spoken about is that the person at the front of the room called "the teacher" is playing a role all the time. Outside this room he or she has a life distinct from classroom instructor. The person who has spent years preparing to teach in a classroom, and is usually paid to do so, has to approach the work with the zest of a stage actor.[26] The fifty or ninety minutes of the class is sacred time, not just time for an ordinary conversation, but for challenging everyone in the room to reflect on their words.[27]

The classroom instructor's lines are not all set beforehand, although a lesson plan is usually helpful. A class meeting that has been carefully planned allows for the feeling of spontaneity and the possibility of redoing the show in the middle of the play. Some contemporary plays that ask, "what is a play?" and "who are the players?" get close to the classroom. If a play in a theater tries to break out from behind the proscenium, an audience unprepared for the experience may be left confused

196

and angry. People entering a classroom should be prepared for exploring what eventually arises in every area of study: Who or what teaches? Who or what decided that history or literature or psychology exist as the subject matter? In the end, the people who entered the class as "students" must demonstrate both in writing and in oral presentation that they could play "teacher." That is what testing and evaluation should be.

The second language in the family of teaching the conversation is "dialectical discussion." The somewhat technical adjective is to highlight that the classroom is different from a local bar or talk at the office coffee machine. The sacred time in the classroom is not for endless bull sessions. Discussion of ideas and their assumptions is what must be structured in classrooms. The careful choice of the topic for discussion, the proper number of people in each group, and the planning of the physical arrangement of the room lead to the most spontaneity and ease in the discussion.

The use of group discussion is highly praised in educational literature. However, much of the praise of discussion groups is simply a vote against "lecturing." That is a bad avenue of approach to using group discussion. Some teachers conclude that if they cannot push it into the students (by lecture) then they will pull it out (by discussion groups). This conclusion is often accompanied by a reference to education's etymology as "to lead out."

Instead of a leading out, dialectical discussion can better be imagined as leading people into the middle of the human race's conversation. Ideas are neither put in nor pulled out; they happen in between the speakers. For each of us as learners, the conversation is at first between great minds who have spent years mastering a "discipline" of ideas. We may have to spend a long time listening carefully to the discussion. Then a four-person group can be a modest embodiment of that human conversation.

Like role playing, discussion is usually spoken of as a technique that the teacher can use. But the teacher, too, is constantly functioning as a member of several groups. Within a school, the group ought to include the faculty's interaction. The faculty as a group ought to stimulate the thinking of individual teachers and protect students if a teacher is irresponsible. The school faculty is a modest representative of the community of scholars that span the human race.

The classroom teacher ought never to lose sight of his or her being in a group of searchers for the truth. The individual teacher can manifest this relation by occasionally reading a passage from a book or an essay. This is where a lecture – say thirty seconds to a minute in length – has a place in the classroom. The teacher can then agree or respectfully disagree with the writer's formulation of the truth. "Dialectical" means going back and forth with the end (purpose) of getting closer to some truth, but without end (termination) in the search for the truth.[28]

Finally, we come to the language most specifically designed for the classroom: academic criticism. In the previous two languages, the meaning of the words is implicitly in question. Here the meaning of words is the question. The grammatical form that academic criticism takes is the interrogative. Who says so? Why? What is presumed? What implications follow? In practice, the teacher varies the grammar and syntax. For example, ironic statements can lighten the tone, while forcing the questioning of an apparent statement of fact.

A teacher often finishes speaking and says, "Are there any questions?" The better teacher tries to start with the student's questions. But asking for questions at the beginning of a class or at the start of a course may be no more effective than asking at the end of the class or the course. The more crucial thing is the teacher's manner of using questions in teaching. If the teacher is asking serious questions, that process will unfreeze the students' questions.[29]

By becoming a questioner, the student becomes a teacher. In Augustine of Hippo's essay "The Teacher," his interlocutor asks, "How in the world do you suppose we learn, if not by asking questions?" Augustine responds, "I think that even then we simply want to teach. Now I am inquiring of you whether you ask a question for any other reason than to teach the person asked what it is you want to know."[30] At the most primordial level of teaching, bodily examples reveal the continuity of teaching and learning; and at the most esoteric level of teaching, the language of questioning reveals that teaching and learning are elements of the same process.

The central element in the classroom is not the idea nor the concept but the word. To walk across the threshold of a classroom, whether in second grade or in a doctoral program, is to expose one's words to public scrutiny. The student's thought remains largely private; they are hidden from the teacher and possibly from the student as well. Words exist in the space between teacher and student with a social and public existence. The teacher's words as well as the student's words are open to question. The main question is not, "Do you agree?" but "What do you mean?" or more importantly "What do the words mean?" The difference between the intended meaning of the speaker and the other meanings of the statement is the main space of academic criticism.

The teacher is the one who is supposed to bring the discipline of academic learning to bear on the inevitable disputes about the meaning of the words. The teacher's criticism is not directed at a person but at words. The teacher unendingly asks,

"Is there a better way to say what you are trying to say?" The person who deserves the name "teacher" must show how to improve the student's skills. In teaching academically, a teacher must use a strange style of bending the words back on themselves so that the student begins to hear his or her own words and recognize their ambiguity.

Where we have the description of great thinkers in classrooms, the initial reaction of a student is commonly one of confusion or anger. The description of Wittgenstein is probably like what happens with most great thinkers. "He taught classes not by lecturing, nor yet by what we usually think of as discussion. Wittgenstein thought aloud before his class."[31] The student becomes a participant in this speaking which is thinking aloud. The student's own words are brought into the thinking aloud with the human race's words. "Mid-wife teachers help students deliver their words to the world, and they use their own knowledge to put the students into conversation with other voices - past and present in the culture."[32]

Teaching in a classroom does not consist of "covering a subject." Books and computers are available for that purpose. What a student should come to a classroom for is to get insight into what he or she has already read. The amount of reading is not a measure of the insight. Jerome Bruner describes a course he took with I. A. Richards that began with the teacher writing on the board: "Gray is all theory/Green grows the golden tree of life." Bruner comments, "The reading time for eleven words was three weeks. It was the antithesis of just reading, and the reward in the end was that I owned outright, free and clear, eleven words. A good bargain. Never before had I read with such a lively sense of conjecture, like a speaker and not a listener, or like a writer and not a reader."[33]

The direct object of "to teach" in the classroom setting is usually "a subject." There is a running debate concerning whether that is the right noun and whether the idea of a school subject is not a false construct. This is a legitimate area for academic criticism. A first question for biology class is "Who says there is such a thing as biology?" The answer will have to include the admission that "biology" is a somewhat arbitrary invention of someone who thought that speaking of a contrast between living things and nonliving things is a helpful way to proceed.to understanding.

Inevitably, the classroom curriculum must be broken down into areas of study. Inventing a lot of new names for these areas might be attractive but that process seldom works. The academic world is constantly, though slowly, altering these names. Biology can be broken down into smaller areas of study; and biology overlaps other sciences that have different approaches. There continue to be people called biologists, chemists, and physicists. That fact does not necessarily mean that high school students should study biology, chemistry, and physics in three different years. A way to get at better questions might be to have biology, chemistry, and physics teachers cooperate in a single curriculum area. The teachers could devise any plan that would stimulate students' thinking about these and other sciences.

P. H. Hirst proposed that to teach a subject is to deal with a "logical grammar."[34] That is, each school subject to be a subject must have a structure of ideas that can be presented by the teacher. Hirst draws his examples from history, physics, and mathematics. John Passmore criticized this way of thinking because it seems inapplicable to much of the school timetable; he cites the examples of typing and cooking as school topics that do not have a distinctive logic. He also thinks that to "teach French" is not done by teaching a logical grammar, and that "history" does not have its own logical grammar.[35] That leaves only physical sciences and mathematics for Hirst's explanation of teaching the logical grammar of subjects in school.

Passmore raises several interesting questions here. They force one to think in narrower terms of what teaching a subject in a classroom means. Can one teach something in a classroom that is not a "subject"? I think that what we need is to complement the teaching of subjects with another kind of teaching, one that goes on inside the school as well as outside. Topics such as typing or cooking do not belong in the classroom, though they may belong in the performance area described below. Similarly, French or English is not the name of a school subject, but French grammar or British literature can be.

As for history not having its own "logical grammar," I think Passmore is correct. But what this example reveals is that the discussion should be about ways of speaking rather than logical structures. A classroom subject is indeed an arbitrary division, but if it is a way of speaking with a long history, then it may be a serviceable if slightly illogical category. And a new subject can push its way into the curriculum if enough people are convinced that it is an important area around which intelligent discussion is possible. The walls of the classroom curriculum are always being pushed through, moved around, torn down, and rebuilt.

Schools in the United States have gone in cycles, saying at one time to students, "We know what is best for you, do this," to saying at another time, "We don't know what is best for you, study anything in any order you wish." Today there may be a better environment for the school advising the student, "We know some things that are good for you, so choose courses in these academic areas."[36]

Performance Areas

The previous discussion focused on a single area, the classroom. The classroom is not an essentially different place for girls or boys, for six-year olds or sixty-year olds, for Africans or South Americans. The activity taking place within the classroom space can be described with some precision. But the second main form of school learning is necessarily in the plural: performance areas. The complexity of performance can be bewildering.

One of the many ambiguities surrounding the word school is whether it refers to an agency under which a set of activities can be organized or whether it means a separate and quite restricted institution of learning. Especially for younger people, the efficient way to reach them is often through the auspices of the school. Important health and government services are made available in school. For example, many children receive their best meal of the day in the school cafeteria. If a child needs medical aid or counseling for emotional distress, the school is likely to be a place for providing help.

If costs are contained, few people complain about these additions to the school. However, the process does create a mentality that the school is an agent for all kinds of social assistance. The result is a constant expansion of topics in the curriculum and additional courses in teacher preparation. If there are 40,000 automobile deaths annually, introduce driver education. If the real estate industry supports racial segregation, integrate society by busing children to school. If sexual diseases are rampant, distribute condoms in school.

The last example, condoms, crystallized the problem more than did many other worthwhile concerns that have been installed in schools.[37] The area of sexual education raises a question about the nature of education and the limits of the school. The importance of the politically volatile issue of condoms is that it forces people to ask theoretically and practically, what is a school? If the relevance to education of sexual activity is only discussed under the rubric of the distribution of condoms, many people object that the school is simply aping the vending machines in a men's room.

What this issue could spark is a discussion of how the classroom's verbal instruction can be appropriately complemented by another kind of learning, one that I have placed in performance areas. Unfortunately, the classroom teaching on human sexuality has never been very strong. Any realistic discussion of sex in the classroom can still cause an uproar from people who think that discussing something is the same as advocating it.

In the case of sexual activity, there is a clear need for contribution from a performance area that might include counseling, artistic exhibitions, and the availability of materials for the protection of health. These approaches should be carried out with careful attention to the age of students. Because the school is always on the verge of being overwhelmed by society's concerns, it would be desirable to supply many worthwhile services and educational experiences by a means other than the school.

Although there are many services and concerns that are of questionable validity for a school to offer, there are performance areas that have rightfully been accepted for many decades as part of school. The three main areas are (1) art (2) job-related work and (3) sports. For young people, each of these areas should be a part of their school education.

Arts. The arts, as we use the term, are central to anyone's lifelong education. Aesthetic education begins before age five and can continue until death. One can learn an an art from an individual teacher outside school, but it makes sense to have the school provide organized teaching of various arts. Any school for young people should have designated spaces for laboratory, studio, or audition hall. How much variety a school can offer depends upon local conditions, including financial considerations, and the availability of teachers. But every school pupil ought to be able to get a taste of some artistic experience.

Many verbal arts have an obvious connection to the classroom. I mentioned earlier that dramatic performance is intrinsic to classroom teaching. A natural overflow is into school plays. Similarly, a debating team or work on a student newspaper staff carries verbal learning into verbal art. Sometimes the artistic projects are restricted to a small group who engage in extracurriculars. However, learning through group projects should be a regular part of the school curriculum. Not everyone is a talented artist; nonetheless, every young person should be able to stand in front of an audience to articulate what he or she knows and to develop a well-shaped argument.

In the previous section, I noted that English or French is not a classroom subject. Learning to speak a language is an art that is not effectively taught in a classroom. For one's first and second language, the classroom's effective use is after you have learned to speak the language. The classroom can be a place to learn grammar and learn to speak the language better. The school library or learning center can supply aids, such as audio recordings. Most effectively, the school can be the organizer of travel to a country where the language is spoken. This foreign country may be a few city blocks away.[38]

Other arts, less verbal in character, should have a place in the school distinct from the classroom. When we are not sure whether something belongs in the classroom, we often insist on its place by attaching the word education (driver education, physical education, drug education). This peculiar twist of language usually has the opposite effect of certifying that the course is not a serious part of education. Sometimes we attach appreciation to various things that do not fit in the classroom, but which we think are a part of everyone's education. Thus, we have courses in art appreciation or music appreciation, but such appreciations have often turned students against appreciating anything but the most banal art.

We need serious courses in the classroom that examine the history and nature of an art. In addition, if there is to be an appreciation of painting, music, sculpture, architecture, pottery, gardening, or woodworking, we need some participation, however amateurish it may be, in the doing of these arts. With some of the arts, one learns solitude and the value of self-discipline. With other arts, one learns the value of teamwork. A band or chorus for children in a school is an invaluable experience of being taught by community, environment, objects, master teacher and fellow apprentices.

Job. The second general area that most schools have some responsibility for is job performance. The classroom instruction for young people needs complementing with the performance of skills that are helpful to holding a job now or in the future. Most students in college and even in high school have part-time jobs so that the school's task is not to initiate work programs but to explore a better relation between existing forms of learning.

The high school or college also must work in cooperation with business institutions, even while being careful to maintain its own autonomy. The business world can sometimes help financially with current technology; sometimes it can supply specialized teaching. The school must ask what realistic experiences of the job world are possible within the school's walls. Where a realistic experience of jobs is not possible, then the school must look beyond itself. The school's performance areas may include connection to a factory downtown or a health center in the neighborhood.

Some schools are predominantly this kind of learning. That makes sense for people training to be better at their current job or retraining if they are unemployed. A trade school is a place that unashamedly announces what its function is. Many such schools produce what they promise, that is, training for existing jobs. Unfortunately, the jobs are often ones of limited skill for the bottom of the economic ladder. If people are to advance in personal satisfaction and social rewards through work, job training must usually be coupled with serious classroom work.

This fact is related to a disastrous split in schools for young people. Since early in the twentieth century, there have been academic schools for those headed for the better jobs and vocational schools for those considered not academically talented.[39] What should be two parts of one school became two schools. Both populations were the poorer for this segregation. Not surprisingly, the students in the vocational schools were financially poorer. Their training was often on outdated equipment and they were prepared for jobs that were either not in the economy or could quickly disappear. The term "vocational," chosen for its religious connotations, was a galling feature of this split that provided power for the rich and a vocation for the poor.

Despite all the limitations of the trade and vocational system, these schools and their dedicated teachers often provide important lessons on teaching. The teacher in the classroom, dealing with literature, science, and history, has to ask, "In what way is this. real work"? In what way do I show these students how to perform, not how to get rich from a job but how to have satisfaction in work? What does hands-on learning mean in a classroom? The schools that have taught manual trades are a helpful reminder. However different the future may be, it will still need people who can make things, fix things that are broken, and take care of complicated services to large populations. If the two-tiered school system is gradually integrated, the academic students might get a more realistic taste of the job experience. Learning to use sophisticated machinery to retrieve information should be a part of everyone's education.[40]

I think it should be clear today that an emphasis upon job preparation need not be gender biased. What Plato envisioned for his upper class is now required for the whole society: equal pay for equal work, and, more important, equal access to all jobs. If the most desirable jobs are to be shared between men and women, then there must be a more equitable sharing of housework and childcare. Plato casually dismisses womanish work in his education for the ideal state.[41] But appreciation of all work and an equitable sharing of the most laborious jobs are necessary for justice between men and women.

In the previous chapter, I called attention to a kind of work, that of service to those in need. The performance area here is generally outside the school but could be organized by the school. Some studies have called for a service requirement in each of the four years of high school with an academic credit for such work.[42] Perhaps that is the only way to get educational attention, but it muddies the distinction between classroom curriculum and school curriculum. The *New York Times Magazine* once published an article entitled "Soup Kitchen Classroom"[43] That title does not help either soup kitchens or classrooms, which are complementary forms of education. The classroom needs protection of its fragile boundaries; and the kitchen is not a place for study but to serve soup.

Few people would object to a program of this kind if it is voluntary. But a school requirement, especially if extended to elementary schools, makes people uneasy. Simply requiring a sixth grader to work in a nursing home could have poor results. But the issue raises interesting questions about having any requirements in schools and how things that are required are designed and carried out.

Service is an area that should be encountered in everyone's education. The student should be supplied with places to work and invited to design how she or he will do the work. The many schools that have such programs know that this service area is not "informal" education. The preparation and monitoring of service work involve at least as much form as classroom instruction.

Sports. Finally, there is sport as a teaching-learning activity deserving of attention. Often, the athletic department is seen as a distraction, or something worse, for the serious business of the school. Much of college and high school athletics is a scandal. Some varsity football teams are simply minor-league teams of the NFL. Hundreds of thousands of black students only have eyes for the 300 slots in the NBA.

High school teams, especially football or basketball and occasionally other sports, can be exaggerated out of all proportion. Nevertheless, when kept under control, sports can teach powerful lessons about living and dying. Often a young person first learns about discipline, motivation, and team effort by participating in sports. School people sometimes hate the athletic department because they suspect that it is the only part of the school that really works, where school has a community spirit and players are fully engaged in what they are doing.

The question for school sports is not how to suppress them but how to extend them to every student. If basketball is only for twelve people in a school, its effect is likely to be distortive. But if the basketball program includes everyone who is interested in playing and has a modicum of ability, it deserves to be recognized as an educational force.

Not surprisingly, the segregation of athletes from nonathletes included a strong gender bias. Women were all but excluded from organized sports. Title IX of the Education Amendment Act of 1972 has brought about remarkable progress in correcting the terrible bias against girls and women in scholastic sports programs. A long way remains but a fairer, if not equal, attention to women in sports is one of the great educational successes of recent times.

I think there is an interesting parallel here between gender bias in the classroom and in the sports arena. I said that emphasis on language in the classroom is not gender-biased. To have voice in the classroom is at least as important to women as to men. Women were mostly silent and often overlooked in classroom practice. But in every classroom subject women can hold their own, even if the evidence is not conclusive whether girls are generally better at some subjects, boys at others.

Performance in the sports arena is a similar case. Women were not present anywhere near as much as men. A call to recognize the importance of sports in teaching may seem biased against women. But the physical education of the human body is at least as important to women as to men. In basketball, soccer, tennis, and golf women often have matches that are more impressive and interesting than men's sports. Women may never match men in some highly valued sport's roles (for example, linebacker) but in other sports with criteria of grace and elegance women may be generally superior. In any case, what Plato once again wished for his upper-class guardians — equality of opportunity in sports — may be coming true for young people.

Chapter Nine: Teaching Morally, Teaching Morality

This last chapter returns to the theme of the first chapter: the dilemma that seems to be inherent to teaching. The intervening chapters have laid out the elements for a solution to that dilemma. Someone who is attentive to the several forms of teaching and the language appropriate to each form can teach morally. Only after that is it possible to teach morality. If teaching were itself an immoral activity, it would be absurd to ask how to teach morality. In this chapter, I review the rise of "moral education" before I summarize the case for teaching morally. I then turn to the teaching of morality in the various forms of education, including classroom instruction in morality.

"Moral education," as a single term with a single referent, was born at the beginning of the twentieth century. Not that the adjective "moral" was a stranger to the term "education." But for the most part, the phrase "moral education" would have sounded redundant. Education since the time of the Greek philosophers was assumed to be a moral undertaking. In the founding of the U.S. public school, morality was a dominant concern.[1]

Toward the end of the nineteenth century, however, the rise of the sciences and the decline of religion aroused a fear that education was becoming amoral. Two opposite corrections were possible. One was to add a remedy called "moral education"; the other was to rethink the moral character of all education. I look briefly at the attempted addition of moral education before examining how all education should be moral.

In the seventeenth and eighteenth centuries, many people hoped that science and religion could work together. The division of the work was that the intellectual class would live by science and the masses would continue to believe the myths of religion. The flaw in this arrangement was that education was located on the side of science. As education along with science advanced, religion was bound to retreat. The foundation of morality in most people's lives was outside or even opposed to education.

Emile Durkheim is one of the inventors of the term "moral education." In his book of that title, published in 1900, Durkheim described the experiment that was underway: "We decided to give our children in our state-supported schools a purely secular moral education. It is essential to understand that this means an education that is not derived from revealed religion, but that rests exclusively on ideas, sentiments and practices accountable to reason only – in short, a purely rationalistic education."[2]

Jean Piaget is the other twentieth-century giant at the origin of moral education. Like Durkheim, Piaget assumed the intellectual bankruptcy of religion as a moral foundation. The title of Piaget's book, *The Moral Judgment of the Child,* indicates the clear and narrow focus of his moral education: judgments made by children. At the beginning of the book, he announces in one sweeping statement: "All morality consists in a system of rules, and the essence of all morality is to be sought for in the respect which the individual acquires for the rules."[3]

If one accepts Piaget's meaning of morality, then the pre-eminent task is that children learn to reason and to judge properly. The child is to discover the rules through interaction with other children, but morality is not a communal affair; it is about the individual and his respect for rules. Moral education thereby moved from the sociologist describing group behavior to the psychologist describing structures of the individual mind.

Piaget expresses strong disagreement with Durkheim for retaining a morality based on "authority." Piaget rejects the preeminence that Durkheim gives to the school. He particularly objects to the premise that "the schoolmaster is the priest who acts as an intermediary between society and the child."[4] For Piaget, adults in general and schoolteachers specifically, tend to get in the way of the child's development of moral judgment. Experiencing a game with rules intrinsic to the game is what the child's judgment about justice requires. Teaching has little part.

According to Piaget, the child who has begun to reason about rules goes through two stages: the first in which rules are thought to be eternally fixed and externally imposed; the second in which rules are seen to be devised by the community for the service of its changing needs. This second stage of autonomous judgment follows upon the capacity to grasp the concept of equality and a concomitant ability to react emotionally to problems of inequity.[5]

After Piaget documents in detail this movement to autonomous judgment, he admits there may be further stages that are not within his purview. As an individual passes from childhood to adulthood, other moral categories, such as care or compassion, may become central.[6] Piaget quotes a precocious thirteen-year old boy, who when asked why he did not hit back after having been hit by another child, replies, "Because there is no end to vengeance."[7]

Lawrence Kohlberg thought that it was logical to try to stretch Piaget's categories beyond where Piaget had firmly anchored them. Kohlberg described his work as "putting patches on Piaget."[8] Beyond the merely conventional morality which Piaget had said can be reached by most adults, Kohlberg postulated a "postconventional" morality, in which the individual goes beyond the observance of rules to a more universal stand.

In 1978 Kohlberg wrote a brief essay that expressed doubt about his whole system. His great hope of a decade earlier for moving students up the ladder to "principled reasoning" had not been realized.[9] The fact struck him forcefully that little boys are prone to lie and cheat. Kohlberg mused that perhaps for some of the population a little indoctrination might not be such a bad thing. After two decades of attacking religions using indoctrination, Kohlberg toyed with the enemy's word.

James Rest, describing the effect of Kohlberg's musings, wrote that for a Kohlbergian it was similar to the first mate hearing that "the captain of the ship has just jumped ship and is headed on another boat in the opposite direction."[10] But then everyone, including Kohlberg, seemed to go back to the business of measuring stages. The collections of Kohlberg's papers, published in the 1980s, show few glimmers of doubt that moral education equals moral development, and that moral development equals the child's power to reason about moral dilemmas.

If Kohlberg had delved more deeply into religious practice, he might have found a richer meaning of education, including education in moral practice. The major traditions are very practical and realistic. None of these religions has been unaware that children lie and cheat. Countermeasures are in place from the beginning so that one does not suddenly have to resort to indoctrination when reasoning does not work. Education in morality begins neither with doctrine nor reasoning but with discipline, ritual and practice.

One reaction to Kohlberg style moral education was by feminist criticism led by Carol Gilligan. Her study, *In A Different Voice*, opened a flood of writing by women that has never stopped.[11] Gilligan introduced a different language of morality, picking up on Piaget's suggestion that care, compassion and responsibility may be important categories that cannot be measured by Kohlberg's moral dilemmas.

A related reaction against Kohlberg was called "character education." One of the leaders of the movement was Thomas Lickona who wrote on "how our schools can teach respect and responsibility," in his book, *Education for Character*. The movement raised a question of whether the classroom is a place for teaching character. One positive feature of Lickona's approach was that he devoted a book to the family's part before writing a book on the school.[12]

A response to Kohlberg, Gilligan and Lickona was William Kilpatrick's *Why Johnny Can't Tell Right from Wrong*. Kilpatrick contrasted two possible courses that might be taught in elementary grades. The first course would deal with dilemmas in which there are no right or wrong answers; teachers would be nonjudgmental and allow students to develop their own value systems. In the second course, the teacher would make a conscious effort to teach specific virtues and character traits. The teacher would express strong belief in the importance of virtues and encourage students to practice them.[13]

Kilpatrick expressed disdain that most schoolteachers, when asked to choose between these two courses, preferred the first. As a classroom instructor, I would choose the first over the second, if those were the only two choices. The first course would probably have little effect while the second would undermine the work of the classroom. But this choice is a false one; neither the first nor the second describes an academic course. The direct object of instruction in a classroom cannot be "specific virtues and character traits."

Looking back nostalgically to the past, Kilpatrick writes, "The idea that the parent is the first and foremost teacher was taken seriously: teachers acted for the parents as trustees of the child 's education." But Kilpatrick does not take seriously his own statement that the parent is "the first and foremost teacher." The second half of his sentence ("teachers acted for parents") contradicts the fact that the parent is a teacher.[14]

Teaching Morally

For addressing the problem of teaching morally I have stepped back from classroom teaching to examine what teaching means in more ordinary situations. Unless these other kinds of teaching are taken seriously, schoolteachers will inevitably be asked to do more than is possible and other than what is ethically defensible. The fundamental meaning of "to teach," as to show someone how to do something, does not immediately connote any moral conflict. Teaching is a gift that calls forth a personal response. If a gift is not received it turns out to be not a gift but an attempted gift. Coercion is a sign that we are not dealing in gift exchange, that is, something which is freely given and freely received.

The most comprehensive teacher is the whole universe, which offers gifts each day. The human being can receive the gift from ocean and desert, mountain and tree, sunlight and star. The individual human can refuse to learn (or be taught), although it is a refusal to accept one's human nature as the preeminently teachable animal. If most humans beings take this attitude toward air, water, topsoil, forest, and earth, then humans will eventually discover that a refusal to be taught is not a long-term option. "Liberation from the soil is not freedom for the tree," wrote Tagore. Liberation from being taught by the gifts in their environment is not freedom for the humans.

Potential moral conflict arises when we move from the universe as teacher to the human community as the teacher. The individual human being cannot reject being taught by the human community. To be a human being is to be in a relation of teaching-learning with the human community. The difficulty, however, is that "the human community" is not directly available. At any particular time and place, what we find are incomplete and imperfect representations of community, for example, one's family.

We do not quibble about the limitations of our community when we are born to this mother and this father. Before one can start raising questions about the deficiencies of one's family, clan, or nation, one must have received life and the basic skills to survive. A particular community says: Here is how to eat, how to speak, how to protect yourself from the cold, how to make things. No one complains that he or she was taught to eat food rather than have the freedom to ingest poison.

The moral problem of teaching emerges when an individual steps forth from the community and is called "the teacher." The authority on which this step is taken is an issue that can never be fully resolved. No one gets appointed as universal teacher, a teacher of all things to all people. Anyone who wishes to play the part of teacher must examine the conditions under which he or she can legitimately teach. Who did the appointing and for how long? What is this teacher appointed to teach? Who are the prospective students?

The answers to some of these questions depend upon the teacher listening to the prospective students. Most particularly, the teacher must ascertain whether the potential learners are ready to learn. Clear signals must provide an affirmative answer that the students are ready at this time and in this place to learn this skill. That is why times and places have been designated to indicate acceptance of the teaching-learning situation. If someone walks across the threshold of a classroom, that is a signal of a willingness to learn in one clearly specified way for a specified period of, say, fifty minutes or two hours. The classroom consent is no more and no less than to expose to critical examination one's written and spoken words on an agreed-upon topic.

Each institution has specified limitations that protect the learner's right to privacy. In a classroom, the learner has a right not to be bombarded with speech inappropriate for the classroom. The learner in a church congregation or the client in a therapist's office has consented to certain forms of speech. A moral crisis arises when institutions overstep their respective boundaries.

Freedom is always a bounded situation. A person exists with a physical body and a psychological makeup that are a precipitate of the past. At each moment the choice is to consent to what is offered or to say no. Sometimes saying no makes available other possibilities; sometimes the no is all that the exercise of freedom means at present. Nonetheless, saying no, whether by a two-year old or an adult, can be the way to preserve one's dignity.

Over against large institutions (banks, business corporations, post office, city hall) the individual can feel powerless. We do not really expect to win individual games with these large foreign powers, but we become dispirited if they run up the score. Children feel much of the time that they are being had by adults. The word "kid" is dismissive and demeaning. Even when adults try to be nice, children are so outgunned that kindness can seem condescending.

School protests are usually a protest against the unfair distribution of power that many young people and some older people feel. They want a say in how their lives flow. School is a place that often focuses resentment, even though the school is usually less repressive than many other institutions. With a few basic changes, students in school can come to see that the school is more on their side than against it.

Very few young people really wish to run a school, but most of them do wish to have some choices in school. Those choices involve space, time, and the forms of learning. Why cannot schools allow students a freedom to move between the school's two main areas of learning, choosing to concentrate on one or the other? Why cannot every student be invited to contribute to the design of courses? Such suggestions may sound like prescriptions for chaos, but any movement in the direction of increased choice can be cautious and measured. The principle of respect for a student's choice should be immediately and clearly affirmed. Young people are likely to be patient if they know that the adults are serious about moving in the direction of increased freedom.

In school, individual teachers should not have to be confronting students daily in a conflict between the right to teach and the student's freedom to learn. The validation of the teacher's work should not rest entirely on each teacher establishing it. The environment and the community should supply the context for supporting the teacher's authority. The professional schoolteacher has a license to teach, which means the freedom to do what seems the best way to proceed with teaching-learning.

If a schoolteacher regularly violates this trust, he or she quite literally loses the ability to teach. Asking classroom instructors to teach character traits or specific virtues is seriously detrimental. The teacher who uses the license responsibly has a right to the support of school administrators, parents, business people, politicians, religious leaders. When the moral authority of a schoolteacher is evident, students learn not by being subservient but by being cooperative.

There are many situations, of course, in which the potential learner cannot foresee what is coming. He or she consents based on trust in the teacher for the process to be started. The possibility that a teacher in a classroom, gymnasium, factory, or church can turn out to be unreasonably demanding or fraudulent points to the need of escape hatches for the learner.

Even the best teachers need places along the way to renegotiate the learner's original consent to join the process. The moral character of teaching-learning never reaches a place so secure that it is invulnerable to corruption. However, the moral universe of teaching does not have to be reconstituted every day. Unless there is evidence to the contrary in particular situations, to teach is a morally good activity.

Teaching Morality

Some kind of morality is always being taught in the activity of showing someone how to live. The explicitness of the concern with morality can vary greatly. Each of the forms of education described in chapter seven teaches morality in its own fashion. Family, classroom, job, and leisure can be examined as teachers of morality.

Family. Relations in the family teach morality every day. The lessons vary according to whether the learner is a two-year old only child, a sixteen-year old oldest of seven, a thirty-year old parent of three, or a seventy-year old grand-parent. Children, however young, are morally educated by routines of daily existence. Long before a child can reflect upon rules of conduct, the child's moral future is profoundly shaped. When moral education is equated with moral reasoning, very young children disappear from the map of moral education.

The child is vulnerable to being miseducated. We have lately become more aware of the violation called child abuse, including abuse of a sexual kind. Rousseau, out of his personal experience, was one of the first writers who began the exposé of child abuse.[15] Other writers quickly followed. We might

220

think that there was a sudden rash of child abuse in the eighteenth century. On the contrary, that century was the beginning of the end of child abuse, even though we have yet to bring about that end. The eighteenth-century's great contribution was to name the reality and thereby make it visible.[16]

One of the especially tragic aspects of child abuse is its self-perpetuating character. Those who are beaten up early in life very often learn their lesson well. Surely, breaking the cycle of child abuse should be central to education in morality, but the issue is beyond the boundary of what in the twentieth and twenty-first centuries has been called "moral education." Children are taught by what they see, hear, touch, and taste. To care for a child and show love teaches care and love. To abuse a child sexually or otherwise is to teach a devastating lesson in violence.

School. As in the family setting, the school does most of its teaching by example. The school can be looked upon as a moral community that shows how virtue is practiced. The school community differs from the family community by having a wider range of examples. Morality is taught in a school by the example of other children and by the lives of administrators, classroom instructors, coaches, counselors and other workers in the school.

Even a small school has a degree of impersonality that sets it in contrast to the family. Durkheim and others believed that the impersonal is not always negative. A child needs the experience of being treated as the most important person in the world; the child also needs the experience of being one among many important beings. School can be a place of fairness, decency, and respect even when hundreds or thousands of pupils are passing through the doors.

Job. A person's job is also an important teacher for nearly all people. The kind of work we do and the way we do it shape our way of life. It is morally debilitating not to be able to have a job, that is, to have tasks that involve intelligence, skill, and training, and which contribute to society's functioning. Money does not have to be involved, although money is a standard sign that the job is valued and that the laborer is respected. Recognition and appreciation of one's efforts are intrinsic elements in the job being real work.

Some jobs wear people down; those jobs that are physical drudgery or mindless repetition teach very little moral sensibility or passion for justice. But most jobs have at least a spark of possibility for being reshaped into work of friendliness, helpfulness, and social improvement. Bank tellers, restaurant waiters, elevator operators, postal workers, taxi drivers, train conductors and at times anyone else, can turn bitter at the limitations of their jobs.

Professional workers are not necessarily better people, but they are people who profess something about the value of their work. They are people who claim to have a calling. They believe, for example, that in a conflict between client and money, the client comes first; otherwise, they have no right to the term "professional."

Since professionals have been graced by some knowledge or skill that a community needs, they must take special pride in doing their work well because the work is worth doing. Professional work is usually more complex and personally fulfilling. It ought to give a moral shape to much of one's life. If one is a writer, actor, philosopher, economist, psychotherapist, one might not ever retire from one's job, though elderhood involves accepting a change in one's physical energies for doing some aspects of the work.

Leisure. In Erik Erikson's scheme of psychosocial development, the last stage of life is characterized by

222

"integrity," a word having strong moral connotations.[17] In chapter seven, I placed wisdom as the value embodied in retirement and leisure activity. By the time one is old, life should have taught the person some semblance of wisdom and moral integrity. This moral teaching should have begun in the infant's playpen and continued throughout school and job. The trials of old age challenge life's earlier teaching and should develop the human individual's receptivity to life, inclusive of death.

The morality of wisdom is the nonattachment to any earthly possession. One is grateful for the day; one enjoys the hour; one lives in the present. Morality is often misunderstood to be a kind of higher selfishness: keep the rules and get greater rewards. The person who morally develops into old age recognizes that we came into this world without possessions and we leave the same way. The deaths of people whom we love remind us of our own mortality. Death is a powerful teacher for those who are ready to learn.

Old age does not guarantee a sudden surge of wisdom. Not every seventy-year old is a Buddhist sage. The leisure activities throughout life, and especially in the older years, lead people down one of two moral paths. Either they become more egocentric in their interests, turned in on their own problems. Or they turn toward greater compassion for human and nonhuman life. The liberation from means-to-end thinking can release in older lives a care for other older people who are worse off, and a concern for the young who share a similar position of vulnerability.

The young and the old often find that they can teach each other about transitions into new life. Sometimes parents and children are locked too closely together; the grandparent has a helpful distance from everyday conflicts. For the child the grandparent paradoxically represents vitality, even in the face of approaching death. The quiet center of retirement's leisure activity seems to be almost contentless, but it is really a revelation of harmony and unity.

Teaching Ethics

Classroom. Two challenges are raised by the issue of teaching morality in a classroom. What light does teaching morality in a classroom throw on teaching anything in a classroom? How does the classroom's part in teaching morality relate to the teaching of morality in and by other educational settings?

Throughout much of the academic world there is belief that it is impossible – or at least academically illegitimate – to teach morality in a classroom. Concerning the teachability of things in a classroom, a spectrum is assumed that has mathematics and physical science at one end; there is no debate on whether physics and calculus are teachable subjects. Moving away from that end of the spectrum, literature, history, and human sciences are also thought to be teachable. But for many people, religion and morality go off the chart. They are thought to be too private, too subjective, too lacking in definite answers.

A first clarification needed is that "morality" is not the most appropriate name for the academic form of teaching morality. The academic subject is best indicated by the term "ethics." In previous centuries, terms such as "moral science" or "moral philosophy" served this purpose. However, ethics has a long history as part of philosophical inquiry.

What is worrisome when people dismiss the possibility of teaching morality or ethics in a classroom is not what they assume about morality, but what they think "to teach" means. An understanding of the teaching of morality/ethics might help to clarify what it means to teach anything. If teaching in a classroom consisted of telling people what is so, then teaching morality/ethics would be a violation of the pupil's right to privacy, conscience, and freedom.

The classroom is not a place for telling people the truth. It is a place for a peculiar kind of conversation. Every question asked, every problem raised has ambiguity built into the formulation. But the ambiguity in the words is not limitless. Through sustained conversation we can hope to narrow misunderstandings even if we cannot reach complete agreement. Teaching morality/ethics means being skeptical of any yes or no as an answer to a complicated moral problem. The teacher's job is to be certain that there are enough voices in the discussion and that the terms of the dispute are carefully reflected upon. This process bears little resemblance to what is characterized as "value-free inquiry."

In contrast to academic teaching as conversation, consider this statement in Stephen Carter's *The Culture of Disbelief*: "It is difficult to resist the impression that some educators simply feel uncomfortable with stating a clear and simple value – they seem to believe that in some way, by telling students what they *should* do (instead of telling them how to do what they want to do) they are engaging in a form of pedagogy best avoided."[18]

I think that "telling students ·what they *should* do" is indeed a form of pedagogy which is best avoided. The classroom teacher has no business telling people what they should do, beyond stating the rules of civility in classroom behavior.

Carter's alternative to telling them what they should do is contained within the parentheses: "telling them how to do what they want to do." I assume that he intends that phrase to be caricature or sarcasm. Actually, it is close to stating the classroom's task of helping students to follow their best lights.

225

However, I would not accept either of his alternatives. The underlying problem here is the assumption that to teach is to tell, and that classroom teaching should consist in teachers telling students what is true and what is false, what is right and what is wrong.

Carter wants students "to be told that abstinence is a good and desirable thing." I would not tell students in a classroom that (sexual?) abstinence is a good and desirable thing. I do not think that teachers should be telling students that abstinence is a bad and undesirable thing. But the academic alternative to both "tellings" is to bring students into the conversation from which the teacher's own opinions and beliefs have emerged.

At the end of that conversation, the student may or may not agree with the teacher. The teacher's success can be measured by whether the student has a better understanding of the issue discussed. To teach ethics is to show a student how to use a language of morality that can improve his or her understanding of the best course of action;

A procedure that is sometimes employed with ethics courses is a debate in which the students take sides.[19] As a technique to get students involved, there is merit to the approach. But if the result is that the pro and con sides simply dig in deeper to defend their respective opinions, the classroom's potential is dissipated. In a few cases (e.g., nuclear war), the yes or no is clear-cut. On ideas of euthanasia, abortion, or sexual codes, the work is to clarify where there might be agreements despite disagreements. If the classroom does not supply a better understanding of what these questions mean, our politics will get hopelessly stalemated. Other issues (feminism, multiculturalism, environmentalism) are not case studies at all but complex movements overlaid with various ideologies. Taking sides on these issues is likely to generate more heat than understanding. A debate needs a single clear focus which comes from reading and interpretation of texts in those areas.

The ethics teacher, like all classroom teachers, needs two points of view. The first is that the position which he or she states is true because it draws upon the richest strands of human history and geography. The second viewpoint is that the teacher's position, as it is stated, is deficient because formulas can always be improved. This dual perspective in the classroom conveys a certainty that one has some hold on the truth and a certainty that one cannot state the whole truth. What the teacher says in academic conversation is asserted as not false and not empty There is always more to learn for the teacher as well as for the taught. The ethics teacher is no worse off here than the science or art teacher. Perhaps the ethics teacher is a little better off in having to admit the duality of perspectives.

At some moments in life it may seem distracting to have more than one perspective. There is nothing wrong with a chant of "peace now," the slogan "a woman's body is her own," or a "gay pride" banner. However, when an emotionally charged issue shows up in the classroom, no orthodoxy can be left unchallenged. In a classroom, every formula on every topic is open to criticism.

Take an extreme case.[20] In 1986 a curriculum *Facing History and Ourselves* was refused funding by a federal agency. The rumor was leaked that the refusal was based on the fact that the curriculum did not give Hitler's side of the story. This rumor was confirmed in 1995 when Newt Gingrich tried to appoint the evaluator, Christina Jeffrey, to be historian of the House of Representatives. Jeffrey had written in her evaluation, "The program gives no evidence of balance or objectivity. The Nazi point of view, however unpopular, is still a point of view and is not presented."[21] When that statement was made public it was met with scorn and disbelief. Actually, there was a valid point to be made here, but Jeffrey's phrasing of the issue as "balance or objectivity," as well as Hitler's view being "unpopular," was a misleading way to make her point.

A curriculum that would provide moral symmetry for Hitler and the victims of the Holocaust would be obscene. Nonetheless, the classroom is a place to examine every viewpoint, even Hitler's. Otherwise, the mode of discourse is preaching, rather than academic criticism. The classroom's contribution to preventing future holocausts is understanding, which involves getting inside the minds of everyone involved in the Holocaust. There are times for memorial services, for protesting bigotry, for preaching love, for legal restraints on neo-Nazis. But when the time for ethics class comes, the relevant question is, do you understand?[22]

We can start asking a five-year-old child, "Do you understand?" but it would be unwise to offer an ethics course in elementary grades. Like religion or psychology, ethics is a difficult academic subject that should not be attempted before many other subjects have been studied. However, ethical questions can surface in every subject of the classroom curriculum. When enough ethical issues have appeared in their historical contexts and practical situations, the strands can be gathered together for reflection on the subject of ethics itself. To teach ethics is to clarify a language for thinking clearly, comprehensively, and consistently about the moral life.

Simply dealing with language may seem to be an ineffective way to get at morality. Is not the point of teaching morality to produce better people? The knock against teaching ethics is like the general complaint against classroom instruction: all talk and no action. With morality the accusation becomes most acute. What is the point of knowing Aristotle's analysis of friendship if it is no help to making friends? I have previously cited Aristotle saying that

228

the way to become virtuous is to grow up in a virtuous community. That might seem to imply that studying ethics is a waste of time. Yet Aristotle gave us our word "ethics" in the naming of two books that provide instruction on the subject.

The key here is not to neglect the rest of education in morality when we directly attend to the teaching of ethics in a classroom. If the rest of a person's education is effective, the teaching-learning of ethics will make a moral contribution to that education. However, if one's education in morality is generally deficient, the teaching-learning of ethics is not likely to reverse the process or substitute for every defect. Aristotle produced his books on ethics for people who were already virtuous and wished to become more so.[23] A classroom environment may overcome some deficiencies in other teaching of morality, but the teacher of ethics cannot expect to produce care, love, kindness, discipline, and honesty by teaching ethics.

The ethics instructor hopes to contribute to the improvement of the human race but signs of moral uplift cannot be demanded of this pupil at this moment. When classroom instruction is aimed at something other than the understanding of spoken and written language, it fails to do what the classroom is set up to do and which usually is not done elsewhere.

As is true of other classroom instruction, the ethics teacher works with the language of the student which is situated within a conversation of the wisest minds available. The choice is not between talk and action. The choice is what kind of talk? Talking is a kind of action; the most appropriate action in a classroom is academic criticism. The temptation is to slide from academic teaching of ethics in one direction to storytelling, lecturing, and preaching or in the other direction toward therapeutic opinionating. Either "I know what is right and I will tell them so" or more likely in U.S. schools: "Let's all express our views and feel

229

satisfied at the end of class." Teaching ethics means finding the formulas or inarticulate fragments that students have and working to improve that language.

The teacher of ethics has a modest position in the teaching of classroom subjects. He or she is likely to be left alone with what is assumed to be an innocuous endeavor. Of course, if the ethics teacher starts preaching revolution or carrying out lab experiments in sexual relations, the course will draw attention because of the misuse of the academic setting.

It can happen, however, that the ethics class, precisely because it is doing its job, can conflict with the society around it and even the school that houses it. The questions raised in ethics class about power relations, justice, and bias are potentially embarrassing for any institution. Both school administrators and ethics teachers should be aware that conflict is inherent to their situation. Good will on both sides can ameliorate but not eliminate conflict.

Take the case of a particularly sharp tension: a military school. John Keegan, a premier historian of warfare, describes teaching in a military college. He calls the vocational side of the student's education "formation," which "aims, if not to close his mind to unorthodox or difficult ideas, at least to stop it down to a fairly short focal length." Keegan says there is also an academic side, "which aims to offer the student not a single but a variety of angles of vision; which asks him to adopt in his study of war the standpoint not only of officer, but of private soldier, non-combatant, neutral observer, industrialist, diplomat, relief worker, professional pacifist – all valid and documented points of view."[24]

Keegan is describing a history course, but the ethical dimension is obvious. The better the historian does his or her job, the more unavoidable are the ethical questions. Keegan's statement that all the views on war and peace are valid and documented means that they exist and can be studied. But what happens if the student officer gets persuaded by the viewpoint of the "professional pacifist"? Is being persuaded of the validity of pacifism a proper education for the man whose formation has everything to do with leading soldiers in battle?

The inference one might draw is that if the academic part of the student soldier's education is adequately developed, it might cause a crisis for the profession. This crisis is not peculiar to the soldiering profession. Suppose law students really examined the value of a lawyer's work from all perspectives? What if land developers started looking at land from a variety of human and nonhuman perspectives?

My concern here is not the morality of soldiering, law, or land development It is rather that we are all in the same position of being trained to act in certain ways before we are able to think out for ourselves how to act. That is the "moral education" we receive when we are very young. Academic instruction can only come later to examine, not necessarily reject, what we have learned in childhood.

Ethics must challenge assumptions in our family life, career, and leisure activities. Teaching ethics, instead of being off the end of the spectrum of academic subjects, is the logical consequence of teaching anything in a classroom. In relation to the overall teaching of morality, the classroom teaching of ethics is a modest part of the whole project, but it is what keeps education in morality from becoming either neutral techniques or conformity to rules. Education, including moral teaching and teaching of morality, is for improving human life, including the relations of men and women, adults and children, and to reshape for the better the human relation to the nonhuman world.

Conclusion

This book has tried to answer a single question: What is the meaning of "to teach?" I have proposed that to teach is to show someone how to do something. I have proceeded by testing out this meaning for determining whether it would open into diverse kinds of teaching and gather the diversity into a consistent whole.

When describing the language of academic criticism in chapter six, I said that the most apt metaphor for it is a legal one: the teacher advocates a case before a jury. The listeners may or may not be convinced by the argument. This book is written in the language of academic criticism, with occasional help from other forms of speech. The reader is a jury member. In my final summation, I would like to present a comparison between the meaning of "teach" in the two philosophical traditions described in the first chapter.

In the first tradition, teaching is the intention of an individual to explain something to a learner, usually a child. This meaning has an appealing clarity within a system of modern ideas on education. In the second tradition to teach is to show someone how to do something, most comprehensively how to live and how to die. This second meaning does not contradict the first; it provides a context for understanding how that first meaning became dominant but why it cannot take us far enough.

I would resist a description of this second meaning as wider or more general. I have not so much tried to expand the meaning of the term as to expand the conversation about that meaning. My method has been retrieval rather than invention. The meaning is already there, although participants in a conversation on teaching may not be aware of it.

The second meaning is not a general or abstract meaning that is out of touch with practical realities. On the contrary, my aim has been to start with a precise and practical meaning, one that is strong enough to bear a variety of forms. The search has not been for a general meaning abstracted from individual cases, but for a (nearly) universal meaning embedded in the particular cases.

The second meaning's most appropriate image, therefore, is not broader *but deeper* and as a result more comprehensive. I started with a *root* meaning rather than a general one. I have tried to ground the meaning of "to teach" in ordinary, earthy, bodily action. A variety of linguistic branches grow from that root meaning. While the root may not always be visible in the branches, the vitality of teaching is still traceable to that root.

In the paragraphs that follow, I will set out a point-by-point comparison of the two meanings of "to teach."

In the first meaning, to teach is to explain; in the second meaning, to teach is to show someone how to do something. The agent of teaching in the first meaning is an individual human being who can give reasons. In the second meaning, the comprehensive agent of teaching is the universe of living beings, including the example of the human community and individuals within the community.

In the first meaning, the necessary note is intention. Where the intent to teach is present, teaching exists; where there is no intention, there is no teaching. In the second meaning, the necessary note is learning. The only proof that teaching exists is that learning exists. Where there is learning, there is teaching; where there is no learning, there is no teaching.

In both meanings, a gap in the continuity of teaching-learning exists. In the first meaning, the gap is between teaching and learning. Two different processes exist: one activity is teaching, the other activity is learning. In the second meaning, the gap is between the individual's intention and what is actually taught and learned. In this case, teaching-learning is a single and continuous process, but not entirely under the control of an individual.

These two gaps lead to two different interpretations of the problem of teaching. In the first, it will be said, "I taught them; they didn't learn." In contrast, the second meaning of teach leads to the problem statement: "I tried to teach them; they did not learn." The response to the first problem statement has usually been to search for psychological causes. The second problem statement is likely to look for answers in economic, political, social – as well as psychological – concerns.

Psychology has made helpful contributions to our understanding of learning. Nevertheless, the almost complete absorption of education's language into psychology has severely limited the discussion of education and teaching. The second meaning opens the conversation to all who teach. It looks for obstacles to teach-learn in the mal-distributions of power between adult and child, men and women, rich and poor, sick and healthy, schooled and unschooled.

When teaching appears to fail in the first meaning, the remedy is to develop better explanations that are aligned with the child's style of learning and stage of development. However, since we cannot trust that people are going to be reasonable all the time, most people need gentle coercion.

In the second meaning, the remedy is also twofold: Find out who and what *are* teaching. Then undertake a redesign of the teaching-learning situation. It may take some time to discover the who and the what of teaching, and our redesigns will always be imperfect. But teaching is the best hope of humanity, and it should not be cast aside for supposedly quicker and more efficient solutions, such as more police and more prison cells. Some coercive power will probably always be with us but should only be used as a protection at the border of teaching, not as a regular substitute for teaching.

The first meaning is reflected in the language of "formal and informal education." Either *the* form is present and we have education, or else we have only something deficient that claims to be education. The dominant image of "formal education" is a school within which there are classrooms and an adult standing before a group of children who are seated at desks.

The second meaning of teaching does not exist in an institution called "formal education"; instead it is found in many forms. Even within the school itself there is more than one form of teaching-learning. If to teach is to show someone how to live, that requires many settings in which adults interact with each other and where children gradually enter these exchanges. I proposed as a pattern of educational forms: family, job, classroom, leisure. To teach is to reshape one of these forms and to reshape the interrelation of these forms.

In the first meaning, teaching is almost entirely restricted to one form of speech: to teach is to tell. Speech has the function of conveying knowledge from one human mind to another, usually from the trained expert to the ignorant child. In the second meaning of teaching, there are several families of languages and many cases within each family.

In the second meaning, teaching begins and ends in silence; between the silences, teachers use a variety of languages. Sometimes speech is used to urge people on to their goal; at other times speech is used to restore a sense of purpose in the learner's life. Speech can also be used to provoke the mind, forcing the learner to go in search of the right questions before he or she can get answers. One setting of education differs from another by the particular mix of languages used. For example, a school and a family over time will include every main form of speech. They will differ in the prominence and the amount of each kind of speech in their respective mixes of teaching languages.

In summary, the second meaning of "teach" is superior on every point. So long as this second meaning is not misunderstood as a kind of soft and sentimental generality, there are no drawbacks to it. It encompasses what most people in the past have meant by teaching and it gives new seriousness to contemporary uses of "teaching" that otherwise receive at most only passing mention.

If the case for this meaning of teaching is so strong, why is there such difficulty in getting a hearing for it and what would be necessary for it to reemerge at center stage? I suggest two main reasons behind the modern era's narrow meaning of "to teach."

1. The meaning of teaching as "to show someone how to live and how to die" has moral and religious connotations. Recent times have been a sea of confusion about both morality and religion, not to mention the relation between them. In philosophical history, as far back as Socrates, and in religious history, including all the world's major religions, the justifying of who teaches and what is taught have been moral issues. The modern world has preferred to avoid as far as possible religious and moral issues. If to teach simply means to give people reasons or to explain things, we seemingly avoid all the bickerings of religion and the uncertainties of morality.

There is nonetheless a moral assumption here, namely, that reasons and explanations are desirable and that no sane person can object to being given reasons. The ideal of universal schooling is based on this assumption. Children are confined to schools because they are not yet reasonable adults.

Schoolteachers are given a license to explain things to children until the children can think for themselves. Children receiving explanations in classrooms is a better alternative than what most children in history have faced. The problem is the reduction of the meaning of teaching to this one, unusual form.

The attempt to avoid all moral and religious issues has not entirely succeeded. Outside a narrowly circumscribed area of mathematics and science, teachers do not rely exclusively on rational explanations based on objective facts. John Dewey in the 1930s could hold out "scientific method" as the ideal for all teaching.[1] Since then, however, it has become obvious that classroom instructors in any discipline, not excluding the physical sciences, have to rely on interpretation of data, and must appeal to imaginative, aesthetic, and subjective considerations.

Reason has proved to be a powerful instrument for the human journey; reason has also proved to be a dangerous power if it eliminates what precedes and surrounds it. As Martin Buber said of consciousness, reason ought to play first violin but not try to be conductor.[2] Reason is at the service of life. Teaching as the giving of reasons should be at the service of teaching people how to live. But if living is the more comprehensive object of teaching, where can we find teachers of how to live? Should we turn our classrooms over to gurus and prophets?

My answer has been twofold. We must protect the classroom against gurus and prophets if these terms connote preaching messages, indoctrinating young minds, and forming disciples. The classroom is a place for thoughtful conversation carried out in measured speech. But that does not mean that religion and morality should be excluded from the conversation. Religion becomes irrational and morality becomes mindless if they are declared unworthy of serious attention in the classroom.

The answer to the question "where do we find teachers of how to live" is that they are already here and doing their job: parents, friends, political leaders and religious activists. If we would recognize them and name them as teachers, we could help them to do their job better.

The assumption in the late nineteenth century that religion was soon to disappear and that "moral education" could be handled with a few new twists has proved to be naive. We need a coalition of teachers – human and nonhuman – to face up to the moral and religious crisis that threatens to tear apart the world.

2. The second underlying issue in the narrowing of the meaning of teaching is the growth of the school system and the better preparation of schoolteachers. For the modern school to fulfill its purpose, full-time "professional educators" were needed. During the last century and a half, it has been assumed that a person called "the teacher," is a member of this group. Teaching is therefore thought to be the work of the "teaching profession." To challenge the meanings of teaching and teacher is to run up against a thick wall of professional control.

There is a certain irony, I realize, in complaining about the control that is exercised by professional educators. Schoolteachers have had a long journey, not yet completed, to be recognized as a profession at all. In the nineteenth century, when school teaching switched from being a man's to a woman's job, many writers described school teaching as an extension of the one profession for which women were suited: motherhood.[3] Since then, schoolteachers (along with nurses) have struggled to go beyond what Amitai Etzioni called "semi-professions" and achieve the full status of a profession.[4]

Becoming a profession looks deceptively easy. Numerous groups take on the trappings of a profession (a code of ethics, a set of credentials, an annual conference, a journal, and so forth) and declare themselves to be a profession. It is another thing, however, for the public to recognize that a group has an area of knowledge and skill under its control and can offer a sustained service to a community.

The difficulty that schoolteachers have had in establishing their professional claim is that most people think they know what teaching a six-year old entails.[5] In contrast, most people are mystified by the talk of lawyers, accountants, and civil engineers. People are correct when they claim some knowledge of how to teach a six-year old; a great many people do have that experience. However, very few people have what it takes to teach a group of six-year olds in a classroom. For that, one needs talent, training, and dedication. If schoolteachers would name their profession more accurately, admitting its continuity with teaching in ordinary life, they would get both support as professionals in a distinctive work and cooperation from parents and others whose work has some similarity.

For most of the past hundred and fifty years, it has been feared that to admit a continuity with ordinary life would weaken the claim to professionalization.[6] And, indeed, the modern professions have depended upon a perception that their work is so arcane that it is beyond the mere lay person's understanding. The medical profession led the way to the top of professional status, paving the way for tax accountants and mortgage closers. But in recent decades a turn seems to have occurred, led again by the medical profession. Having succeeded in isolating their esoteric knowledge from the laity, physicians found themselves losing the trust of the public and being hit with malpractice suits.

Physicians have been pressed to redesign their relation to other professionals and to the (medical) laity. The emerging result is a new configuration, centered on health not medicine, in which the physician is still a central player but is part of a team. Included in that team is the patient who must learn about health and what to do for his or her body. In the health professions, there can be many concentric circles of expert knowledge but there is no room for any group called "laity," that is, people totally ignorant of their health concerns.

The schoolteachers who had seemed to trail behind in the modern professional world may turn out to have an advantage. The link to teaching in ordinary life can place the schoolteachers into immediate relation with the adults and children being served. Every profession in the future must be a teaching profession in which the aim is to share knowledge rather than hide it in impenetrable jargon. Those who are skillful at instruction are a key to the reformation of professional life.

My resistance to the control of "teaching" by professional schoolteachers is not meant as a disparagement of teaching in school. I believe there is no greater profession in the world of work. However, the case for this profession needs strengthening in U.S. society. The language we have inherited, mainly from the nineteenth century, tends to flowery praise of teachers but not enough economic and political support for the work of schools and their teachers.

I have proposed that schoolteachers let go of the one word they have in their grasp: teaching. They must stop talking about the "teaching profession" and include the school as the place where they are experts in teaching. That may seem asking for professional educators to commit suicide, but they could have a stronger profession.

If we start with teaching as showing someone how to do something, school people are challenged to examine their special ways of teaching. Both classroom instructors and performance coaches have a fund of experience that needs to be tapped. They need linguistic help to draw from that experience and get help for their work. If this were to happen, we would be on the way to combining the best meaning of teaching with a more solidly grounded profession of school teaching.

INDEX

Frye, Northrop, 81, 254
funeral rite, 120

G

Gadamer, Hans-Georg, 76
Gettysburg Address, 90
Gilligan, Carol, 214
Glaser, Elizabeth, 167
Gopnik, Alison, v
Gordon, Ruth, 134
Gorer, Geoffrey, 130
gossip, 82-83.
Graham, Patricia, 190
grandchildren, 175-76
grandparent, 163, 168, 223

H

Hamlet, 131-32
have a nice day, 113
Havel, Vaclav, 88-89
Havelock, Eric, 134
Hegel, Georg, 126, 135
Hirst, P.H., 201
Holocaust, 118, 141, 228
Holt, John, 13
horses, 38
human design, 43
Hume, David,110

I

Illich, Ivan, 14-15
impersonality, 221
infant, v, xi, 9, 32, 40, 47, 44, 51, 59, 66, 122, 167, 223
instruction, 32, 35, 58, 59, 183, 190-91
ironic question, 141-42

irony, 3-4, 50, 238

J

Jaeger. Werner. 248
Jenniger, Philip, 141-42
Jesus, v, 135, 180, 217, 234

K

Kant, Immanuel, 10, 101, 139
Keegan, John, 230, 272
Kerferd, G.B., 260
Kermode, Frank, 128
Kilpatrick, William, 215-16
King, Martin Luther, Jr, 94-95
Kliebard, Herbert, 180
Kohlberg, Lawrence, 213-15
Kolakowski, Leszek, 76
Krishnamurti, 47
Kübler-Ross, Elisabeth, 120
Kushner, Howard, 121

L

language games, viii
languages of teaching, 151
laborious jobs, 174, 208
Lash, Nicholas, 249
lecture, 85-91, 194-98
Lickona, Thomas, 215
Lincoln, Abraham, 95, 195
Lowe, John, 51, 250
Luther, Martin, 94, 99, 100

M

Malcolm X, 37, 251
Malinowski, Bronislaw, 256
Marshall, George, 97-89
Martin, Jane, 91, 167
Marx brothers, 132
Marx, Karl, 126,135
master stories, 81-82
meanings of education, 153, 160
Meier, Deborah, 256
mentor, 189-90
mid-wife, 156
Mill, John Stuart, 137
Montessori, Maria, 47-50,169,171
moral education, 211-215, 231
Morgan, Edmund, 262
Morgan, Michael, 248
mothers, v, vi, 1, 9, 80, 167
mourn, 114-22
movies, 44, 84
Murrow, Edward, 91
myth, 81-83, 148

N

native peoples, 118
Needleman, Jacob, 28, 251
Neill, A.S.,14
Niebuhr, Reinhold, 110
Nietzsche, Friedrich, vii, viii, 20, 125
nonhuman animals as teachers, 19, 30, 68
nonverbal teaching, 35, 37
Nuland, Sherwin, 35, 120

O

Oakeshott, Michael, 25-27, 140

puns, 132-33

R

S

Title IX, 209
to child one's parents, 34, 167
to parent, 5, 34, 167
Tolstoy, Leo, 47-49
Tom, Alan, 189
trade school, 206
traditional rituals, 98
trust, 46-47, 59, 84, 102, 116, 219, 238
truth and meaning, 127-28
"to parent", 5, 34,

V

Vlastos, Gregory, 3
vocational schools, 207

W

Waiting for Godot, 132
Wallant, Edmund, 122
Wees, W.P., 248
welcome, 111-14
Westbrook, Robert, 257, 266, 268
what a school is, 179
Whitehead, Alfred North, 75
Whittle, Chris, 195
willing, ix, 25, 28 32, 54. 125, 167, 217
Wills, Garry, 90, 255
Wittgenstein, Ludwig, viii, 7-8, 27-28, 103, 106, 130, 200
Wollstonecraft, Mary, 9
work, pro bono, 172

Notes

Introduction

[1] Alison Gopnik. *The Philosophical Baby* (New York: Farrar, Straus and Giroux, 2009), 5.

[2] Jacques Barzun, *Teacher in America* (Bostonm MA: Little, Brown and Co., 1945), 10.

[3] Gilbert Highet, *The Art of Teaching* (New York: Vintage Books, 1954), 157.

[4] Steven Pinker, *The Language Instinct* (New York: Morrow, 1994), 39.

[5] Gary Shapiro, "The Writing on the Wall: The Anti-Christ and the Semiotics of History," in *Reading Nietzsche*, ed. Robert Solomon and Kathleen Higgins (New York: Oxford University Press, 1988), 199.

[6] Ludwig Wittgenstein *Philosophical Investigations,* 3rd ed. (New York; Macmillan, 1968).

[7] Arthur Lovejoy and Franz Boas, *Primitivism and Related Ideas in Antiquity* (New York: Octagon, 1965), 109.

[8] Wittgenstein, *Philosophical Investigations,* par. 241.

Chapter One

[1]Michael Morgan, *Platonic Piety* (New Haven, CT: Yale University Press, 1990), 7-31.

[2] *The Sophistic Movement* (Cambridge: Cambridge University Press, 1981); for the statement of Protagoras, see Plato, *Protagoras,* 316, 324-25.

[3] Plato, *Apology* 21b.

[4] Gregory Vlastos, *Socrates: Ironist* and *Moral Philosopher* (Ithaca, NY: Cornell University Press, 1990), 33; see also Werner Jaeger, *Paideia: The Ideals of Greek Culture* (New York: Oxford University Press, 1971), 2:171-72: "It is true that the new *paideia* is not teachable as the sophists understood teaching: so Socrates was right to say that he did not teach men - not by giving them information. But by asserting that virtue must be knowledge and making his way toward that knowledge, he took the place of those false prophets of wisdom, as the only real educator."

[5] W. P Wees, *Nobody Can Teach Anybody Anything* (New York: Doubleday, 1971).

[6] Johann Comenius, *The Great Didactic,* ed. M. W. Keatinge (New York: McGraw Hill, 1931), 51.

[7] John Locke, *Some Thoughts Concerning Education* (New York: Dover, 2007), sec. 85, 68.

[8] Jean-Jacques Rousseau, *Emile* (New York: Basic Books, 1979).

[9]Rousseau, *Emile,* 37-39.

[10] Rousseau, *Emile,* 21

[11] Rousseau, *Emile,* 370-72

[12] Rousseau's novel which was called *Les Solitaires* was never completed.

253

[13] Mary Wollstonecraft, *A Vindication of the Rights of Woman,* ed. Charles Hagelman Jr. (New York: Norton, 1967), 233.

[14] Jane Martin, *Reclaiming a Conversation* (New Haven, CT: Yale University Press, 1985), 69.

[15] Immanuel Kant, "What is Enlightenment?" *Foundations of* the *Metaphysics of Morals* (New York: Macmillan, 1990), 83.

[16] Nicholas Lash, "Teaching or Commanding?" *America,* Dec. 13, 2010, 17-20.

[17] Johann Pestalozzi, *Leonard and Gertrude* (Charleston, SC: Nabu Press, 2010).

[18] John Holt. *How Children Fail* (New York: Putnam, 1964); *Learning all the Time* (Boston, MA: De Capo, 1990). The subtitle is: "How Children begin to read, write, count and investigate without being taught."

18 Carl Rogers, *Freedom to Learn* (Columbus, OH: Merrill, 1969), 153.

[20] A. S. Neill, *Summerhill* (New York: St. Martin's Press, I 992), 101.

[21] Neil Postman, *Teaching as a Subversive Activity* (New York: Delta, 1971). One of his later books which is often referred to today is *Amusing Ourselves to Death* (New York: Peter Lang, 2014).

[22] Ivan Illich, *Deschooling Society* (New York: Harper and Row, 1971).

[23] John Lowe, *The Education of Adults: A World Perspective* (Paris: UNESCO, 1975), 14.

[24]Friedrich Nietzsche, *Beyond Good and Evil* (New York: Penguin Books, 1973), 45. Nietzsche himself did not seem to apply his own teaching to himself when he talked of being a teacher. He seems to have tried too directly to make disciples and was constantly disappointed; for a discussion of Nietzsche as teacher, see Leslie Thiele, *Friedrich Nietzsche and the Politics of Soul* (Princeton, N.J.: Princeton University Press, 1960), 165-82.

[25] Alan Tom, *Teaching as a Moral Craft* (London: Longman, 1984), 55; for a more positive assessment of this tradition, see Michael Dunkin and Bruce Biddle, *The Study of Teaching* (New York: Holt, Rinehart and Winston, 1974).

[26] Gilbert Ryle, *The Concept of Mind* (New York: Barnes and Noble,1949),149-52; Israel Scheffler, *The Language of Education* (Springfield, IL: Charles Thomas, 1960),,. 42.

[27] Aristotle, *Physics,* vii: 4; Thomas Aquinas, *The Disputed Questions of Truth* (Chicago, IL: Henry Regnery, 1952), Question XI: The Teacher.

[28] David Elkind, *Children and Adolescents* (New York: Oxford University Press, 1970), 99.

[29] Michael Oakeshott, *The Voice of Liberal Learning,* ed. Timothy Fuller (New Haven, CT: Yale University Press, 1989), 44.

[30] Marjorie Boyle, *Erasmus on Language and Method in Theology* (Toronto, ON: University of Toronto Press, 1977), 83.

[31] Ludwig Wittgenstein, The *Blue and Brown Books* (New York: Harper and Row, 1964), 16.

[32] Gary Snyder, *The Practice of the Wild* (San Francisco, CA: North Point Press, 1990), 23; on trees and forests as teachers, see Brian Walsh, Marianne Karsh, and Nick Ansell, "Trees,

Forestry and the Responsiveness of Creation," *Cross Currents* 44 (Summer 1994): 149-62.

[33] Jacob Needleman, *A Sense of the Cosmos* (Garden City, NY: Doubleday, 1975), 56; for a similar view in Islamic tradition, Seyed Hossein Nasr, *Ideals and Realities of Islam* (Boston, MA: Beacon Press, 1972), 139.

[34] Niko Tinbergen, "War and Peace in Animals and Man," *Science,* 160(June 28, 1960), 1412-1413.

[35] For dogs teaching other dogs, see Elizabeth Marshall Thomas, The *Hidden Life of Dogs* (Boston, MA: Houghton Mifflin, 1993).

[36] Eugene Daley, *Father Feelings* (New York: Morrow, 1978), 65.

[37] Sherwin Nuland, *How We Die* (New York: Knopf, 1994), 1; see also Elisabeth Kübler-Ross, *On Death and* Dying (New York: Macmillan, 1969), preface: "We have asked him [the dying patient] to be our teacher so that we may learn more about the final stages of life with all its anxieties, fears and hopes."

[38] John Locke, *Some Thoughts Concerning Education* (Cambridge: Cambridge University Press, 1972) , par. 82, 182.

[39] Malcolm X, The *Autobiography of Malcolm* X (New York: Ballantine Books, 1973), 333-34.

[40] Page Smith, *Killing* the *Spirit* (New York: Viking Books, 1991), 203; Neill, *Summerhill,* 138: "I have said it many times and say it again, that you cannot teach anything of importance. Math, English, French, yes, but not charity, love, sincerity, balance, or tolerance."

[41] Aristotle, *Nicomachean Ethics*, 1103 a, 33.

[42] Hannah Pitkin, *Wittgenstein and Justice* (Berkeley, CA: University of California Press, 1973), 57.

Chapter Three

[1]Allan Janik and Stephen Toulmin, *Wittgenstein's Vienna* (New York: Simon and Schuster, 1973), 182-83.

[2]Susan Walker, *Speaking of Silence: Christians and Buddhists on the Contemplative Way* (New York: Paulist Press, 1987), 172.

[3] J. Krishnamurti, *Commentaries on Living. Second Series* (Wheaton, Il: Theosophical Publishing House, 1958), 83, 138.

[4] Leo Tolstoy. *Tolstoy on Education*, ed. Alan Pinch and Michael Armstong (Rutherford, NJ: Fairleigh Dickinson University, 1982), 84.

[5] Tolstoy, *Tolstoy on Education,* 246.

[6] Maria Montessori, *Education for a New World* (Madras, India: Kalakshetra, 1959), 66.

[7] Sylvia Ashton-Warner, *Spinster* (New York: Simon and Schuster, 1959); *Teacher* (New York: Simon and Schuster, 1963); *Spearpoint: Teacher in America* (New York: Knopf, 1972).

[8] Ashton-Warner, *Spinster*, 45.

[9] Lowe, *The Education of Adults,* 95.

[10] Paulo Freire, *Pedagogy of the Oppressed* (New York: Herder and Herder, 1970), 59, 67.

[11] B. F. Skinner, "Behaviorism at Fifty," in *Behaviorism and Phenomenology,* ed. T.W. Winn (Chicago, IL: University of Chicago Press, 1964), 90-91.

[12] George Dennison, *The Lives of Children* (New York: Random House, 1969), 89.

[13] Aristotle, *Nicomachean Ethics,* 1103a, 34,

[14] Margaret Donaldson, *Children Minds* (New York: Norton, 1979), 32, 261.

[15] Richard Burton, John Brown and Gertrude Fischer, "Skiing as a Model of Instruction," in *Everyday Cognition*, ed. Barbara Rogove and Jean Lave (Cambridge, MA: Harvard University Press, 1993), 129-50.

[16] Donald Schön, *The Reflective Practitioner* (New York: Basic Books, 1983), 21-69.

[17] Adam Phillips, *On Kissing, Tickling and Being Bored* (Cambridge, MA: Harvard University Press, 1993), 30: A sixteen-year-old describing the experience of learning to swim says: "I knew I was safer out of my depth because even though I couldn't stand, there was more water to hold me up." The therapist comments: "For the boy the risk of learning to swim was the risk of discovering that he, or rather his body would float. The heart of swimming is that you can float. Standing within his depth, apparently in control, was the omnipotence born of anxiety; the opposite of omnipotence here was not impotence, as he had feared, but his being able to entrust himself to the water."

Chapter Four

[1] I adopt here and in the following chapters the idea of family resemblance for groups of languages that are related. The claim is not that they have a common essence but that there are qualities that link the family members together. See, Wittgenstein, *Philosophical Investigations*, par. 64.

[2] John Dewey, *Human Nature and Conduct* (Carbondale, IL: Southern Illinois University Press, 1988), 159: "An end is a device of intelligence in guiding action, instrumental to freeing and harmonizing troubled and divided tendencies."

[3] Wayne Booth, *Modern Dogma and the Rhetoric of Assent* (Notre Dame, IN.: University of Notre Dame Press, 1979), 125.

This book was influential in beginning the attempt to recover the positive, rich meaning of rhetoric

[4] Hans-Georg Gadamer, *Truth and Method* (New York: Seabury Press, 1975), 247.

[5] Leszek Kolakowski, *Modernity on Trial* (Chicago, Il: University of Chicago Press, 1990), 126.

[6] Quoted in John Thornhill, *Making Australia* (Newtown: Omnibus, 1992), 194..

[7] Northrop Frye, *The Educated Imagination* (Bloomington, IN: Indiana University Press, 1964), 64..

[8] In Moliere's novel, *Le bourgeois gentilhomme* (Paris: Presses Pocker, 1992).

[9] On the value of gossip, see John Sabini and Maury Silver, *Moralities of Everyday Life* (New York: Oxford University Press, 1982),89,106.

[10] Kenneth Eble, *The Craft of Teaching* (San Francisco, CA: Jossey-Bass, 1976), 42.

[11] Eble, *The Craft of Teaching,* 43.

[12] George Marshall, "Harvard Commencement Address," *George C. Marshall Foundation,* June 5, 1947.

[13] Robert Hughes, *Culture of Complaint* (New York: Oxford University Press, 1993), 72.

[14] Robert Wilken, *John Chrysostom and the Jews* (Berkeley, CA: University of California Press, 1983), 106.

[15] Matthew Fox, *Breakthrough* (Garden City, NY: Doubleday, 1980).

[16] Robert Pattison, *On Literacy* (New York: Oxford University Press, 1982), 71.

[17] Perry Miller, *Errand into the Wilderness* (New York: Harper, 1964), 175-83.

[18] Garry Wills, *Lincoln's Gettysburg Address* (New York Touchstone Books, 1993), 175.

[19] Quoted by Nat Hentoff in *The Village Voice*, March 12, 1985, 3.

[20] Augustine of Hippo, "Christian Instruction," in *Saint Augustine* (New York: Fathers of the Church, 1947), 194: "They must be persuaded not that they may know what should be done, but to do what they already know they should do."

[21] Philip Rieff, *Fellow Teachers* (New York: Harper and Row, 1973), 2.

[22] Martin Luther King Jr., *I Have a Dream: Writings and Speeches that Changed the World* (San Francisco, CA: Harper, 1992), 101-6.

Chapter Five

[1] Mary Douglas, *Natural Symbols* (New York: Pantheon Books, 1970), 73.

[2] Philip Rieff, *The Triumph of the Therapeutic* (New York: Harper and Row, 1966).

[3] Cyril Houle, *Design of Education* (San Francisco, CA: Jossey-Bass, 1972), 29.

[4] Kant, *Foundations of the Metaphysics of Morals*, 9.

5 Bronislaw Malinowski coined the term *phatic* communion for this yes or uh-huh, that is, a type of speech in which ties of union are created by the mere exchange of words. See

Bronislaw Malinowski, "The Problem of Meaning in Primitive Language," in C. K. Ogden and I. A. Richards, *The Meaning of Meaning* (New York: Harcourt, Brace, Jovanovich, 1989), 296-336.

[6] Wittgenstein, *Philosophical Investigations,* par. 133

[7] Ludwig Wittgenstein, *Tractatus-Logico-Philosophicus* (London: Routledge and Kegan Paul, 1971).

[8] Thomas Aquinas, *De Potentia*, 7,5 ad 14; *Summa Theologiae,* Ia, prologue

[9] Frank Tobin, *Meister Eckhart: Thought and Language* (Philadelphia, PA: University of Pennsylvania Press, 1986), 80, 167; Reiner Schurmann, *Meister Eckhart: Mystic and Philosopher* (Bloomington, IN: University of Indiana Press, 1978), 213.

[10] Plato, *Republic,* 518 c,d,e.

[11] Comenius, *The Great Didactic,* 52

[12] Wittgenstein, *Philosophical Investigations,* par. 23, 12.

[13] James Hillman, *Suicide and the Soul* (New York: Harper, 1975), 124.

[14] Albert Camus, *The Plague* (New York: Vintage Books, 1972), 236.

[15] Martin Buber, quoted in Maurice Friedman, *Martin Buber's Life and Work: The Middle Years 1923-1945* (New York: Dutton, 1983), 325.

[16] The well-known prayer of Francis of Assisi is, "It is in giving that we receive; it is in pardoning that we are pardoned; it is in dying that we are born to eternal life."

[17] Hannah Arendt, *The Life of the Mind: Thinking* (New York: Harcourt, Brace, Jovanovich, 1978), 143.

[18] Standing, *Maria Montessori*, 310; John Holt, *How Children Fail*, 44: "Do children really need so much praise? When a child after a long struggle, finally does the cube puzzle, does he need to be told that he has accomplished something? Doesn't he know without being told, that he has accomplished something? In fact, when we praise him, are we not perhaps horning in on his accomplishment?"

[19] David Hume, *An Enquiry Concerning the Principles of Morals* (Chicago IL: Open Court, 1960), 121.

[20] Robert Westbrook, *John Dewey and American Democracy* (Ithaca, NY: Cornell University Press, 1991), 180.

[21] Fyodor Dostoyevsky, *The Brothers Karamazov* (New York: New American Library, 1952), 538.

[22] Arendt, *The Life of the Mind: Thinking*, 5.

[23] Gabriel Moran, *Uniqueness: Problem or Paradox in Jewish and Christian Traditions* (Maryknoll, NY: Orbis Books, 1982), chap. 4.

[24] Arendt, *The Human Condition*, 241.

[25] Sogyal Rinpoche, *The Tibetan Book of Living and Dying* (San Francisco, CA: Harper, 1992), begins with the author being taught about death; the term teaching appears on almost every page of the book.

[26] Samuel Beckett, *Waiting for Godot* (New York: Grove Press, 1954), 57.

[27] Miguel Unamuno, *Tragic Sense of Life* (Princeton, N.J.: Princeton University Press, 1972), 20.

[28] Daniel Levinson, *The Seasons of a Man's Life* (New York: Knopf, 1978); Nuland, *How We Die*.

[29] Geoffrey Gorer, *Death, Grief and Mourning* (Garden City, NY: Doubleday, 1965), 111.

[30] Kübler-Ross, *On Death and Dying;* Philippe Aries, *The Hour of Our Death* (New York: Knopf, 1981); Nuland, *How We Die.*

[31] S. J. Connolly, *Priest and People in Pre-Famine Ireland* (New York: St. Martin's Press, 1982), 159.

[32] Harold Kushner, *When Bad Things Happen to Good People* (New York: Avon Books, 1981), 90.

[33] Samuel Beckett, *Endgame* (New York: Grove Press, 1958), 53.

[34] Edmund Wallant, *Children at the Gate* (New York: Harcourt, Brace and World, 1964), 144.

Chapter Six

[1] Richard Rorty, *Essays on Heidegger and Others* (New York: Cambridge University Press, 1991), 12.

[2] Hannah Pitkin, *Wittgenstein and Justice* (Berkeley, CA: University of California Press, 1972), 297.

[3] Peter Elbow, *Embracing Contraries* (New York: Oxford University Press, 1987), 267-84.

[4] Friedrich Nietzsche, *Birth of Tragedy and Genealogy of Morals* (Garden City NY:, Doubleday, 1956), 163.

[5] Georg Hegel, *Philosophy of Right* (Chicago, IL: Encyclopedia Britannica, 1952), 12-13.

[6] Karl Marx, "Concerning Feuerbach," in *Karl Marx: Early Writings* (London: Penguin Books, 1992), 423.

[7] Ray Monk, *Ludwig Wittgenstein: His Life and Work* (New York: Free Press, 1990), 533.

[8] Stanley Fish, "There's No Such Thing as Free Speech and It's a Good Thing, Too," in *Debating P.C.*, ed. Paul Berman (New York: Dell, 1992), 237.

[9] Ludwig Wittgenstein, *On Certainty* (New York: Harper Torch, 1972), par. 433: "The philosopher must give the circumstances in which this expression functions"; par. 229: "Our talk gets its sense from the rest of our actions." *Philosophical Investigations,* par. 489: "Ask yourself: on what occasion, for what purpose, do we say this? What kind of actions accompany these words? (Think of a greeting)."

[10] Benedict Spinoza, *A Theologico-Political Treatise* (New York: Dover, 1951), 101: "We are at work not on the truth of passages, but solely on their meaning....In order not to confound the meaning of a passage with its truth, we must examine it solely by means of the signification of the words, or by a reason acknowledging no foundation but Scripture."

[11] Frank Kermode, *The Genesis of Secrecy* (Cambridge, MA: Harvard University Press, 1979), 122.

[12] Plato, *Thaetetus,* 189e.

[13] Martin Buber, *I and Thou* (New York: Scribner's, 1970), 69.

[14] Steven Cavell, *Must We Make Sense!* (Cambridge: Cambridge University Press, 1969), 157.

[15] Mel Gussow, conversation with Tom Stoppard, *New York Times*, August 8, 1992, 28.

[16] Peter Farb, *Word Play: What Happens When People Talk* (New York: Knopf, 1974), 24-26.

[17] Richard Gilman, *The Making of Modern Drama* (New York: Farrar, Straus and Giroux, 1974).

[18] Eric Havelock, *Preface to Plato* (Cambridge, MA: Harvard University Press, 1963), 208; G.B. Kerferd, *The Sophistic Movement* (Cambridge: Cambridge University, 1981), 59-67.

[19] Michel Foucault, *The Order of Things* (New York: Pantheon, 1970).

[20] Fernand van Steenberghen, *Thomas Aquinas and Radical Aristotelianism* (Washington, D.C.: Catholic University of America Press, 1980); Josef Pieper, *Guide to Thomas Aquinas* (San Francisco, CA: Ignatius Press, 1991), 83.

[21] Ronald Beiner, *Political Judgment* (Chicago, IL: University of Chicago Press, 1953), 152.

[22] John Stuart Mill, *On Liberty* (New York: Norton, 1975), 36; Aristotle, *Topics,* 101 a, 35: "The ability to raise searching difficulties on both sides of a subject will make us detect more easily the truth and error about several points that arise."

[23] John Dewey, *Characters and Events* (New York: Holt, 1929), xi.

[24] Michael Oakeshott, *The Voice of Liberal Learning* (New Haven, CT: Yale University Press, 1989), 115.

[25] Leo Straus, preface to *Spinoza: The Jewish Expression* (New York: Macmillan, 1950).

[26] *New York Times*, November 12, 1988, 8.

[27] Ian Buruma, *The Wages of Guilt: Memories of War in Germany and Japan* (New York: Farrar, Straus and Giroux, 1994), 239; for a summary of the whole episode, 239-49.

[28] Carol Gilligan, *In a Different Voice* (Cambridge, MA: Harvard University Press, 1982); Mary Belenky, Blythe Clinchy, Nancy Goldberger and Jill Tamie, *Women's Ways of Knowing* (New York: Basic Books, 1986).

[29] Gsbriel Moran, *America in the United States and the United States in America* (Indianapolis, IN: iUniverse, 2018).

Chapter Seven

[1] Jacques Barzun, *Begin Here: The Forgotten Conditions of Teaching and Learning* (Chicago, IL: University of Chicago Press, 1991), 3.

[2] Leo Tolstoy, "On the Education of the People," in *Tolstoy on Education,* 66: "How can this be? The demand for education is present in every human being; the people love and seek education as they love and seek air to breathe. The government and society have a burning desire to educate the people, and in spite of all the force, the cunning devices and obstinacy of governments and educated classes, the common people constantly declare that they are not content with the education offered to them and, step by step, give in only to force."

[3] David Elkind, *The Child and Society* (New York: Oxford University Press, 1979), 107.

[4] Rousseau, *Emile,* 42.

[5] *The Compact Edition of the Oxford English Dictionary* (New York: Oxford University Press, 1971), 1:833: Education is "the process of nourishing or rearing a child or young person, an animal."

[6] Edmund Morgan, *The Puritan Family* (New York: Harper, 1966), 88.

[7] Locke, *Some Thoughts Concerning Education,* 51, says that he is writing for "an ordinary Gentleman's Son"; Rousseau, *Emile,* 357, chides Locke: "I do not have the honor of raising a gentleman"; however, at the beginning of the book he says, "I will not be distressed if Emile is of noble birth" (52).

[8] John Dewey, *School and Society* (Chicago, IL: University of Chicago Press, 1990), 6-29.

[9] John Dewey, "My Pedagogic Creed," in *John Dewey on*

Education, ed. Reginald Archambault (Chicago, IL: University of Chicago Press, 1974), 32.

[10] N.E.S. Grundtvig, *Tradition and Renewal* (Copenhagen: Danish Institute, 1983); Basil Yeaxlee, *Lifelong Education: A Sketch of the Range and Significance of the Adult Education Movement* (London: Castile and Co., 1929);Grattan Hartley, *American Ideas about Adult Education, 1760-1951* (New York: Teachers College Press, 1959).

[11] Bernard Bailyn, *Education in the Forming of American Society* (New York: Norton, 1962)..

[12] Lawrence Cremin, *American Education: The Colonial Experience, 1607-1783* (New York: Harper, 1970); *American Education: The National Experience, 1783- 1876* (New York: Harper, 1980), and *American Education: The Metropolitan Experience, 1876-1980* (New York: Harper, 1988).

[13] Bailyn, *Education in the Forming of American Society,* 14.

[14] Lawrence Cremin, *Public Education* (New York: Basic Books, 1976), 27.

[15] John Dewey and Arthur Bentley, *Knowing and the Known* (Boston, MA: Beacon Press, 1949); in this book Dewey prefers the term *transformation* to *interaction,* the word he had used throughout his earlier writings. I think both terms can be helpful rather than the first replacing the second.

[16] Plato, *Republic,* Book V.

[17] Shoshana Alexander, *In Praise of Single Parents: Mothers and Fathers Embracing the Challenge* (Boston, MA: Houghton Mifflin, 1994).

[18] Emile Durkheim, *Education and Sociology* (Glencoe, Ill.: Free Press, 1956), 91.

[19] For a description of the positive relation of schoolteacher and

parental teacher, see Deborah Meier, *The Power of Their Ideas* (Boston, MA: Beacon Press, 1995), 26 - 27, 51-53.

[20] Jane Martin, "Excluding Women from the Educational Realm," *Harvard Educational Review*, 52 (May 1982), 133-48.

[21] Sara Ruddick, *Maternal Thinking* (Boston, MA: Beacon Press, 1989), 72-73.

[22] Hillary Rodham Clinton, *It Takes a Village* (New York: Simon and Schuster, 1996), 108. The book only occasionally addresses the theme of its subtitle: *Lessons Children Teach Us*. "Parents discover that this modeling behavior is a two-way street. How many times have you watched a child and thought: If only I could bottle that energy. Spending time with children elevates our perceptions and energizes us."

[23] Eliot Daley, *Father Feelings* (New York: Morrow, 1978), 65: "There are a variety of ways to child one's parents"; Michael Lewis and Leonard Rosenblum, *The Effect of the Infant on Its Caregiver* (New York: John Wiley and Sons, 1974). Maria Montessori, *The Child in the Family* (Chicago, IL: Regnery, 1970). Paulo Freire and Ira Shor, *Pedagogy for Liberation* (Granby, MA: Bergen, 1972).

[24] *New York Times,* July 14, 1992, 18.

[25] Maria Montessori, *The Child in the Family* (Chicago IL: Regnery, 1970).

[26] Paulo Freire and Ira Shor, *Pedagogy for Liberation*, 172.

[27] Quoted in Standing, *Maria Montessori,* 345.

[28] Irene Lilley, *Friedrich Froebel: A Selection from His Writings* (Cambridge: Cambridge University Press, 1967).

[29] Howard Gardner, *The Unschooled Mind* (New York: Basic Books, 1991), 55; for a skeptical view of the enthusiasm for

apprenticeship, see Oakeshott, *Voice of Liberal Learning*, 92.

[30] For some examples, see Clinton, *It Takes a Village*, 193-201.

[31] Plato, *Republic*, 536c.

[32] Schön, *Reflective Practitioner*, 299.

[33] Josef Pieper, *Leisure, the Basis of Culture* (New York: Mentor Books, 1952),

[34] Hannah Arendt, *Human Condition*, 131.

[35] Witold Rybczynsk, *Waiting for the Weekend* (New York: Penguin Books, 1991); Juliet Schor, *The Overworked American: The Unexpected Decline of Leisure* (New York: Basic Books, 1991).

Chapter Eight

[1] Herbert Kliebard, *The Struggle for the American Curriculum, 1893-1958* (Boston MA: Routledge and Kegan Paul, 1986), 254.

[2] Theodore Sizer, *Horace's School* (Boston, MA: Houghton Mifflin, 1992), 11.

[3] George Spindler, ed., *Doing the Ethnography of Schooling* (New York: Holt, Rinehart and Winston, 1982); Peter Woods, *Inside Schools: Ethnography in Educational Research* (New York: Routledge and Kegan Paul, 1986); Mike Rose, *Possible Lives* (Boston, MA: Houghton Mifflin, 1995); Meier, *The Power of Their Ideas*, 161-73.

[4] John Dewey, "The Child and the Curriculum," in *Dewey on Education*, ed. Martin Dworkin (New York: Teachers College Press, 1959), 96-106.

[5] John Dewey, *Esperience and Education* (New York: Collier Books, 1963).

269

[6] Sylvia Farnham-Diggery, *Schooling: The Developing Child* (Cambridge, MA: Harvard University Press, 1990), 95.

[7] John Dewey, *Democracy and Education* (New York: Free Press, 1966); the index to the book supports my statement that Dewey seldom uses the verb "to teach." The occasional use of "teacher" is almost always the equivalent of professional educator; for example: "When the parent or teacher has provided the conditions which stimulate thinking" (160).

[8] John Passmore, *Philosophy of Teaching* (Cambridge, MA: Harvard University Press, 1980), 26; Gardner, *The Unschooled Mind,* 127.

[9] Plato's view in *The Republic* is that philosophy is best studied after the age of 50. Aristotle and Thomas Aquinas agreed with this view.

[10] Dewey, *Democracy* and *Education:* on environment as teacher, 18-19; on lifelong education, 51; on the interdependence of the adult and the child, 44, 50.

[11] Dewey, "My Pedagogic Creed," 30.

[12] Dewey," My Pedagogic Creed," 32.

[13] George Counts, *Dare the Schools Build a New Social Order?* (New York: Amo Press, 1969), 9-10; on the problem of indoctrination in the writings of George Counts, see Gerald Gutek, *The Educational Theory of George* S. Counts (Columbus, OH: Ohio State University Press, 1970), 115-34.

[14] Westbrook, *John Dewey and American Democracy,* 506.

[15] Theodore Sizer, *Horace's Compromise* (Boston MA: Houghton Mifflin, 1985),
120-30.

[16] Herbert Kohl, *Growing Minds:* On *Becoming a Teacher* (New York: Harper and Row, 1984), 80: "Most students in our foolishly competitive schools feel that they are in a battle with

their teachers and that when students fail teachers succeed, and when students succeed they do it despite their teachers. Teaching well implies the opposite – our only success lies in how well our pupils do.

[17] Alan Tom, *Teaching as a Moral Craft* (New York: Addison-Wesley Longman, 1984), 142; see also Harold Stevenson and James Stigler, *The Learning Gap* (New York: Touchstone Books, 1992), 158: "Curiously, we deny our teachers the apprenticeships that are commonly accepted as effective means for other professionals."

[18] Standing, *Maria Montessori*, 216.

[19] Michael Polanyi, *Personal Knowledge* (Chicago,IL: University of Chicago Press, 1958), 53.

[20] On the metaphor of coaching applied to teaching, see Sizer, *Horace's Compromise*, 99-108.

[21] Patricia Graham, S.O.S. (New York: Hill and Wang, 1992), 118. She provides no page number in her footnote for this reference. I think she might be referring to page 17 of Donald Schön's *Educating the Reflective Practitioner* (San Francisco: Jossey-Bass, 1987), where Schön is describing a section of John Dewey's work.

[22] Foucault, *The Order of Things*.

[23] Ernest Boyer, *High School: A Report on Secondary Education in America* (New York: Harper and Row, 1983), 201.

[24] Dewey, *Democracy and Education*, 38.

[25] *New York Times*, July 20, 1992, 35.

[26] J.Katz and M. Henry, *Turning Professors into Teachers* (New York: Macmillan, 1988), 128, quoting one professor: "To speak as though someone is listening is something teachers may not do. They may present facts and give a list of information but they are not speaking as if someone is out

there. I know from my theater background that you can't get away with that – when you are playing to an audience you have to appeal to them. You can't just get up there and give some information."

[27] Northrop Frye, *The Great Code* (New York: Harcourt, Brace, Jovanovich, 1982), xxi: "Information does have to be conveyed in teaching, of course, but for the teacher the imparting of information is again in a context of irony, which means that it often looks like a kind of game."

[28] Alasdair McIntyre, *Three Rival Versions of Moral Enquiry* (Notre Dame, IN.: University of Notre Dame Press, 1990), 233: "Knowing how to read antagonistically without defeating oneself as well as one's opponent by not learning from the encounter is a skill without which no tradition can flourish."

[29] Frye, *The Great Code,* 15; see also Wittgenstein, *Blue and Brown Books,* 451: "In philosophy it is always good to put a *question* instead of an answer to a question. For an answer to a philosophical question may easily be unfair; disposing of it by another question is not."

[30] Saint Augustine, "The Teacher," in *The Fathers of the Church* (Washington, DC: Catholic University of America Press, 1967), 59:7.

[31] Pitkin, *Wittgenstein and Justice,* 241; for another description of Wittgenstein teaching, see Monk, *Ludwig Wittgenstein,* 289; see also the description of John Dewey teaching in Westbrook, *John Dewey and American Democracy,* 378-79: The student, Irwin Edman, says that on first impression Dewey "seemed to be saying whatever came into his head next, and at one o'clock on an autumn afternoon to at least one undergraduate what came next did not always have a very clear connection with what had just gone before." Eventually, however, Edman concluded: "I had been listening not to the semi-theatrical repetition of a discourse many times made before – a fairly accurate description of many academic lectures – I had been listening to a man actually *thinking* in the presence of the class. To attend a lecture of John Dewey

was to participate in the actual business of thought."

[32] Belenky et al., *Women's Ways of Knowing,* 219.

[33] Jerome Bruner, *Toward a Theory of Instruction* (Cambridge, MA: Harvard University Press, 1967), 104.

[34] P.H. Hirst, "The Logical and Psychological Aspects of Teaching a Subject," in *The Concept of Education,* ed. Richard Peters (London: Routledge and Kegan Paul, 1967), 59.

[35] Passmore, *Philosophy of Teaching,* 32.

[36] Sizer, *Horace's School,* 183.

[37] Explaining the policy of the New York City public schools in providing condoms, Joseph Fernandez said in *Tales Out of School* (Boston, MA: Little Brown, 1992), 245: "My course, I thought was clear. The school system has a moral responsibility to its children. Its children were dying, and although many would die no matter what we did, if we did nothing the numbers would be apocalyptic."

[38] Henry Perkinson, *Teachers without Goals, Students without Purposes* (New York: McGraw-Hill, 1992), 26: "Teachers and schools should never claim that they will teach students how to read, or how to write, or how to speak French, or to perform any skill. The only logical, practical and moral claim educators can make is that they will help students become better readers, better writers, better speakers of French, or better performers of some specific skill."

[39] Michael Katz, *Class, Bureaucracy, and Schools,* 2nd ed. (New York: Praeger, 1973), 164- 65; for John Dewey's argument against this split, see "Education versus Traditional Training," *New Republic,* May 8, 1915, 8-14.

[40] Harvey Kantor, "Managing the Transition from School to Work: The False Promise of Youth Apprenticeship," *Teachers College Record,* 95 (Summer 1994): 442-61, is very suspicious of the enthusiasm for apprenticeship expressed by politicians. If

the new apprenticeship is simply a redoing of the old vocational school for the academic castoffs, then apprenticeship would be a false hope. John Dewey was on the right track early in the century in talking about vocational aspects of education rather than vocational schools; see Dewey, *Democracy and Education,* 316.

[41] Plato, *Republic,* 455c.

[42] Boyer, *High School,* 202-15.

[43] *New York Times Magazine,* September 27, 1992, 37- 42.

Chapter Nine

[1] Michael Katz, *The Irony of Early School Reform* (Boston, MA: Beacon Press, 1968); Carl Kaestle, *The Evolution of an Urban School System: New York City, 1750-1850* (Cambridge, MA: Harvard University Press, 1974).

[2] Durkheim, *Moral Education,* 18-19.

[3] Jean Piaget, *Moral Judgment of the Child,* 191.

[4] Durkheim, *Education* and *Sociology,* 87 - 90.

[5] Piaget, *Moral Judgment of the Child,* 191.

[6] Piaget, *Moral Judgment of the Child,* 309, 324.

[7] Piaget, *Moral Judgment of the Child,* 323.

[8] Lawrence Kohlberg in his speech before the American Psychological Association in 1978; see *Psychology Today,* February 1979, 57.

[9] Lawrence Kohlberg, "Moral Education Reappraised," *The Humanist* 38 (November 1978), 13- 15.

[10] James Rest, "Basic Issues in Evaluating Moral Education Programs," in *Evaluating Moral Development,* ed. Lisa Kuhmerker and others (Schenectady, NY: Character Research Project, 1980), 5-6.

[11] Carol Gillligan, *In a Different Voice.*

[12] Thomas Lickona, *Raising* Good *Children* (New York: Bantam, 1987); and his *Educating for Character* (New York: Bantam, 1991).

[13] William Kilpatrick, *Why Johnny Can't Tell Right from Wrong* (New York: Simon and Schuster, 1992), 93-94.

[14] Kilpatrick, *Why Johnny,* 255-56.

[15] Philip Greven, *Spare the Child* (New York: Vintage Books, 1952), 184-85.

[16] Richard Sennett, *The Fall of Public Man* (New York: Knopf, 1997), 94.

[17] Erikson, *Childhood and Society,* 268-69.

[18] Stephen Carter, *The Culture of Disbelief* (New York: Basic Books, 1993), 201; see also Amitai Etzioni, *The Spirit of Community* (New York: Crown, 1993), 205: "Educators, however, regularly require students to attend all kinds of classes, from foreign-language courses to math. Why not require them to attend classes that will teach them civility?" The answer to Etzioni's question should be obvious. Math and foreign languages can be studied in school as subjects; civility is not the name of that kind of thing. "Civics" is a word invented in the 1890s for schoolchildren; it has never had academic substance. If the issue were to be confronted, it would be found that civics can only be preached in elementary grades, not academically taught. Civility might be learned in school by the study of history or literature; far more important is that civility is learned by school being a civil place.

[19] Steven Satris, ed., *Taking Sides: Clashing Views* on *Contemporary Moral Issues,* 5th ed. (Guilford, CT: Dushkin, 1996).

[20] My comments are not a criticism of this curriculum. The authors are aware of the need to provide multiple perspectives. See Margaret Strom and William Parsons, *Facing History and Ourselves: Holocaust and Human Behavior* (Watertown, MA.: Intentional Education, 1982).

[21] *New York Times,* January 10, 1995, A8.

[22] Sometimes writers who understandably wish to call attention to the Holocaust do not see that their way of insisting on this in schools is self- defeating. Robert Goldman, in an essay entitled "Don't Be Calm about the Holocaust," addresses "teachers, preachers, parents" with the admonition: "Boredom, calm, understanding are not for the Holocaust. Deep anger,
disgust and rejection are what it generates among decent people." I agree that boredom does not belong in the classroom, but calm usually does, and understanding is the indispensable goal. See *International Herald Tribune,* August 17, 1994, 6.

[23] Aristotle, *Ethics*, 1180a: "In order to be a good man, one must first have been brought up in the right way and trained in the right habits . . . "; 1095a: "For those who regulate their impulses and act in accord with principle, a knowledge of these subjects will be of great advantage."

[24] John Keegan, *The Face of Battle* (New York: Viking Books, 1976), 23-24.

Conclusion

[1] John Dewey, *Experience and Education*, 88.

[2] Martin Buber, *Eclipse of God* (New York: Harper Torch, 1952).

[3] Redding Sugg, *Motherteacher:* The Femininization *of American Education* (Charlottesville, VA: University of Virginia Press, 1978).

[4] Amitai Etzioni, *The Semi-Professions and* their *Organization* (New York: Free Press, 1969); for the history of the profession of school teaching, see Donald Warren, ed., *American Teacher: Histories of a Profession at Work* (New York: Macmillan, 1989).

[5] Deborah Meier *The Power of Their Ideas*, 139: "We think we know all about teaching; after all, by the time we become adults we've had prolonged contacts with more teaching situations than those of any other occupation."

[6] R. K. Kelsall and Helen Kelsall, *The Schoolteacher in England and the United States* (London: Pergamon, 1969), 147: "One obvious moral to be drawn from the experience of other professions is that, if status is to be maintained or enhanced, practitioners must not be seen to be engaged on any duties which less highly trained people could perfectly easily perform."

CPSIA information can be obtained
at www.ICGtesting.com
Printed in the USA
BVHW071342120820
586216BV00004B/99